Digitalization and Firm Performance

Milena Ratajczak-Mrozek ·
Paweł Marszałek
Editors

Digitalization and Firm Performance

Examining the Strategic Impact

palgrave
macmillan

Editors
Milena Ratajczak-Mrozek
Department of International Marketing
Poznań University of Economics and Business
Poznań, Poland

Paweł Marszałek
Department of Money and Banking
Poznań University of Economics and Business
Poznań, Poland

ISBN 978-3-030-83359-6 ISBN 978-3-030-83360-2 (eBook)
https://doi.org/10.1007/978-3-030-83360-2

This Palgrave Macmillan imprint is published by the registered company Springer Nature Switzerland AG
The registered company address is: Gewerbestrasse 11, 6330 Cham, Switzerland

Acknowledgements

We would like to thank all contributors for their commitment and cooperation.

The book was financed within the Regional Excellence Initiative programme of the Minister of Science and Higher Education of Poland, years 2019–2022, grant no. 004/RID/2018/19, financing 3,000,000 PLN.

Contents

Contributors

Chiara Ancillai Department of Management, Università Politecnica Delle Marche, Ancona, Italy

Teodora Cristina Barbu Bucharest University of Economic Studies, Bucharest, Romania

Iustina Alina Boitan Bucharest University of Economic Studies, Bucharest, Romania

Alejandra Cabello National Autonomous University of Mexico, Mexico City, Mexico

Cosmin Cepoi Bucharest University of Economic Studies, Bucharest, Romania

Mehmet Demiral Department of Economics, Niğde Ömer Halisdemir University, Niğde, Turkey

Özge Demiral Department of International Trade and Logistics, Niğde Ömer Halisdemir University, Niğde, Turkey

Héctor Díaz-Rodríguez National Autonomous University of Mexico, Mexico City, Mexico

Aleksandra Hauke-Lopes Department of International Marketing, Poznań University of Economics and Business, Poznań, Poland

Luca Marinelli Department of Management, Università Politecnica Delle Marche, Ancona, Italy

Paweł Marszałek Poznań University of Economics and Business, Poznań, Poland

Federica Pascucci Department of Management, Università Politecnica Delle Marche, Ancona, Italy

Raluca Crina Petrescu Bucharest University of Economic Studies, Bucharest, Romania

Dawid Piątek Poznań University of Economics and Business, Poznań, Poland

Michał Pilc Poznań University of Economics and Business, Poznań, Poland

Cristina Poncibò Department of Law, University of Turin, Turin, Italy

Valéry Psyché Université TÉLUQ, Montréal, QC, Canada

Milena Ratajczak-Mrozek Department of International Marketing, Poznań University of Economics and Business, Poznań, Poland

Miriam Sosa Metropolitan Autonomous University, Mexico City, Mexico

Katarzyna Szarzec Poznań University of Economics and Business, Poznań, Poland

Diane-Gabrielle Tremblay Université TÉLUQ, Montréal, QC, Canada

Marcin Wierzeczycki Department of International Marketing, Poznań University of Economics and Business, Poznań, Poland

Katarzyna Woźniak Poznań University of Economics and Business, Poznań, Poland

Beata Woźniak-Jęchorek Poznań University of Economics and Business, Poznań, Poland

Qing XU Université Côte d'Azur-GREDEG-CNRS, Valbonne, France

Amina Yagoubi Université TÉLUQ, Montréal, QC, Canada

List of Figures

List of Tables

1

Introduction: Digitalization as a Driver of the Contemporary Economy

Paweł Marszałek and Milena Ratajczak-Mrozek

One of the most important determinants shaping economic and social life in recent decades has been technological progress. Together with other factors (such as globalization, or social and climate change), it has radically changed the way of doing business, the organization of companies, individual industries and the entire economy (Barbrook, 2007; Caputo et al., 2021; Reis et al., 2018; Sennet, 2006; Thurow, 1996). Modern technologies have also influenced human behaviour, people's incentives and decision-making processes, intensifying—somewhat paradoxically—the number of mutual, often direct interactions between individual entities (Gobble, 2015). All these factors have changed the

P. Marszałek (✉)
Department of Money and Banking, Poznań University of Economics and Business, Poznań, Poland
e-mail: pawel.marszalek@ue.poznan.pl

M. Ratajczak-Mrozek
Department of International Marketing, Poznań University of Economics and Business, Poznań, Poland
e-mail: milena.ratajczak-mrozek@ue.poznan.pl

M. Ratajczak-Mrozek and P. Marszałek (eds.), *Digitalization and Firm Performance*,
https://doi.org/10.1007/978-3-030-83360-2_1

model of social life and cultural patterns which, in turn, has obviously had an impact on the way companies and markets function.

Rapid changes of technology, mainly in the field of information and communication technologies (ICT), have influenced the competitive position of individual sectors of the economy, as well as entire countries, business models and the behaviour of market process participants. The scale of these changes was so significant that some authors argued a "New Economy" was emerging (Jorgensen & Stiroh, 1999; Nakamura, 2000; Oliner & Sichel, 2000). This is manifested in the different production processes and the allocation of goods and services, as well as in changes in the hierarchy and organization of individual elements of a given economy.

The phenomenon of the New Economy, usually identified with the transition—due to the increased importance of knowledge and information, the development of ICT and the commercialization of the Internet—from an industrial economy to a technology-based economy, with the dominant role of services (Gordon, 2000; Nakamura, 2000), has usually been treated as an unequivocally positive phenomenon. Appreciating the role of new technologies, as well as a proper theoretical foundation and an "improved" institutional framework for economic policy, the era of general macroeconomic stability was proclaimed. It was also emphasized that thanks to new technologies it was possible to make economic entities more rational and to bring individual markets closer to the state of perfect competition (Goodfriend, 2007; Jorgenson & Stiroh, 1999).

Even the Global Financial Crisis of 2007–2009, and the resulting recession, social tensions and debt crises in many countries did not stop the further development of new technologies or the expansion of the scope of their application. The Internet, technologies, mobile devices, social networks and technological platforms are developing so quickly that the technological revolution is even referred to as the next industrial revolution—the fourth one, in fact (Rifkin, 2011; Schwab, 2016).

One of the most important aspects and dimensions of economy 4.0 is the digitalization process. As Gartner's Glossary (2021) defines it, digitalization is "the use of digital technologies to change a business model and provide new revenue and value-producing opportunities; it is the process of moving to a digital business". The process should not be identified with digitization, which is just a conversion of data and processes. Digitization describes the pure analogue-to-digital conversion of existing data and documents (e.g. scanning a photograph or converting a paper report to a PDF file), not changing the data itself—it is simply about data being encoded in a digital format. It provides more efficiency (digitized data can be used to automate processes and enable better accessibility), but does not seek to optimize business processes or data as a whole. Thus, the meaning of digitalization is much broader than digitization, as the process can also be identified with qualitative change and specific transformation. Digitalization embraces the ability of digital technology to collect data, establish trends and make better business decisions. It is about "the use of new digital technologies (social media, mobile, analytics or embedded devices) to enable major business improvements" (Fitzgerald et al., 2014, p. 2). In consequence, the process changes, or even disrupts, the way that markets, firms and financial institutions function.

As Tekic and Koroteev (2019, p. 684) underline, "digital transformation is a multifaceted phenomenon in that it has different aspects/implications for different companies". The adoption of new technologies becomes necessary for survival and being competitive (Caputo et al., 2021; Rachinger et al., 2019). What is fascinating about digitalization is that it affects all companies, sectors and markets, regardless of the degree of their digital advancement. Even highly traditional companies and industries with a high level of manual labour are facing digital challenges and need to learn how to handle digital solutions. Therefore, for some companies and sectors, digital transformation may mean the adoption of new modes of production, while for others it might involve using social media for the purposes of advertising and selling.

Among technologies and processes that are a manifestation of digitalization, and which are of particular importance for the economy, management and finances, primarily include the so-called Big Data, distributed ledger technology (DLT), Artificial Intelligence (AI), Internet of Things (IoT), augmented reality, blockchain, FinTech, InsurTech, RegTech, cryptocurrencies and the so-called cashless economy.

Big data is involved wherever a large amount of digital data is accompanied by the need to acquire new information or knowledge. The availability of large amounts of real-time data opens up opportunities for companies to apply new statistical methods, improve economic forecasts and make profitability and risk assessments along with quick feedback (Bakshi, 2012; Bartosik-Purgat & Ratajczak-Mrozek, 2018; Warner & Wäger, 2019).

Blockchain is a form of DLT, in other words, a decentralized database that exists in many identical copies for individual users. It can be used for secure and forgery-proof logging of all kinds of transactions. Thanks to this technology, transactions between many entities can be easily and automatically settled, which makes it applicable in virtually all industries: financial and insurance, but also the energy and oil industry, environmental protection, advertising, health protection and public administration (Narayanan et al., 2016).

The most popular use of blockchain currently concerns finance and is associated with the so-called cryptocurrencies, i.e. a special case of virtual currency, often perceived—rather exaggeratedly—as money of the future. Cryptocurrencies, being so far rather a tool of speculation and not having the status of money in principle, can, however, form the basis for the creation of local currency systems, as well as enable the transition to the so-called cashless economy, i.e. a situation in which cash, at best, is only a tiny fraction of the money supply (EBC, 2012: Popper, 2016).

RegTech is the application of the latest technologies for regulatory purposes. Solutions in this field are designed to support the collection, interpretation and reporting of data in order to meet regulatory needs. The growing importance of this issue may be associated with the global financial crisis of 2007–2009, which resulted in a sharp increase in the number of new regulations. Although it has other applications, RegTech is a specific complement to FinTech and InsurTech—the use of modern technologies in institutions and financial transactions. FinTech and InsurTech have radically changed the way financial institutions operate, including banks. For the latter, the term "Bank 4.0" has even started to be used, denoting a new way of segmenting clients and shaping relationships with them, distributing banking products, banking risk management, modelling the offer, etc. (Carney, 2017; Fostering Innovations, 2020; King, 2018);

Augmented reality, AI and IoT, in turn, found greater use outside the financial sector. Augmented reality is defined as an enhanced version of reality created by the use of technology that overlays digital information on an image of something being viewed through a specific device, or, more simply, a system connecting the real and computer-generated world. It reflects the fusion of digital technology with reality, where images from the "real" world are synchronized with 3D and animated computer graphics (Correia Loureiro et al., 2020).

IoT describes the network of physical objects—"things"—that are embedded with sensors, software and other technologies for the purpose of connecting and exchanging data with other devices and systems over the Internet. Such things can be for instance household appliances, lighting and heating products, and even wearables (Atzori et al., 2010; Wortman & Fluchter, 2015).

AI refers to the simulation of human intelligence in machines that are programmed to think like humans and mimic their actions and thinking, but much more efficiently. The term AI can be also understood as any machine that exhibits the traits associated with a human mind such as learning and problem-solving. It is assumed that AI is able to rationalize and take actions that have the best chance of achieving a specific goal. A subset of artificial intelligence is machine learning, referring to the concept that computer programs can independently and automatically learn from and adapt to new data (Acemoglu & Restrepo, 2018).

The technologies described above change the shape and functioning of individual sectors of the economy and also affect the shape and intensity of interrelations between organizations and other actors in economic and social life. They also create new attitudes, behaviours and communication patterns of consumers, employees and investors. One group especially empowered by digitalization is modern consumers. Due to access to numerous media, consumers are becoming information-empowered and are much more interconnected (Alamäki & Korpela, 2021). Through these processes they are able not only to communicate with each other but also to communicate directly with companies and influence their activities (Matarazzo et al., 2021).

Thus, through digitalization the existing forms and intensity of market and non-market relations are transformed, and consequently—the efficiency, effectiveness and results of business processes. Digitalization especially changes existing business models (Caputo et al., 2021; Luz Martín-Peña et al., 2018; Rachinger et al., 2019). These diversified, new forms of business models are "characterized by decreased reliance on physical elements" (Caputo et al., 2021, p. 490) and may concern a broad spectrum of digital solutions, such as offering a digital product, reliance on digital channels of sale or the robotization of manufacturing processes. As a result of digitalization, if handled correctly, companies should be able to optimize their operations and obtain better operational efficiency and business performance (Ribeiro-Navarrete et al., 2021), which also results in the co-creation of value.

The pioneers in the business application of new technologies have been entities from the financial sector. Banks, insurance companies and investment funds have applied new technologies naturally, so to speak, thereby fostering the development of digital devices and instruments. Yet, digitalization has very quickly proven to be of the utmost importance also with regard to firms from other industries that operate on different markets. Moreover, electronic channels and innovations have also fostered closer ties between production, trade and service companies, and the financial institutions cooperating with them.

To sum up in more detail, one might identify the subsequent channels through which digitalization has had an impact on the economy: (1) digital technologies allow firms to transcend the boundaries of space, providing them with access to a larger, sometimes even global markets, and are thus claimed to be the drivers of growth and competitiveness; (2) digitization strongly influences the strategies of firms and has had a significant impact on resources and the processes taking place both internally in firms and in markets and the economy. At the same time, the adoption of new technologies imposes some challenges for management, requiring new business models and strategies; (3) digitalization leads to consumer empowerment, equipping them with new means of influencing firms, as well as leading to increased expectations; (4) digitalization causes profound changes in the labour market, introducing new production solutions, replacing human work with robotics solutions, which creates additional pressure on firms and in turn changes the way markets operate; (5) digitalization changes the face of the financial markets and institutions, as new forms of financial instrument are created, new forms and methods of payments emerge, and the scale and speed of payments and settlements increases; and (6) the dissemination of new technologies and the consequences of this process has also become an important factor on macroeconomic level, influencing countries' digital and international competitiveness. Therefore, digitalization may be considered in the context of both challenges and opportunities set by digital technologies for business models and business operations (e.g. production, logistics, marketing activities) and markets, as well as the main driver of growth and competitiveness for markets and firms/businesses.

As a consequence of the processes mentioned above, the markets driven by technological revolutions are constantly changing. Digitalization can be seen as a crucial factor that should be taken into account when one considers management on both the micro-level (companies and markets) and macro-level (economic policy and regulations). Therefore, in the present book we adopt the interdisciplinary approach, as it provides a comprehensive view of digitalization, its manifestations, features and impact on both individual firms and economic systems as a whole. The book contributes to the present state of knowledge by offering evidence on how digitalization and digital technologies are impacting markets, firms and financial institutions. Throughout the book we identify and highlight the challenges resulting from digitalization, as well as the opportunities connected with this process. Challenges and opportunities are important elements that are taken into account in managerial decisions and are also subject to intensive research. The thorough and comprehensive analysis of these factors and phenomena, which this book aims to pursue, can be important for grasping the current and future directions of research and managerial practice.

The book comprises 11 Chapters. The authors apply various methods (quantitative and qualitative) and approaches in their research, considering the investigated problems on different levels of analysis—micro, mezzo and macro. Such diversity provides us with a broad perspective on the problem of digitalization and at the same time gives us a wider audience for our research results. In subsequent chapters the authors bring closer various aspects of digitalization, identifying the opportunities and challenges presented by new technologies.

The first three chapters focus on how digitalization challenges the management of modern companies, which nowadays are more interrelated than ever before and function within business networks and ecosystems. In Chapter 2, Psyché, Tremblay and Yagoubi discuss the functioning of the artificial intelligence (AI) ecosystem and the contribution of technology service providers, both to this ecosystem and to specific firms in the process of digital transformation. During digital transformation, some companies, especially in the manufacturing sector, are facing difficulties with starting to modernize their facilities. The biggest identified challenges are a wariness of technological changes and concerns about data protection. However, the process of digital transformation can be facilitated by the wider AI ecosystem, including technology service providers.

In a similar vein, in Chapter 3 Hauke-Lopes, Ratajczak-Mrozek and Wieczerzycki present a case study of business cooperation anchored in a digital platform which impacts the value creation and appropriation processes in small companies' network relationships. The presented research shows that digitalization and the need to adopt certain digital solutions, services and software apply not only to IT-related sectors, but also to highly traditional (analogue) sectors, where it is not fully possible to replace the human factor and manual labour with digital solutions. Not every company is capable of carrying out full digital transformation. The introduction of digitalization to such companies poses challenges for management and their operations which, if handled correctly, through cooperation, may result in some opportunities as well. The presented research indicates that network relationships created through a digital platform result in the creation and appropriation of financial, knowledge, personal and operational value.

In Chapter 4, Ancillai, Marinelli and Pascucci also discuss the impact of digitalization on highly traditional businesses. These companies need to keep up with technological development to be able to compete with innovative firms, even if the introduction of digital solutions may be more challenging for them than in the case of IT-related companies. The research provides a thorough analysis of a digital-driven innovation in a business model in a product/service firm, thereby showing how data can act as an enabler of change and innovation in more traditional organizations.

Network relationships and cooperation between organizations translate into the macroeconomic situation of entire countries, and the processes related to digitalization are global in nature. Therefore, in Chapter 5 Demiral and Demiral compare higher digitally-competitive countries (HDCCs) and lower digitally-competitive countries (LDCCs) in terms of the export performance associated with digital-intensive Information and Communications Technology (ICT) goods. They examine the effects of economic structure, globalization and governance indicators on the export performance of these goods.

Similarly, adopting the international cross-boundaries perspective in Chapter 6, Poncibo discusses the case of digital (smart) contracts in international trade and finance by considering, specifically, smart contracts. These contracts represent a typical example of the digitalization of cross-border business transactions and, in the absence of legal certainty, the chapter notes that economic operators and financial traders are increasingly relying on smart contracts, which are primarily characterized by a reliance on technology, to manage their international digital transactions. Poncibo's analysis is an example of an interdisciplinary approach, as the author considers the economic construct of smart contracts from a legal perspective.

Digitalization causes profound changes in the labour market, introducing new production solutions, which may cause fears that human work will be replaced with robotics solutions. Therefore, in Chapter 7 Pilc, Woźniak-Jęchorek Woźniak and Piątek compare the public messages formulated by employer associations and trade unions concerning the Fourth Industrial Revolution (or Industry 4.0) in France, Germany, Poland and the UK. The results indicate that in the case of Industry 4.0 there is one message with regard to which employer associations and trade unions are in agreement. It states that to help the manufacturing sector benefit from Industry 4.0 the government should invest much more in workers' skills.

Issues associated with human capital and workers' skills are also the subject of research conducted in Chapter 8. Here, Díaz-Rodríguez, Sosa and Cabello employ a graph theory approach, while analysing the impact of digitalization on talent migration flows and on the human capital skills required for work in the financial industry. The empirical analysis, drawing on the Digital Data for Development database (2015–2019), unveils the labour market dynamics in the financial industry. The authors' findings suggest that digitalization influences the human capital of financial institutions in a twofold way—both qualitative and quantitative change—such that the financial sector has become a pole of attraction for talent, and labour skills have increased and become specialized in this sector.

The next two chapters concentrate on the monetary aspects of digitalization. Xu (Chapter 9) and Marszałek and Szarzec (Chapter 10) consider the impact and consequences of the process on payments and the entire monetary system, respectively. As was already mentioned, the financial domain has enthusiastically implemented new technologies. In Chapter 9, focusing on the specific cases of two regions, Xu analyses how the successful adoption of mobile payment technologies differed in East Asia and East Africa. To this end, the author presents a classification of the different development paths of mobile payment operational models in the two regions and then considers the consequences of different methods for implementing the digitalization of payments.

In Chapter 10, Marszałek and Szarzec take a general, macroeconomic view, assessing inevitability of transition—being a consequence of the continuous dematerialization of money caused by digitalization and new technologies—to the cashless economy. The authors discuss the definitions and origins of the cashless economy, its features, determinants and understanding from both the micro- and macroeconomic points of view. On that ground they identify key advantages and disadvantages of the cashless economy, considering the perspectives of different stakeholders. To conclude, they argue that the result of cost–benefit analysis of the cashless economy is ambiguous, which means its full adoption is not inevitable.

One of the most currently hyped—but at the same time controversial—manifestations of the new technologies are cryptocurrencies, which are treated as form of specific, private digital currency. In the last chapter, Chapter 11, Barbu, Boitan, Petrescu and Cepoi run a threshold analysis to attempt to identify the financial drivers of the price of Bitcoin, the most popular cryptocurrency, in times of economic and policy uncertainty. From their results it is evident that the relationships between Bitcoin price and bond yields from China and Japan are robust and statistically significant only in times of low economic or political uncertainty. This stands in contrast to German bond yields, which negatively influence the Bitcoin price in periods of economic or political turbulence. The chapter demonstrates that Bitcoin is a versatile financial product, which may act either as a diversifier or as a hedge asset, depending on investors' behaviour and risk appetite.

The chapters presented in the book show that digitalization is a factor that permeates and consolidates all economic processes in the contemporary economy. It creates numerous linkages and feedback mechanisms between individuals, companies, policymakers and supervisors. Moreover, digitalization is manifested not only in the economic dimension, but is visible also in social, cultural or legal spheres. For this reason, digitalization should be viewed as interdisciplinary phenomenon which impacts the micro, mezzo and macro levels of economic activity. Precise description and assessment of this phenomenon requires an interdisciplinary approach, combining economics, management, sociology and law, as digitalization is, as was already stressed, a phenomenon reaching far beyond economic life.

This complexity and multithreading of digitalization, as well as linkages and interdependencies between the individual spheres of economic and social life it generates, are presented synthetically in Fig. 1.1. Furthermore, it also illustrates the dependencies between the individual chapters of the book, which pertain to individual aspects of digitalization's influence.

Thus, digitalization, in changing the shape of economic and social relations, can be perceived as a specific driver of contemporary economies. It reshapes markets and monetary and political hierarchies, influencing at the same time incentives and behaviour of economic agents. This process is still ongoing and dynamic, since it received an additional boost from the COVID-19 pandemic. Looking to the future,

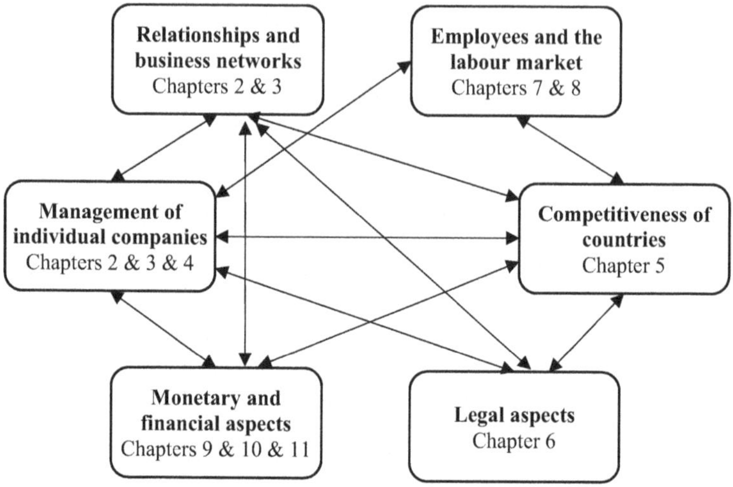

Fig. 1.1 Digitalization—areas of influence and interdependencies

we do hope that this book has captured at least a small part of contemporary digitalization, its impact on and linkages with the economy, management and finance, and that it will help us to have a better understanding of this extraordinary phenomenon.

Acknowledgements The study has been financed within the Regional Initiative for Excellence programme of the Minister of Science and Higher Education of Poland, years 2019–2022, grant no. 004/RID/2018/19, financing 3,000,000 PLN.

References

Acemoglu, D., & Restrepo, P. (2018). The race between man and machine: Implications of technology for growth, factor shares, and employment. *American Economic Review, 108*(6), 1488–1542.

Alamäki, A., & Korpela, P. (2021). Digital transformation and value-based selling activities: seller and buyer perspectives. *Baltic Journal of Management, 16*(2), 298–317.

Atzori, L., Iera, A., & Morabito, G. (2010). The internet of things: A survey. *Computer Networks, 54*(15), 2787–2805. https://doi.org/10.1016/j.comnet.2010.05.010

Bakshi, K. (2012). *Considerations for big data: Architecture and approach.* In 2012 IEEE, Aerospace Conference, Big Sky Montana. pp. 1–7. https://doi.org/10.1109/AERO.2012.6187357

Barbrook, R. (2007). *Imaginary futures: From thinking machines to the global village.* Pluto Press. ISBN-13: 978-0745326603.

Bartosik-Purgat, M., & Ratajczak-Mrozek, M. (2018). Big data analysis as a source of companies' competitive advantage: A review. *Entrepreneurial Business and Economics Review, 6*(4), 197–215. https://doi.org/10.15678/EBER.2018.060411

Caputo, A., Pizzi, S., Pellegrini, M. M., & Dabić, M. (2021). Digitalization and business models: Where are we going? A science map of the field. *Journal of Business Research, 123*, 489–501. https://doi.org/10.1016/j.jbusres.2020.09.053

Carney, M. (2017). *The promise of FinTech—Something new under the Sun?* Speech given at the Deutsche Bundesbank G20 conference on "Digitising finance, financial inclusion and financial literacy", Wiesbaden.

Correia Loureiro, S. M., Guerreiro, J., & Ali, F. (2020). 20 years of research on virtual reality and augmented reality in tourism context: A text-mining approach. *Tourism Management, 77*. https://doi.org/10.1016/j.tourman.2019.104028

Fitzgerald, M., Kruschwitz, N., Bonnet, D., & Welch, M. (2014). Embracing digital technology: A new strategic imperative. *MIT Sloan Management Review, 55*(2), 1.

Fostering innovation and competitiveness with FinTech, RegTech, and SupTech. (2020). Marchewka-Bartkowiak, K., & Boitan I. A. (Eds.). IGI Global. https://doi.org/10.4018/978-1-7998-4390-0

Gartner's Glossary. (2021). *Digitalization.* https://www.gartner.com/en/information-technology/glossary/digitalization

Gobble, M. M. (2015). Regulating innovation in the new economy. *Research-Technology Management, 58*(2), 62–67.

Gordon, R. J. (2000). Does the "new economy" measure up to the great inventions of the past? *The Journal of Economic Perspectives, 14*, 49–74.

Goodfriend, M. (2007). How the world achieved consensus on monetary policy. *Journal of Economic Perspectives, 21*(4), 47–68. https://doi.org/10.1257/jep.21.4.47

Jorgenson, D. W., & Stiroh, K. J. (1999). Information technology and growth. *American Economic Review, 89*(2), 109–115. https://doi.org/10.1257/aer.89.2.109

King, B. (2018). *Bank 4.0: Banking everywhere, never at a bank*. Wiley.

Luz Martín-Peña, M., Díaz-Garrido, E., & Sánchez-López, J. M. (2018). The digitalization and servitization of manufacturing: A review on digital business models. *Strategic Change, 27*(2), 91–99. https://doi.org/10.1002/jsc.2184

Matarazzo, M., Penco, L., Profumo, G., & Quaglia, R. (2021). Digital transformation and customer value creation in Made in Italy SMEs: A dynamic capabilities perspective. *Journal of Business Research, 123*, 148–2963. https://doi.org/10.1016/j.jbusres.2020.10.033

Nakamura, L. I. (2000). Economics and the new economy: The invisible hand meets creative destruction. *Federal Reserve Bank of Philadelphia Business Review*, July–August, 15–30.

Narayanan, A., Bonneau, J. Felten, E., Miller, A., & Goldfeder, S. (2016). *Bitcoin and cryptocurrency technologies: a comprehensive introduction.* Princeton University Press. ISBN 978-0-691-17169-2.

Oliner, S. D., & Sichel, D. E. (2000). The resurgence of growth in the late 1990s: Is information technology the story? *Journal of Economic Perspectives, 14*(4), 3–22. https://doi.org/10.1257/jep.14.4.3

Popper, N. (2016). *Digital gold. The untold story of bitcoin.* Penguin.

Rachinger, M., Rauter, R., Müller, C., Vorraber, W., & Schirgi, E. (2019). Digitalization and its influence on business model innovation. *Journal of Manufacturing Technology Management, 30*(8), 1143–1160. https://doi.org/10.1108/JMTM-01-2018-0020

Reis, J., Amorim, M., Melão, N., & Matos, P. (2018). Digital transformation: A literature review and guidelines for future research. In Á. Rocha, H. Adeli, L. P. Reis, & S. Costanzo (Eds.), *Trends and advances in information systems and technologies.* WorldCIST'18 2018. Advances in intelligent systems and computing (Vol. 745). Springer. https://doi.org/10.1007/978-3-319-77703-0_41

Ribeiro-Navarrete, S., Botella-Carrubi, D., Palacios-Marqués, D., & Orero-Blat, M. (2021). The effect of digitalization on business performance: An applied study of KIBS. *Journal of Business Research, 126* (July 2020), 319–326. https://doi.org/10.1016/j.jbusres.2020.12.065

Rifkin, J. (2011). *The third industrial revolution: How lateral power is transforming energy, the economy, and the world*. Palgrave Macmillan.

Schwab, K. (2016). *The fourth industrial revolution.* Penguin.

Sennet, R. (2006). *The culture of the new capitalism.* Yale University Press. Retrieved June 14, 2021, from http://www.jstor.org/stable/j.ctt1nq6w.

Tekic, Z., & Koroteev, D. (2019). From disruptively digital to proudly analog: A holistic typology of digital transformation strategies. *Business Horizons, 62*(6), 683–693. https://doi.org/10.1016/j.bushor.2019.07.002

Thurow, L. C. (1996). *The future of capitalism: How Today's economic forces shape tomorrow's world*. Nicholas Brealey Publishing.

Warner, K. S. R., & Wäger, M. (2019). Building dynamic capabilities for digital transformation: An ongoing process of strategic renewal. *Long Range Planning, 52*(3), 326–349. https://doi.org/10.1016/j.lrp.2018.12.001

Wortman, F., & Fluchter, K. (2015). Internet of Things. *Business & Information Systems Engineering, 57*(3), 221–224. https://doi.org/10.1007/s12599-015-0383-3

2

Digital Transformation: An Analysis of the Role of Technology Service Providers in Montreal's Emerging AI Business Ecosystem

Diane-Gabrielle Tremblay, Amina Yagoubi, and Valéry Psyché

Introduction

Over the past years, there has been much interest in the sources of innovation and integration of Information Technologies (IT) and other technologies within organisations. One of the main concepts that has attracted interest is that of Open Innovation, which draws attention to the role of various stakeholders and to the concept of entrepreneurial ecosystems. Recently, several studies have focused on the concept of business or entrepreneurial ecosystems (EEs) (Brydges & Pugh, 2021).

D.-G. Tremblay (✉) · A. Yagoubi · V. Psyché
Université TÉLUQ, Montréal, QC, Canada
e-mail: diane-gabrielle.tremblay@teluq.ca

A. Yagoubi
e-mail: amina.yagoubi@teluq.ca

V. Psyché
e-mail: valery.psyche@teluq.ca

M. Ratajczak-Mrozek and P. Marszałek (eds.), *Digitalization and Firm Performance*,
https://doi.org/10.1007/978-3-030-83360-2_2

In the context of Industry 4.0 and the accelerated development of new technologies, companies are increasingly facing the need to make a digital shift. With Artificial Intelligence (AI), on the one hand, they must value their data, but on the other they must also introduce AI into their business, and this is a challenge for many of them, to which service providers can contribute, as we will see further on. In the face of these new developments, many companies are unfortunately not ready to make a digital shift and need the help of expert consultants who are in fact service providers. This is why we are seeing more and more suppliers appear in this economic and technological business ecosystem. They offer AI solutions thanks to software and customised support.

The objective of this chapter is to close a research gap concerning the functioning of the AI ecosystem and the contribution of technology service providers, both to this ecosystem and to specific firms in the process of digital transformation. We address the role of technology service providers in the digital transformation of businesses, but also the composition of the wider AI ecosystem and the support it provided for business digitalisation, as they are interrelated.

In this chapter, we analyse the role of these AI solution service providers. In particular we seek to determine how and to what extent stakeholders can contribute to digitalisation in various firms and to identify how they help companies move forward in this direction. In our research, we identified the actors who are present to support firms in AI solution integration and determined their role in this transformation in the city of Montreal in particular, and the province of Québec more generally, as some stakeholders intervene at the provincial level globally. It is through in-depth qualitative research that we explore the dynamics of valuing the emerging ecosystem and its stakeholders, including the providers of technology and AI solutions. Thus, we conducted a qualitative survey based on the meeting of 3 focus groups, 3 co-construction meetings on Zoom and Miro, and 25 semi-structured interviews with experts, throughout 2020. This allows us to report on the dynamics of key players and their contribution in supporting firms in with AI solution integration and digital transformation in general.

The chapter is structured as follows. We first present the theoretical perspectives and identify the knowledge gap. We then present the methodology used for data collection, as well as their treatment. Then, following a thematic analysis of our interviews, we present the results of our qualitative analysis on what is needed from AI project managers and technology service providers to help companies to make their digital shift. Indeed, some companies and industries are having difficulty with starting to modernise their facilities, especially in the manufacturing sector; many are wary of technological changes and worried about data protection, amongst other preoccupations.

Theoretical Perspectives

There are two concepts which are at the base of our theoretical contribution as well as our empirical investigation. The first concept is that of Open Innovation, and the second is that of Enterprise Ecosystem.

Open Innovation

Theory on open innovation involves knowledge coming from various sources, especially the integration of knowledge from external sources, from outside of specific firms, in order to foster innovative knowledge and lead to creative ideas and innovation (Chesbrough, 2003, 2006, Chesbrough et al., 2006). Open innovation theories refer to the idea that external knowledge and competencies can be integrated into a firm. Open innovation requires firms to be open to external ideas and knowledge, to eliminate the obstacles to innovation or digitalisation, opening up to sources of information and knowledge sharing.

Open innovation may be all the more important in smaller firms, considering their limited resources (human and capital). Indeed, smaller firms have less internal knowledge and research capacity, and they have to access external sources of information, knowledge and networks. (Chesbrough, 2003) The novelty and diversity of knowledge that can be accessed through this open innovation process is clearly an important source of competitiveness, technology integration and business development (Chesbrough, 2003, 2006; Chesbrough et al., 2006; Trott, 2009).

New technologies can thus be accessed and integrated, and products, new processes, new markets and other forms of innovation can thus be developed.

Providers of AI solutions and software can be part of the network of sources of knowledge. Indeed, these important players support the digital transformation of firms which often do not have the means to have an AI department.

These service providers and other stakeholders will help Industry 4.0 and manufacturers either to undertake the digital shift if they have no data or to attain digital maturity.

Business Ecosystem

It is evident that the organisation of a business ecosystem is essential for bringing together stakeholders and creating interaction with different stakeholders (Esty & Winston, 2009; Freeman, 1984, 1994, 1999). This is a fundamental source of added value. On the one hand, this allows players to make themselves known, but also to develop links and business opportunities, for example in R&D.

> *Inside an ecosystem, the different stakeholders' roles are not fixed, but are dynamic and dependent on characteristics of the local environment, but there are certain stakeholders in an ecosystem that play a crucial role (Peltola, Aarikka-Stenroos, Viana, & Mäkinen, 2016).* (Bonollo & Poopuu, 2019, p. 6)

Such a business ecosystem involves the contribution of a network of key, strategic players and niche players (Bonollo & Poopuu, 2019; Boutillier & Uzunidis, 2010), for example, suppliers, companies, organisations, governments at various levels, Technology Transfer Centre, Research Centre, etc. It appears important to foster relationships "between institutions (scientific, technological, industrial, commercial, financial, political), private and public (companies, research and engineering laboratories, administrations, etc.)" (Boutillier & Uzunidis, 2010, p. 4) and cross-industry collaboration (Lu et al., 2014, p. 4579).

With the deployment of technological and digital ecosystems, there are no longer strong boundaries between industries. We find common characteristics in all business ecosystems (ES), a concept developed by Moore (1996, 2006), which can be summarised as follows:

- The actors are heterogeneous and can be companies (suppliers, producers, etc.), institutional bodies, interest groups, or shareholders, etc. They can belong to one or many ecosystems.
- Business ecosystem actors belong to different business sectors. This situation is reinforced in the context of convergence between several industries: information technology, telecommunications and media that are restructuring around ICT and the Internet (Gossain & Kandiah, 1998; Isckia, 2009). The very notion of industry seems to be disappearing, to a certain extent.

Also, a business ecosystem (ES) is a strategic response of companies of all sizes, which have to adapt rapidly to new technological and economic challenges and to new customers' needs, by offering innovative solutions (Moore, 1993). In this regard, it is important to analyse the roles of stakeholders within this ecosystem and in companies, but especially in the technological development of Industry 4.0 and smaller firms, which often lag in their digital transformation.

Finally, a business ecosystem is similar to the entrepreneurial ecosystems (EEs) defined by Spilling (1996) as composed of a "complexity and diversity of actors, roles and environmental factors that interact to determine the entrepreneurial performance of a region or locality" (Brydges & Pugh, 2021, p. 3). The EE also encompasses different stakeholders (private/public) working together to support new business development in a municipality or region. Both concepts are closely related, but the entrepreneurial ecosystem puts the accent on entrepreneurs and entrepreneurial dynamics.

We now present the methodology of the research in order to fill the knowledge gap concerning the roles and intervention of stakeholders in the process of digitalisation and the introduction of AI in Montreal firms.

Methodology

As part of our project on the definition of the AI ecosystem and the construction of an AI project management competency framework, our methodology is of a qualitative nature (Miles & Huberman, 1994). We conducted a knowledge synthesis (Cooper,1984, 1988; Kitchenham, 2004). This synthesis helped us to prepare the interview guide for a large consultation (i.e. interviews and focus group) with experts from the Quebec AI ecosystem. We have adopted an exploratory, inductive and prospective approach to the evolution of companies and their business models in the context of AI.

The procedure mentioned above allows us to understand the challenges and the reality reported by experts and analysts of the AI ecosystem in Montreal and more generally the Québec province. We thus conducted interviews and did focus groups with firms. Also, work with experts was carried out after the completion of this initial data collection stage, which allowed us to establish an inventory of the scientific, governmental and paragovernmental literature. This step is particularly important in qualitative research, which most of the time uses literature reviews to collect the main data needed for a research project or for triangulation with other data collection techniques (Paillé & Mucchielli, 2008; Kiron 2017; Staples & Niazi, 2007; Mace & Petry, 2010).

Interviews

For the interviews with the experts, we aimed to build a sample as representative and varied as possible of the AI business ecosystem in Montreal (contractors, consultants, AI solution providers, companies, governments advisors dealing with Industry 4.0, researchers, unions advisors at Quebec public service, researchers, etc.).

In order to manage and reflect this diversity, we have developed two interview guides: one for business stakeholders; the second for private/public organisations; and other intermediary actors. According to our sampling technique (Van Der Maren, 1987), we conducted a census of key players in the AI sector by exploiting our networks and word of mouth, but also by researching AI experts on LinkedIn.

Fieldwork took place from March 2020 to September 2020. We conducted semi-directional expert interviews (1–2 h) using the comprehensive interview methodology (Kaufmann, 1996) with 25 recruited AI experts involved in Industry 4.0, who agreed to answer our questions on a voluntary basis. The codification «Org» (Org1, Org2, …) in the qualitative analysis refers to organisations and «Ent» (Ent1, Ent2, Ent3…) refers to Enterprises.

All the interviews were recorded and transcribed. We used NVivo software for the qualitative analysis of verbatim: the thematic breakdown of data; the creation of significant nodes, and then we subjected the survey material to a content analysis (Miles & Huberman, 1994) to identify key and emerging themes from the verbatim analysis (2020–2021). These themes were also discussed in the focus groups.

Working Groups and Focus Groups (FG)

We organised 3 Working groups to mobilise the members of the project Alma and Bois-de-Boulogne colleges) as well as some experts from the AI ecosystem in Montreal. We also led some focus groups within these meetings on the following subjects: FG1: Competencies of an AI Project Manager, April 29, 2020; FG2: Data Governance, Cyber Security and Ethics, May 26, 2020; and FG3: Data Governance, Cyber Security and Ethics, June 10, 2020. All were organised by videoconference on Zoom (3 h for each session) with experts.

In each working group, the experts made short oral presentations in order to initiate an open focus group on the subject matter. Throughout each focus group session a researcher was present to coordinate and animate the discussion group.

All these sources of information (literature review, working groups, focus groups and interviews) were used for data analysis. In the following sections, we describe the results on the AI ecosystem as it appears from our literature review, and then we centre on the results of interviews and discussion groups.

The AI Ecosystem in Canada

In recent years, AI has become a fast-growing economic sector in Canada. There has been a phenomenal rise in the number of AI companies created, and the number of investments in these companies continues to grow (Mantha et al., 2019). However, we see that it is mainly the providers of AI solutions and software that are becoming important players: "We see that the number of net-new companies is falling, start-up funding is switching to later in the lifecycle and AI solution providers are taking a rapidly increasing share of the overall enterprise solutions market" (Mantha et al., 2019: Executive Summary).

In parallel with the business sector, Canada is a world leader in AI research, and in the province of Quebec there are many major players, research centres, training centres, companies, etc. Some data confirm this trend (Mantha et al., 2019: Table of Contents): 70 major companies have AI research laboratories in Canada. AI research contributes 50% of the business solutions of Canadian companies; "Canada remains in the top 5 in terms of the number of researchers creating a major impact in AI" (Mantha et al., 2019: Executive Summary).

In addition, several initiatives are being developed in Canada in terms of digital, data and AI governance. One is Canada's AI policy, led by the Canadian Institute for Advanced Research (CIFAR, n.d.), founded in 1982, which establishes strategic plans for digital and AI development at the national and international levels. The organisation has an annual budget of $41 million, with more than 400 researchers—including 20 Nobel Laureates—across more than 130 institutions (CIFAR, n.d.). CIFAR has contributed to two important initiatives. The first initiative led by the Standards Council of Canada (SCC) is the creation of a committee which participates in consultations and debates in the ecosystems that set such standards: the collective of the Canadian Data Governance Standardization Collaborative. This Collective coordinates the work, accelerates the creation of standards, reports on the national situation regarding the standardisation of data management and makes recommendations (CDGSC, 2019). The second initiative is Canada's Digital Charter, which brings together 10 principles (CDC, 2019, p. 18) and new ideas, for example, addressing hate and extremist language on digital platforms (CDC, 2019: Principle 9); access to open, modern, easy-to-use and high-performing government digital platforms (CDC, 2019: Principle 5); regulation of the digital economy to foster healthy competition among businesses, but also to ensure that consumers are the main beneficiaries of the thriving market (CDC, 2019: Principle 6). At the international level, starting in 2019, CIFAR also participates in disseminating the Organisation for Economic Cooperation and Development (OECD) principles on human-centred AI and well-being. These principles are based on five main criteria (OECD, 2019) in connection with an AI sensitive to laws and human rights, democratic values, cybersecurity issues, transparency and responsibility.

Industry 4.0 and Artificial Intelligence

We retain the definition adopted by the Department of Economy and Innovation of Québec (MEI—Ministry of Economy and Innovation, 2016) of the concept of Industry 4.0, the fourth industrial revolution, in terms of processes and digital transformation:

> *Data and object connectivity is the defining component of Industry 4.0. Connectivity of software, equipment, data, massive data to be processed and cybersecurity become essential elements for creating intelligence in a manufacturing system capable of greater adaptability in production and more efficient allocation of resources.* (PAEN, 2016a, Foreword)

This transformation requires facing several challenges: developing new skills, supporting industry in this transition, ensuring data security and meeting investment needs (MESI, 2017; PAEN, 2016a).

Oberer and Erkollar (2018) are of the view that too often technology does not reach its full potential in companies because it is poorly understood and controlled by the members of the organisation. They call for the emergence of a digital culture (Oberer & Erkollar, 2018); a culture that can emerge through leadership 4.0. This leadership is characterised by several competencies, such as "high-level willingness and ability for change, encouraging high-level agility between the market, customer, partners, and employees, and deliberating promotion; the ability to create a transparent framework for information distribution, counting on employees' and teams' collectable debt of self-responsibility, and proactive behaviour; knowing that innovation is learnable, being able to transform old structures through the use of multidisciplinary teams, and creative processes and flexible work environments" (Oberer & Erkollar, 2018, p. 6).

"Artificial intelligence helps to improve human capabilities, automate manual tasks, solve problems, make better decisions while building on emerging technologies including autonomous vehicles, digital assistants or data mining" (MEI, 2016). The benefits to companies of developing AI in their business are numerous. For example, it allows them to improve their productivity; perform tasks that were impossible to do before, such as anticipating future customer purchases, create new jobs, reduce costs by improving operations, respond to the specific needs of a niche clientele and to improve their competitiveness (MEI, 2018). However, the integration of new disruptive technologies (Rydning, 2018) such as AI, into Industry 4.0 represents a real challenge for societies, as it has important impacts on employment and work (Rocheleau-Houle, 2019), but also a challenge for the success of the digital transformation of companies. Indeed, as many firms do not have the internal knowledge to master the process of digital transformation, they need support in this, including on the ethical dimensions or social responsibility issues (Dilhac, 2018). As we will see further on, external service providers and experts can support them in this process. This requires support from the government, but also from a set of players in the AI ecosystem.

Results from Interviews and Discussion Groups

We now present the results of interviews on the AI business ecosystem in Montreal and elements on Québec's IA strategy.

The AI Business Ecosystem in Montreal

Concerning the AI ecosystem, in Montreal, our interviewees indicate there is a strong labour shortage ... in technology positions, specialized employees (Ent6), such as data science experts (Ent4), machinists (Ent6). There are several AI trainings, workshops and webinars (in universities, CEGEPs and other organisations) to initiate or train people in data science (Ent3) in order to develop Industry 4.0.

> IVADO or MILA, etc., for example are very good, they will create new jobs, for Industry 4.0 in the future... It's all well and good to put this on, but it takes people who are able to support the updates, then the implementation [...]. If you outsource your knowledge, you put vulnerability in your factory (which is) in the hands of a consulting firm that could disappear. So we need to have some internal intelligence, and that means training more talent in data science and hiring those talents. (Ent3)

Scale AI is a leader in the AI business ecosystem, receiving government support: $230 million from the Government of Canada and $53 million from the Government of Quebec. The Scale AI Innovation Centre, Canada's AI supercluster, supports the transition to AI in terms of support and programs, including tailored training for companies, projects and initiatives, and accelerating start-ups: They work with companies on AI programs. They work with the accelerators to help staff integrate AI. They plan and work with university trainers to do the training that can be subsidised (Org3).

Figure 2.1 indicates some of the players in the AI ecosystem in Montreal in the training field. It includes universities, research centres, some actors in the health sector and the like.

On the manufacturing side, the Salon Bleu event connects manufacturing companies with suppliers of AI solutions or consultants. The government supports this event. Salon Bleu is a manufacturing online fair where service providers can present what they do in artificial intelligence for 4.0 manufacturers. It allows them to connect manufacturing companies with technology suppliers. In fact, it is an online trade show in the smart manufacturer sector here (Ent3).

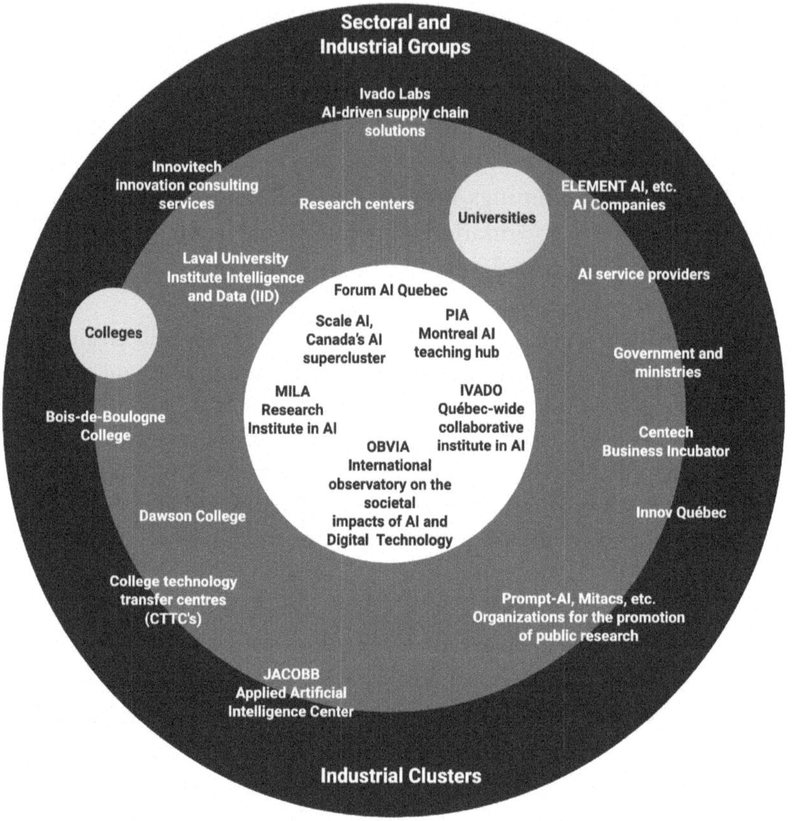

Fig. 2.1 Montreal's AI ecosystem

The manufacturing sector is represented by the Industrial Automation Cluster (REAI), which has existed for 15 years in order to democratise these technologies and map out the different stakeholders: Who gets what, when, how in a process of transformation?

The AI ecosystem in Montreal is made up of many stakeholders who reach out and are named by the interviewees. This is the case of the IVADO institute, Mila, the largest AI research institute in the world (Ent6); Element AI, Scale IA, the supercluster; IVADO Labs; the International Observatory on the Societal Impacts of the Digital and AI (OBVIA); universities and research centres; colleges: Dawson and Bois-de-Boulogne in particular; the Pôle montréalais d'enseignement supérieur en intelligence artificielle (PIA—Montreal universities and colleges group on AI); Innovitech, which supports innovation; the JACOBB: Centre for Applied Artificial Intelligence; Network of College Centres for the Transfer of Technologies (or CCTTs); Centech: Business Incubator for training and support for SME-Montreal companies; Innov Québec: a government-funded non-profit organisation serving businesses that want to accelerate their innovation projects; Prompt-AI and Mitacs: organisations for the promotion and funding of public research, etc.

In terms of the university research community, research labs are proving to be resources for companies that develop partnerships. Companies need IA technologies which come from basic research laboratories in order to develop applied research with them and then create new solutions. In terms of fundamental research development, Montreal can count on the international reputation of Yoshua Bengio, pioneer of deep learning and professor at the University of Montreal, scientific director of Mila.

Thus, in the business community working in AI, there are two categories of companies: companies that are "purely AI", which means that they produce AI technologies in partnership with the university research community to provide services for others. And then there are companies that adopt the AI solutions provided by the first category. Also, an organisation called Bonjour Start-up Montreal supports an important ecosystem of start-ups that covers the entire AI ecosystem.

Quebec Industry 4.0 Stakeholders and Digital Maturity

Although there are delays in the digital maturity of companies and industries in Quebec, some sectors are leaders in AI: aerospace is very advanced (Bombardier, Pratt & Whitney for example are companies that are very advanced); life sciences (medical equipment, etc.); video games and other sectors follow, such as agri-food, building, mining and logistics. In addition, there are niche markets in AI, regardless of the sector, such as ecology, or luxury goods (Ent1).

However, this is not the case for many small firms and manufacturing companies for which Industry 4.0 and AI are often seen as buzzwords (Ent3; Ent4; Org2). The idea that AI is a buzzword is echoed by many who refer to "AI marketing" (Org3). Too many small firms and manufacturing companies' managers still do not think that AI can offer some answers in the digitalisation process. Some refuse to implement AI and are weary of it because they do not see the use of it. The general impression that comes out is that AI is not the solution to all ills and that sometimes things that have been around for 30 years are better for some applications than AI technology. However, they still recognise that new ways of doing things need to be adopted if they want to be part of Industry 4.0, and that new AI-based technologies need to be taken seriously, even if we should not only look at AI solutions.

We see that "there are factories that currently have 200 million sales, but they are still running and managing their business with Excel files… Why? Because they have always done it like this" (Org2).

While Industry 3.0 is characterised by robotics and automation (Ent6), many manufacturing companies in Quebec do not have a digital strategy, few integrated technologies and do not know what Industry 4.0 is. That amounts to 55% of them. Then 32% say they have never heard of it, while 13% have incorrect knowledge of it (MESI, 2017, p. 7). In fact, for most of them:

> *[They are] either still managing with manual manufacturing processes (i.e., they are still at the level of maturity known as 'artisanal') or managing with processes supported by several tools that are not fully integrated (i.e., they are at the level of maturity known as 'disciplined'). In addition, there is still only a minority with an Industry 4.0 digital plan or strategy.* (MESI, 2017, p. 33, our translation)

"The delay may depend on several factors, but in general it is the digital maturity that is not there or there is some mistrust towards certain technologies" (Org2). This delay is mainly explained in this way: Quebec and Canadian manufacturing SMEs are struggling to implement these systems. There is a lot of data available in manufacturing companies, it is just that they are not collected. So that's where the Internet of Thing

(IoT) comes in to help, but they have to choose the right sensors, the right technology providers. Another challenge with the IoT is perhaps the right use of the Internet. Indeed, even today, most manufacturing companies are having a hard time migrating their data to the cloud because they do not want their data to end up in cloud solutions. Maybe it is due to a lack of trust in cloud technologies.

As a data scientist told us, another problem is that there is a lack of massive data in manufacturing SMEs. Indeed, the data are not created automatically, while it is often online transactions, then online data capture, which will form a large enough inventory of data to be able to perform some analyses. "So, considering the level of maturity, often, there will be a very strong correlation between digitalisation and the maturity of automating services or using artificial intelligence. It is still very rare that we will see manufacturing companies who will go over the digitisation of the user experience or the employee experience to do any form of automation at all" (Ent5).

However, as we see with the 2020–2021 pandemic, even the most resilient companies have had to switch to digital, telework, etc., so the digital shift of those companies was may be just a question of time, and the COVID-19 pandemic has accelerated some efforts to adapt. These efforts could lead to new business opportunities with AI.

Québec's Digital Strategy

To address this digital lag, the Government of Quebec is launching a digital strategy (PAEN, 2016b) to raise awareness of new technologies and their benefits, to encourage companies to make their digital shift (CEFRIO, 2016) with a program called: *The roadmap for digital maturity.*

The roadmap for digital maturity and Industry 4.0 rests upon the Quebec government's digital economy action plan[1] and Quebec's Digital Strategy (PAEN, 2016a, 2016b). In the figure presented in the document,[2] the authors refer to functions, sectors of the company and each

[1] "AI is not represented because in 2016, we did not yet talk much about AI" (Org1).

[2] Refer to the document: "Roadmap for Digital Maturity & Industry 4.0". Government of Quebec (PAEN, 2016a, p. 17).

function can be very basic (bottom of the pyramid), or very advanced (top of the pyramid) […]. The ideal is to be at the top in the five sectors (Org1). The roadmap was developed in 2016, when there was not much mention of AI but it gives indications as to the progress of firms in new technologies, which should eventually include AI. As one interviewee mentioned:

> AI, I would see it at the end in 6th position because that would be to integrate or extract knowledge from the data we have. Once we have improved all the functions: management, production, manufacturing, services … once everything is integrated, automated, etc. […] that we have set up systems that can exchange information, AI would be the meta layer at the top which will extract knowledge from all this data that comes from everywhere. It really is knowledge. (Org1)

The government is helping manufacturing and business make a digital shift before technology and AI are implemented (Org1). This is the case with the Industry 4.0 Audit Program (CRIQ, n.d.) of the Economics and Innovation Department of the Government of Québec, which funds audits carried out by private consultants/auditors or accredited by the government to companies that request them. These audits make it possible to identify company problems, analyse and optimise processes, draw up a balance sheet, propose solutions, establish a diagnosis, and then, finally, propose a digital plan with improvement, implementation projects to achieve digital maturity.

The Roadmap for Digital Maturity and Industry 4.0 measures the level of integration of business technologies, by presenting the different steps to follow in order to arrive at the ideal for Industry 4.0 (Org1):

> The difference with the 4.0 audit is that we have really achieved a degree of integration. It is that all these systems can talk to each other, exchange information so that I can make the best use of the data I have. So, the data […] that these systems use, we can make exchanges, but the exchanges are configured automatically to exchange this information to better exploit the data. So either to improve its way of doing things, go further, increase its turnover, increase its sales. So it's an optimal exploitation of all the data that [the company] has, […] by having all these systems integrated

> and making them talk to each other. That's really what we're aiming for in Industry 4.0. It's really reaching a level of automation beyond the systems that are already implemented, it's really going further. (Org1)

Even if different sectors do not understand the meaning of Industry 4.0 and which sectors are targeted, the government is inviting all sectors to develop without distinction, in addition to the manufacturing sector. However, the Government Roadmap for Digital Maturity remains difficult to access for entrepreneurs who find it too complicated and are somewhat discouraged by this vision.

Industry 4.0 and AI Integration

In terms of achieving 4.0 status, many companies do not know how to go about it, or what to do first, especially traditional industries or firms (Org3).

> The challenge is really at the level of the entrepreneur, at the level of his technological maturity, of education. An investment must be made, firms must devote a budget that may seem risky for them. (Ent6)

Indeed, depending on the digital maturity, it is necessary to identify the needs, objectives and priorities at the business level in order to propose a digital development plan (Org3). Many are unfamiliar with the manufacturing sector. To get into AI, you have to know the industry, its problems (Ent3).

It is recommended for every company that hopes to integrate AI solutions should do the following:

> [start] with proof of concept, controlled bench tests where you isolate a process from the chain and you know you might crash, but it's going to be a test bed. So the worst thing you can do, in my opinion, for a manufacturing company is to say: 'Well, perfect, we're going to put temperature sensors on all our machines, in all the plants and we want to use AI to detect when a temperature variation is problematic for my machines.' This is a recipe for disaster, in my opinion … to lose a lot of

> money in systems… It reminds me of the 1990s and 2000s. Everyone wanted ERP and one out of three companies used it more or less. (Ent3)

The idea is to start with pilot projects offered by AI solution providers, they are inexpensive and include customer training and follow-up. We see here the role of solution providers, which we will explain more in the next section. As mentioned by (Ent6):

> Our goal is for the customer to test the technology to remove the fear of investing in case it doesn't work. The pilot project lasts three months and does not cost too much, a few thousand dollars. They have concrete results. […] At the end of the three months, the system is normally in place, they know how to use it by themselves. So they pay a licence based on the number of machines to get the solution, to collect the data and do the tracking on the machine. It is supported, so if they have technical problems or need advice, we're available. But normally beyond the three months, it is in place, it is fewer services and it works. (Ent6)

In the end, "managers of companies who are interested in implementing technologies are motivated by the improvement of their production processes (74%) or management (72%). Two thirds (63%) see this revolution as an opportunity to improve their products and services and 59% their business model" (MESI, 2017, p. 7).

Quality control solutions are important for the manufacturing sector because one of the biggest problems is quality control (Ent3). But also the supply chain, the optimisation of production chains, even of logistics chains (Ent1); predictive maintenance to reduce the maintenance costs (Ent1), to detect a future anomaly (Ent6), for example, to know when will a machine breakdown, then plan their maintenance, plan their activities accordingly (Ent5). There is also the automation of very time-consuming tasks, for example (Ent1). This is only possible with a minimum of digital maturity, an ERP system, for example (Ent6).

AI Solution Providers

Many companies offering AI solutions are service providers (software sales, etc.); this is a new expertise in a niche market, increasingly fragmented. We find that it is full of small actors (Ent1), this is exactly what happened in computing in the last 20 years (Ent1). That is why more and more SMEs and even large companies are currently doing business with suppliers because they do not have the in-house resources or expertise. Our interviews show that technological solution providers are essential in the business ecosystem and our research highlights the role of these organisations in the development of digitalisation and AI in firms, especially small ones.

> What happens is a bit like what happened in Big Data 10 years ago. Since this is a new topic [AI], it is often small businesses that represent the main sources of entrepreneurship and try to create wealth, and eventually sell off to bigger firms. (Ent1)

There are several reasons why companies outsource AI solutions externally; two important reasons are mentioned:

> The first is the risk that a company, I'm going to take BNP, it's not going to have fun increasing its size. If they have to hire 50 data scientists and 100 data engineers, etc., of course, they don't. She prefers to take claimants, press the button to say 'thank you, goodbye' when things are not going well. So that's the first completely logical reason. And the second reason is that even these people don't want to go there. The data scientists don't want to go to BNP. They want to go to a small box where they have more freedom, [because their corporate culture] is not the culture of the big groups. (Ent1)
>
> When the market becomes very [balanced], customers will then internalize. So they don't buy that from suppliers anymore. They do it themselves because they know how to do it very well, it is very well marked, the mistakes and the mess have already passed. So they take fewer risks by internalizing. (Ent1)

To help companies implement AI, vendors typically offer customers beginner solutions: "[simple] app to show that it works and this give companies the confidence and desire to say: Here, it works, so I'm going to invest fairly more!" (Ent1).

AI Solution Providers communicate with experts from client companies, for example, if the AI Solution is for productivity, they will look for people at the operational level (Production Manager, Plant Manager); if they are SMEs, they are addressed to the President or Chief Executive Officer (Ent6). They are the ones who have an interest in our solutions, so they are our interlocutors. If it is a larger company, sometimes there is a person specifically responsible for Industry 4.0 or continuous improvement (Ent6), this is the case for example at Bombardier (Ent6). On the other hand, the needs of this type of key resource may be increasing: there may be a need for Industry 4.0 or continuous improvement managers in Industry 4.0 in the future (Ent6).

However, there can be bad experiences, with the development of solutions with suppliers, which is what pushes some to change suppliers along the way or to develop their technologies internally. This is the case of an interviewee who delivered Excel or PDF files to his clients at the beginning of his activity, then he decided to develop an application to allow customers to connect, while having the project to integrate AI in the future. After a first failure with a service provider, a software development agency (Ent4), his company changed its strategy.

> Even though I was the product manager […], the fact that I didn't have enough technical skills to challenge my supplier and that my supplier didn't ask enough business questions [to my company], it was a failure. Now, for example, with the new suppliers, they are much closer to us, they ask many more questions based on our reality and we are the same, internally, we have developed much more fluid communication tools to communicate with them. So it was quite a learning process. (Ent4)

This recruitment company has the project to inject AI functionality to further automate, but also to increase its AI knowledge through training, etc. (Ent4). This is why good collaboration between the supplier and the customer is essential to provide adequate solutions taking into account the customer's business reality, but it is also important that the customer has a better knowledge of the proposed technologies and solutions.

To democratise technologies, the group of firms in industrial automation (REAI or Regroupement des entreprises en automatisation industrielle) is developing "collaborative automation cells" (Org2) with partners and suppliers. This makes it possible to accompany "small enterprises, with few internal resources" (Org2), which do not have time to transform.

> It becomes a collaborative relationship between the company and the suppliers who also work together... I'm in the process of matching suppliers together so that they have a value chain. It is like building a plant that processes raw materials, which are in this case manufacturing companies. I am mapping stakeholder ecosystems, making them work more together [...] and allowing them to sell better. (Org2)

Discussion

Although the business ecosystem of AI in Montreal makes it possible to promote the environment locally and internationally, it is still rather recent and some denounce a gap between the production of ecosystem knowledge and the practical needs of businesses (Ent1).

For example, a few interviewees hold a similar view to this one: "This whole ecosystem was created from scratch a few years ago and it is a great achievement. It maintains itself very well. It is an example of success for the rest of Canada and the world, but on the other hand, the concrete business applications are not there yet" (Ent1).

However, in Quebec and Canada, the governments (federal and provincial) support the AI ecosystem, which remains a promising sector. Montreal is the stage of "a great collaboration between governments, all the sectors of AI" (Org3).

While a number of small firms are lagging and some manufacturing firms are resisting the introduction of technology, and especially AI, their digital maturity could allow them to remain competitive in a global economy where technological performance is increasingly important. As mentioned by an expert in the manufacturing industry, even if companies can continue to function, and even to succeed, they must transform themselves as quickly as possible:

> What Quebec's manufacturing companies must understand is that they are not in competition with each other. They compete with China, Germany and the USA, which are 75-80% automated. How do you want to fight and impose yourself, when you [with your 20-person team], you have only manual processes? … We are also in a world of digital transition. Often the big fear is "Ah! Robots, machines will replace humans!" […] It will replace the human in [jobs with repetitive tasks]. Are we not also going to develop high value-added jobs that will use the full potential of the human brain? (Org2)

The fear of job loss with the advent of robots and automation is a real issue and in many industrialised nations there are no real plans to deal with redundancies and ensure some form of income security for those laid off or pushed out of work by technology. This is an extremely important issue, which we cannot address here, but it raises the question of ethical regulation of the deployment of AI in the perspective of a responsible company, and of businesses' social responsibility in general. Moreover, the incorporation of AI into the business models of start-ups can present many surprises and challenges. The world of work will surely change with AI, and it is already changing, but the qualities required to build a business (degree, knowledge, expertise, etc.) may also change in the future.

Our interviews show that technological solution providers are essential to support this transition to AI, and our research highlights the role of these organisations in the development of digitalisation and AI in firms, especially small ones. However, they also need to understand small businesses and their needs, as well as the transformations to be supported in the labour force. As mentioned above, they play a role in open innovation and the development of the business ecosystem.

Conclusions

To conclude, let us analyse and synthesise the various elements which in our view fill a research gap on the role of solution providers and experts in contributing to innovation and AI solutions in the context which can be qualified of Open Innovation. Our research shows how these actors intervene through an Open Innovation strategy in the context of the business ecosystem and confirms the importance of the role of these actors, and the importance of a diversity of actors and stakeholders, in the AI Business Ecosystem (Tremblay & Yagoubi, 2017a, b).

While some authors (Mazaud, 2006) argue that pivot firms are crucial to the development of an ecosystem, Barbaroux (2014) finds that the IT ecosystem comes from "a technological breakthrough brought about by a community of public and private organisations; this community brings together researchers and other organisations, and then large commercial firms are relegated to the periphery" (Yagoubi & Tremblay, 2017, p. IX).

This diversity of actors is what we see in the AI business ecosystem in Montreal, which is in some ways an emerging ecosystem, and is therefore not mature (Lu et al., 2014), but the main actors appear to be in place, as we saw in the previous pages; they intervene in various fields such as training and research, as we saw above. The issue of stakeholders, and particularly the diversity of stakeholders and actors, is thus at the heart of the AI ecosystem's dynamics. We are seeing a multiplication of collaborations or partnerships on various projects concerning AI in various sectors including the health and financial sectors, to name only the major ones. This appears to confirm the dynamism of the AI ecosystem, even if some challenges remain ahead, including the issue of employment and the impact on jobs, as well the effect of this AI ecosystem on training and professional development, which needs to be addressed, but goes beyond the object of the present chapter.

In terms of future research, it will be important to address these employment and training issues, but it would also be interesting for research to focus on changing stakeholder roles or the emergence of new key players in the AI ecosystem. Indeed, these roles are affected by new issues related to the evolution of the ecosystem and disruptive technologies.

References

Accenture. (2018). *Artificial intelligence, genuine impact*. Public services in the era of artificial intelligence. Accenture Consulting, 12 p. Accessed May 10, 2020. https://www.accenture.com/_acnmedia/pdf-75/accenture-ai-genuine-impact-pov-final-us.pdf

Barbaroux, P. (2014). Innovation disruptive et naissance d'un écosystème: Voyage aux origines de l'internet. *Revue d'économie industrielle, 146*, 27–59.

Bonollo, N., & Poopuu, P. (2019, may). *The impact of digital platforms on roles and responsibilities in value creation among stakeholders of an ecosystem* (Master thesis, Jönköping University, International Business School). Accessed April 10, 2021. http://hj.diva-portal.org/smash/get/diva2:1321065/FULLTEXT01.pdf

Boutillier, S., & Uzunidis, D. (2010). *Innovation et proximité entreprises, entrepreneurs et milieux innovateurs* (Innovation and proximity entreprises, entrepreneurs and innovative milieus) (No. 10). Research Network on Innovation, 22 p.

Brydges, T., & Pugh, R. (2021). Coming into fashion: Expanding the entrepreneurial ecosystem concept to the creative industries through a Toronto case study. *The Canadian Geographer/Le Géographe canadien*, 1–22.

CDC. (2019). *Canada's digital charter in action: A plan by Canadians, for Canadians*. Report of Government of Canada, Innovation, Science and Economic Development Canada, 1–22. Accessed February 20, 2021. https://www.ic.gc.ca/eic/site/062.nsf/vwapj/Digitalcharter_Report_EN.pdf/$file/Digitalcharter_Report_EN.pdf

CDGSC [Canadian Data Governance Standardization Collaborative]. (2019, November 26). *Canadian data governance standardization collaborative*. Standards Council of Canada. Accessed July 5, 2020. https://www.scc.ca/fr/programmes-phares/gouvernance-des-donnees

CEFRIO. (2016). *Prendre part à la révolution manufacturière ? - Du rattrapage technologique à l'industrie 4.0 chez les PME*. Rapport technique, 31 p.

Chesbrough, H. (2006). Open innovation: A new paradigm for understanding industrial innovation. *Open innovation: Researching a new paradigm, 400,* 0–19.

Chesbrough, H. W. (2003). *Open innovation: The new imperative for creating and profiting from technology.* Harvard Business Press.

Chesbrough, H., Vanhaverbeke, W., & West, J. (Eds.). (2006). *Open innovation: Researching a new paradigm.* Oxford University Press on Demand.

CIFAR. (n.d.). *About CIFAR.* Canadian Institute for Advanced Research. Accessed April 20, 2021. https://cifar.ca/our-story/

Cooper, H. M. (1984). *The integrative research review: A systematic approach. Applied social research methods series.* Sage.

Cooper, H. M. (1988). Organizing knowledge syntheses: A taxonomy of literature reviews. *Knowledge in Society, 1*(1), 104–126.

Dilhac, M.-A., et al. (2018). *The Montreal declaration for a responsible development of artificial intelligence.* Montreal, QC.

Dwivedi, Y. K., Hughes, L., Ismagilova, E., Aarts, G., Coombs, C., Crick, T., Duan, Y., Dwivedi, R., Edwards, J., Eirug, A., Vassilis Galanos, P., Ilavarasan, V., Janssen, M., Jones, P., Kar, A. K., Kizgin, H., Kronemann, B., Lal, B., Lucini, B., ... Williams, M. D. (2019). Artificial Intelligence (AI): Multidisciplinary perspectives on emerging challenges, opportunities, and agenda for research, practice and policy. *International Journal of Information Management, 57*(101994), 1–47.

Esty, M., & Winston, E. (2009). A stakeholder framework for analyzing and evaluating corporate social performance. *Management Review, 5*(2), 45–56.

Freeman, R. E. (1984). *Strategic management: A stakeholder approach.* Pitman.

Freeman, R. E. (1999). Divergent stakeholder theory. *Academy of Management Review, 24*(2), 233–236.

Freeman, R. E. (1994). The politics of stakeholder theory: Some future directions. *Business Ethics Quarterly, 4*(4), 409–421.

Gossain, S., & Kandiah, G. (1998). Reinventing value: The new business ecosystem. *Strategy & Leadership, 26*(5) Chicago, (Nov/Dec 1998): 28–33. https://doi.org/10.1108/eb054622

Kiron, D. (2017). What managers need to know about artificial intelligence. *MIT Sloan Management Review.*

Kitchenham, B. (2004). Procedures for performing systematic reviews. *Keele, UK, Keele University, 33*(2004), 1–26.

Leone, D., Schiavone, F., Appio, F. P., & Chiao, B. (2021). How does artificial intelligence enable and enhance value co-creation in industrial markets?

An exploratory case study in the healthcare ecosystem. *Journal of Business Research, 129*, 849–859.

Lu, C., Rong, K., You, J., & Shi, Y. (2014). Business ecosystems and stakeholders' role transformation: Evidence from Chinese emerging electric vehicle industry. *Expert Systems with Applications, 41*(10), 4579–4595.

Mace, G., & Pétry, F. (2010). *Guide d'élaboration d'un projet de recherche en sciences sociales*. De Boeck Supérieur.

Mantha, Y., Yune, Y. J., Henderson, P., & Lin, W.-W. (2019). *2019 Canadian AI ecosystem*. Jfgagn. Accessed February 7, 2021. https://jfgagne.ai/fr/carte-de-lecosysteme-de-lia-en-2019/

MEI—Ministry of Economy and Innovation. (2016). *Industrie 4.0: les défis de la quatrième révolution industrielle*. Government of Quebec. Accessed May 7, 2020. https://www.economie.gouv.qc.ca/bibliotheques/bulletins/bulletin-espace-conseils-pme/archives/

MEI—Ministry of Economy and Innovation. (2018). *L'intelligence artificielle: pourquoi la PME manufacturière devrait-elle en tirer profit?* Government of Quebec, SME Advice Area. Accessed May 7, 2020. https://www.economie.gouv.qc.ca/bibliotheques/outils/gestion-dune-entreprise/industrie-40/lintelligence-artificielle-pourquoi-la-pme-manufacturiere-devrait-elle-en-tirer-profit/

MESI—Ministry of Economy, Science and Innovation. (2017, June). *Industrie 4.0. Enquête auprès des entreprises manufacturières du Québec*. Analysis report, project team MESI and CEFRIO, pp. 1–35.

Mazaud, F. (2006). De la firme sous-traitante de premier rang à la firme pivot. Une mutation de l'organisation du système productif «Airbus». *Revue D'économie Industrielle, 113*, 45–60.

Miles, M. B., & Huberman, A. M. (1994). *Qualitative data analysis: An expanded sourcebook* (2nd ed.). Sage.

Moore, J. F. (1993). Predators and prey: A new ecology of competition. *Harvard Business Review, 71*(3), 75–86.

Moore, J. F. (1996). *The death of competition. Leadership and strategy in the age of business ecosystems*. Harper Business.

Moore, J. F. (2006). Business ecosystems and the view from the firm. *The Antitrust Bulletin, 51*(1), 31–75.

Oberer, B., & Erkollar, A. (2018). Leadership 4.0: Digital leaders in the age of industry 4.0. *International Journal of Organizational Leadership*, 1–9.

OECD. (s.d. a). (2019). What are the OECD Principles on AI ? Consulted on July 4 2021, https://www.oecd.org/goingdigital/ai/principles/

PAEN [Digital Action Plan]. (2016a, October). Plan d'action en économie numérique. Feuille de route industrie 4.0. *Quebec's digital strategy*, Ministry of Economy, Science and Innovation (MESI), Government of Quebec, 1–52.

PAEN [Digital Action Plan]. (2016b). Plan d'action en économie numérique. Pour l'excellence numérique des entreprises et des organisations québécoises. *Quebec's digital strategy*, Government of Quebec, pp. 1–78.

Paillé, P., & Mucchielli, A. (2008). *L'analyse qualitative en sciences humaines et sociales*. Armand Colin.

Rocheleau-Houle, D. (2019). *Les effets de l'intelligence artificielle sur le monde du travail* [The effects of artificial intelligence on the world of work]. Commission de l'éthique en science et en technologie, Quebec Government, 1–54. Accessed May 20, 2020. https://www.ethique.gouv.qc.ca/assets/documents/IA_travail/CEST_effets_intelligence_artificielle_travail_A.pdf

Rydning, D. R. J. G. J. (2018). *The digitization of the world from edge to core*. International Data Corporation.

Spilling, O. (1996). The entrepreneurial system: On entrepreneurship in the context of a mega-event. *Journal of Business Research, 36*(1), 91–103. https://doi.org/10.1016/0148-2963(95)00166-2

Staples, M., & Niazi, M. (2007). Experiences using systematic review guidelines. *Journal of Systems and Software, 80*(9), 1425–1437.

Tremblay, D. G., & Yagoubi, A. (2017a). Business model and wearables: What convergence and collaboration in the area of connected objects and clothing? *Journal of Human Resource and Sustainability Studies, 5*(1), 101–124.

Tremblay, D. G., & Yagoubi, A. (2017b). "From open innovation to crowd sourcing: A new configuration of collaborative work?" in *American Journal of Industrial and Business Management, 7*(3). http://file.scirp.org/pdf/AJIBM_2017033115053775.pdf (AJIBM).

Trott, P., & Hartmann, D. (2009). Why 'open innovation' is old wine in new bottles. *International Journal of Innovation Management, 13*(4), pp. 715–736. https://doi.org/10.1142/S1363919609002509

Van der Maren, J. M. (1987). L'Interprétation des données dans la recherche qualitative: actes du colloque. In *Actes de colloque*. Université de Montréal, Faculté des sciences de l'éducation.

Voss, E., & Rego, R. (2019). *Digitalization and public services: A labour perspective.*

Yagoubi, A., & Tremblay, D. G. (2017). L'innovation numérique et technologique dans le secteur vêtement-mode: Les politiques publiques en soutien à la création d'un écosystème d'affaires intersectoriel. *Innovations, 2*, 153–193.

Yagoubi, A., Tremblay, D.-G., & Psyché, V. (2021). *What skills are required for an AI project manager?* Development of a skills framework. Research report for the PIA-CO1 project. Montréal: Université Téluq. 80 p.

3

Digitalisation and the Process of Creating and Appropriating Value by Small Companies – the Network Approach

Aleksandra Hauke-Lopes, Milena Ratajczak-Mrozek, and Marcin Wierzeczycki

Introduction

Digitalisation inevitably changes the way companies and economies function (Lechman, 2017). However, companies cannot face the challenging external pressure posed by the ongoing digital transformation on their own and to stay competitive they need to establish and develop business relationships. These relationships—usually long-term, created with various actors, like suppliers, customers or intermediaries—enable the development of commitment and trust, and the exchange

A. Hauke-Lopes (✉) · M. Ratajczak-Mrozek · M. Wierzeczycki
Department of International Marketing, Poznań University of Economics and Business, Poznań, Poland
e-mail: aleksandra.hauke-lopes@ue.poznan.pl

M. Ratajczak-Mrozek
e-mail: milena.ratajczak-mrozek@ue.poznan.pl

M. Wierzeczycki
e-mail: marcin.wieczerzycki@ue.poznan.pl

M. Ratajczak-Mrozek and P. Marszałek (eds.), *Digitalization and Firm Performance*, https://doi.org/10.1007/978-3-030-83360-2_3

of resources. As a result, they facilitate and support the value creation. Value, viewed in terms of the financial and non-financial outcomes of cooperation, is the effect of resource interactions among different network actors (Ford et al., 2017). Thus, created value is afterwards appropriated by network actors. Value appropriation, that is, actions undertaken by actors to capture the jointly created value (Chou & Zolkiewski, 2018), allows actors to compete and face the demands posed by the external environment (Ellegaard et al., 2014). However, value appropriation may encounter tensions and problems stemming from different network positions or actors' bargaining power (Baraldi & Lind, 2017; Corsaro, 2019).

Value creation and appropriation are interrelated, and both are crucial for a company's development. However, studies on value creation and appropriation in network relationships tend to focus more on the former or fail to distinguish between the two at all (Chou & Zolkiewski, 2018; Miguel et al., 2014). Few studies focus on both sides of the equation, that is, value creation and value appropriation, in network relationships, granting them the same amount of attention (Ritala & Tidström, 2014). As a result, there are calls for further research and the integration of appropriation in value analysis (Shi et al., 2019).

The development and adaptation of new technologies, particularly ongoing digitalisation, impact value creation and value appropriation interactions—by expanding their scope, improving their efficiency and accessibility, as well as grounding them in data (Autio, 2017). We assume that this impact may be particularly important for small and medium-sized enterprises (SMEs). These companies may, on the one hand, seize the opportunities brought by digitalisation in terms of relationship development (Joensuu-Salo et al., 2018) and cost-effectiveness (Quinton et al., 2018) which also may positively influence the SMEs' performance (Eller et al., 2020). On the other hand, the impact of digitalisation may be negative, since SMEs may lack some of the resources (Bouwman et al., 2019) or managerial competencies (Lobonţiu & Lobonţiu, 2014) that are needed to properly adjust their business models to the technological changes, which creates and even bigger gap between them and larger companies. Therefore, digitalisation may impact the cooperation and relationship development of SMEs, and the value creation and value appropriation by these companies, both positively and negatively. Although a few studies have been conducted published (e.g. Heim et al., 2019; Jeansson et al., 2017; Li et al., 2009), the literature still lacks empirical research on the impact of digitalisation on value creation and value appropriation in SME relationships. To fill the existing research gap, the aim of our chapter is to identify how digitalisation impacts the value creation and appropriation processes in small companies' network relationships.

We base our analysis on the case study of a digitalised small company operating in Poland. We carry out a detailed analysis of two network relationships of the focal SME, which are assessed each time by both partners within the relationship. Thanks to this approach we gain insight into consistencies and discrepancies in the assessment of the value created and appropriated within each relationship and the impact of digitalisation. We complement the information from 14 interviews with an analysis of secondary sources, such as companies' reports. This enabled us to obtain the complete picture of digitalisation and its impact on the value in the analysed network relationships.

The chapter is structured as follows. First, we conduct a literature review on value creation and value appropriation in the network relationship. Then we present the literature concerning digitalisation and its impact on value creation and appropriation, focusing on SMEs. In the subsequent section, we analyse the focal digitalised SME and its network relationships. In the next part of the chapter, the results obtained from the case study are presented, followed by managerial recommendations and conclusions.

Value Creation and Appropriation in Network Relationships

Value is the "raison d'être of collaborative customer–supplier relationships" (Anderson, 1995, p. 348). The commonly agreed understanding of value sees it as a trade-off between the actor's benefits and the sacrifices that were made during the process or that were the outcomes of interactions (Ellegaard et al., 2014; Kähkönen et al., 2015; Yan &

Wagner, 2017). Such value is always subjective and based on the actor's evaluation. Value can be also viewed as the result of "combining and recombining resources, coordinating activities and connecting individuals within and across businesses" (Ford et al. 2017, p. 30). This perception of value indicates the importance of network relationships, that is, the repetitive, usually long-term interactions between actors (network entities), resources and activities (Håkansson & Snehota, 2017).

In order to embrace its multidimensional character, value should be analysed taking into account both financial and non-financial elements (Corsaro & Snehota, 2010; Ellegaard et al., 2014). With the aim of facilitating the empirical analysis, in the chapter we focused on four dimensions of value proposed by Biggemann and Buttle (2012): personal value (customer-retention, recommendations), financial (efficiency, market share), knowledge value (innovation, idea-creation) and strategic value (long-term planning, extended network).

We agree with Corsaro (2019, p. 99) that "value is the main anchor of management decisions" and as such is vital for network actors. That is why a growing number of studies are shifting from value as an object of exchange towards the significance of actors in value-creating processes (Corsaro, 2014). It is even postulated that "a buyer–supplier relationship is a platform for value creation, and value creation through collaboration and networking has become the new objective of relationship management" (Kähkönen et al., 2015). The value created by actors in a network relationship is then appropriated among them. Value appropriation, meaning actions undertaken by network actors in order to seize the created value (Chou & Zolkiewski, 2018), is measured as the amount of the net value (i.e. total outcomes minus total inputs) that an actor is able to capture (Wagner et al., 2010). The amount of appropriated value depends, among other things, on the actor's position in the network, as well as their bargaining power, resources and indirect relationships (Baraldi and Lind, 2017; Corsaro, 2019).

Value creation and value appropriation are two interrelated processes (Corsaro, 2014; Ellegaard et al., 2014; Wagner et al., 2010). It is stressed that "value creation is a prerequisite for value appropriation, while value appropriation is the purpose of the participation [in the collaborative relationship]" (Zhao et al., 2014:122). While value creation is the result of collaborative outcomes decreased by inputs, value appropriation shows the amount of value overtaken be a company. As a result, the greater the amount of value appropriated by one actor, the less is left for other network actors (Wagner et al., 2010). The inequality of the value appropriated by the actors within a relationship may result in feelings of inequity, tensions, misunderstandings and frustrations (Corsaro, 2014). Problems may also arise when the actor does not obtain enough monetary inflows to find it satisfactory to continue the value creation processes (Baraldi and Lind, 2017). According to the research, collaborative relationships, based on trust, satisfaction, communication, commitment and information exchange, can help create and appropriate superior value in business markets (Wagner et al., 2010).

The Impact of Digitalisation on Value Creation and Appropriation – the SME's Perspective

Digitalisation, defined as "the adoption of Internet-connected digital technologies and applications by companies" (Pagani & Pardo, 2017, p. 185), has been a major factor behind the so-called fourth industrial revolution. While there is a consensus that digital technologies redefined the way in which businesses and consumers interact and exchange value (Yadav & Pavlou, 2014), the exact nature of this change in regard to SMEs still has not been fully identified and remains a subject of discussion in the literature.

It is argued that SMEs could potentially become the benefactors of the digital transformation, thanks to the tendency of digital technologies to level the playing field, which can support intelligence gathering, cost reduction and audience extension (Quinton et al., 2018), nullifying at least some of the traditional advantages held by larger companies and allowing SMEs to better compete against them. According to some studies (Behera et al., 2015; Nguyen et al., 2015), digitalisation can indeed have a positive impact on SMEs, by allowing improved brand and image development, better customer acquisition, customer service and competitiveness. In some cases, it also allows SMEs to reach new business opportunities, build closer relationships with other entities (network actors) and enhance business processes (Joensuu-Salo et al., 2018). There is also evidence of digitalisation improving the financial performance of SMEs (Eller et al., 2020; Joensuu-Salo et al., 2018).

However, there are many challenges and barriers that make it significantly harder for SMEs to reap the rewards of digitalisation. It has been established that digitalisation challenges existing business models (Clauss et al., 2019) and can even result in the change of company's identity (Gioia et al., 2013), but SMEs are held back in that regard by having significantly less time and resources to experiment with their business models and implement new strategies in order to adapt their operations to new technologies (Bouwman et al., 2019).

Another major problem is the lack of human capital equipped with the necessary digital competencies. In some countries and sectors there simply are not enough qualified employees with the knowledge and skills required to effectively utilise digital technologies (Eller et al., 2020; Ingaldi & Ulewicz, 2020). Particularly important in the context of SMEs are the digital competencies of the company managers (who in these types of companies usually double as owners) (Lobonţiu & Lobonţiu, 2014). Such owner-managers have a tremendous impact on the adoption of digital technologies in the company (Quinton et al., 2018). Therefore, a low level of knowledge in that field displayed by the owner-manager can significantly hinder the chances of properly utilising digital technologies to the benefit of the company.

In some cases, such as in the production-focused sectors, the barrier preventing SMEs from adopting digital technologies stems from the improved efficiency itself. Some companies do not possess enough materials and/or potential customers to utilise the production capacity provided by digital technologies and modern machines, which results in digitalisation not being a viable option for them from the economic point of view (Ingaldi & Ulewicz, 2020).

The impact of digitalisation on companies is not limited to their internal activities and processes, but also concerns their capabilities for creating and appropriating value in relationships with other actors—companies or otherwise—or within entire networks of said relationships. It can be said that digital technologies transform the value-creation logic (Joensuu-Salo et al., 2018). They "boost the value co-creating ability of those interactions by enhancing (through easier accessibility and efficiency), extending (beyond the core exchange of goods and services) and enriching them (through greater data intensity)" (Autio, 2017, p. 4).

However, this above-mentioned impact has seen little critical elaboration in the context of SMEs. Meanwhile cooperation and network relationships could potentially help to mitigate the negative effects of the already mentioned barriers preventing SMEs from capitalising on the benefits of digitalisation. For instance, through cooperation with bigger partners, SMEs can gain resources, reach, knowledge and information and decrease the risk inherent to innovation (Ullrich et al., 2018) as well as overcome the problems with commercialisation inherent to companies of this size (Lee et al., 2010). This makes the creation of network relationships a viable approach to creating value in a digital economy.

Considering the conducted literature analysis, there is a potential for digital technologies to be harnessed by SMEs in a way that enhances their ability to both create and appropriate value in relationships with other entities. We further elaborate on this potential with our study. Our conceptual framework is based on the assumption that digitalisation impacts the value creation and appropriation processes of small and medium enterprises (Fig. 3.1). We want to investigate how value is

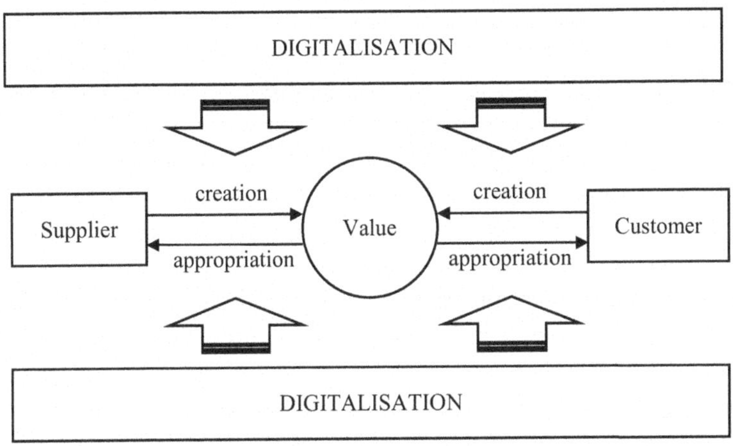

Fig. 3.1 Conceptual framework

created in the network relationships, how it is then appropriated by small companies, and what the impact of digitalisation on that process is.

Method

We adopted a case study research method (Yin, 2009) since it is recommended for analysis aimed at understanding interactions and actors' behaviours on business-to-business markets (Woodside & Wilson, 2003). The case study also allows us to gain insights into "contemporary phenomenon, which is difficult to separate from its context, but necessary to study within it to understand the dynamics involved in settings" (Halinen & Törnroos, 2005, p. 1286).

We base our analysis on the case study of a focal digitalised small company operating in Poland. This company (which we refer to as Alpha company) operates as an online platform for confectionary shops and final customers, by allowing online ordering of cakes. The focal company Alpha was chosen for the analysis as it has the characteristics of a typical digitalised SME (being an online platform provider and a small company). Our detailed analysis covers two network relationships of the focal small company Alpha. The two other companies under analysis, also being small companies, are the direct co-operators of the focal company (Alpha): company Beta is the customer, a confectionary shop that produces and delivers cakes, and the company Gamma is the supplier of IT solutions and support for company Alpha.

We conducted a longitudinal qualitative study based on a semi-structured interview form. The research was conducted between 2015 and 2020, which allowed us to obtain a comprehensive view on the network relationships and the value processes that occur during cooperation. In order to ensure the value of the findings (Salo, 2012), on each occasion we investigated both partners within the relationship, that is, the relationship between Alpha and Beta companies and the relationship between Alpha and Gamma companies. The interviews were held personally, via telephone or Skype. Altogether 14 interviews were performed, with co-owners and managers from company Alpha and different actors cooperating with the focal company Alpha. These interviews were conducted with a total of 7 companies, which allowed us to gain broader insight into the way focal company Alpha operates and how it creates and shapes its network relationships. The interviews lasted between 30 minutes to 2 hours each. Each interview was recorded (with the consent of the interviewee) and fully transcribed. The transcripts were the basis for further analysis.

In order to ensure triangulation, additional data was collected from secondary sources (Woodside & Wilson, 2003; Yin, 2009). The secondary data included industry reports about the confectionary industry and documents provided by company Alpha: financial and sales reports, reports concerning key customers and the network picture visualised by the co-owner. The secondary sources allowed us to obtain a broad picture of the network relationships of the focal company and the analysed industry.

In the study, the abductive research approach (Dubois & Gadde, 2002) was adopted. The data was further analysed through the constant comparative method (Thomas, 2011). To assure the research reliability, three investigators analysed the transcripts of the interviews independently. Also, meetings and discussions concerning the research data were organised. The empirical research was conducted until data saturation was reached.

The empirical analysis concerns Alpha's network relationship with an IT service provider (Beta) and Alpha's relationship with one of its confectioneries (Gamma) in terms of value creation and the impact of digitalisation on value creation and appropriation in these network relationships.

Results and Analysis

Company Alpha

Company Alpha is a Polish online multi-sided platform that allows final B2B and B2C consumers to order cakes via the internet and have it delivered to any location in Poland. Thus, the platform of company Alpha connects final customers with confectionary shops in Poland. In 2020, 533 confectionaries were cooperating with Alpha company, realising about 20.000 orders per year.

Alpha's cooperation with confectioneries is facilitated by a dedicated digital panel for exchanging information on orders. Order processing is highly standardised for all confectioneries—after the final customer places an order online, the confectionery that is closest to the place of the delivery receives electronic documents related to the contract (including the printed image of the cake, which is transmitted to confectioners making the cake), they are also provided with standardised packaging in the colours and logo of the company Alpha. Also, the payments between confectioneries and Alpha are made through the platform. One of the confectioneries is Gamma company, which is also analysed in the case study.

An additional service offered by Alpha to the confectioners is the possibility to create their own online store based on Alpha's technology and hosted on the confectioners' webpage. This solution enables the sale of goods for confectioneries' own account through their website. Confectioneries can freely manage their offer, prices and promotions, while Alpha receives a commission.

The technological solutions offered by Alpha company are being developed by the IT supplier—Beta, a small Polish company. Beta is an important supplier tasked with the development of the platform's technological solutions.

Alpha's co-owners perceive value as an increase in the company's financial value in terms of Discounted Cash Flow (DCF) and as a value of the technology produced. According to co-owner 1, the commercialised technology creates a value that can be translated into financial value. Also, for co-owner 2 the financial outcomes are important while assessing value. However, she added that value is primarily assessed as an element of the service that allows Alpha company to stand out from the competition in terms of offering something new and surprising to the final customer. Another element contributing to the creation of value for Alpha, indicated by co-owner 1, is the ability to attract and retain customers. Therefore, the company is intensively developing advertising and communication channels with final B2B and B2C customers.

The number of final customers who make purchases translates into an increase in sales, and this is also perceived as a value for Alpha.

Alpha–Beta Relationship Analysis

Value Creation in the Alpha–Beta Network Relationship

Beta is an important supplier who is responsible for the development of the platform's technological solutions—as the co-owner 1 of Alpha emphasises, "on the agility level [of the IT provider] rests our ability to achieve the assumed sales objectives". The development of IT infrastructure for communication with confectioneries is extremely important for the company. As co-owner 2 of Alpha points out, it allows the company to coordinate and supervise the sales process, and to respond promptly to emerging problems.

The relationship between Alpha and Beta companies started on the initiative of Alpha company and was strongly grounded in the previous network relationship between the members of both companies. Since Beta had previously developed a similar e-commerce platform for the Alpha's owners' other business venture, the extension of this cooperation to the new endeavour seemed natural. The already existing IT solution required only slight adjustments in order to properly function within the new context of the confectionery industry. Therefore, Alpha knew that it would be much more efficient price- and time-wise to cooperate with Beta on this project as well, rather than finding a new partner, who would require precise instructions pertaining to the required functions and characteristics of the system that Alpha needed.

Both companies in the relationship put emphasis on the fact that the relationship is characterised by some amount of informality, resulting from how long-lasting the cooperation has proved to be (having been established around ten years ago). Along with Beta's knowledge of all the particularities of the industry that Alpha operates in (including both the e-commerce and confectionary sectors), this streamlines the communication between both companies to a large extent. In particular, Alpha's co-owner 2 claims that "our meetings can sometimes be downright comical, since we barely exchange some monosyllables, and it is all it takes for us to understand each other perfectly. At the beginning of the cooperation, the same meeting would have had to last eight hours rather than the mere half an hour that is sufficient at this stage".

Both companies utilise an array of different communication methods. They mostly rely on e-mail, phone and face-to-face meetings. On average the representatives meet (personally) once a week, but both informants stressed that the exact amount of contact varies, depending on the number of projects currently being developed by both companies. During some months (usually July and August), when no new solutions are being introduced, the communication tends to slow down. A factor that leads to more frequent communication is problem solving—if there are bugs or errors in the code, communication usually intensifies. That is also a situation which usually requires face-to-face meetings. At the same time, Beta's informant owner/manager also claimed that the overall communication during the COVID-19 pandemic has been less intense than usual.

Both companies consider each other as important partners. From Beta's perspective, Alpha constitutes 10–30% of their total operations (with 10% covering the maintenance work alone). For Alpha itself, Beta is the main IT service provider (with the only other one being a SEO agency). Both sides are quite unanimous in their assessments of their own and the partner's dependency on the other company. They believe that the hypothetical ending of their network relationship would create issues for both sides. For Alpha, according to both companies, it would take a lot of time to establish a relationship with a new IT services provider and familiarise this new partner with the particular challenges of the market niche occupied by Alpha. For Beta, according to informants from both companies, a significant revenue source would be lost. As a Beta representative puts it, Alpha "is one of our biggest customers, which allows us to develop. They also provide us with some form of safety".

To sum up, both companies appropriate significant amounts of financial value from their mutual relationship. On the one hand, it serves as a direct source of revenue for Beta, for which Alpha is a major buyer. On the other hand, Alpha's entire business model and its efficiency rely on the dedicated technological solutions provided by Beta. That being said, both companies obtain additional value from the cooperation. Beta's representative underlines that the company gained access to some new business opportunities thanks to their relationship with Alpha. According to the informant, "it happened once or twice that they recommended our services to someone and that resulted in some new projects". In other words, Beta appropriates strategic value as well.

According to Alpha's co-owner 2, the additional value stemming from cooperation with Beta is related to the knowledge of technological trends, which Beta shares with Alpha from time to time (knowledge value). Moreover, according to Beta's informant, Alpha appropriates more value in the relationship due to Beta's willingness to go an extra mile for them: "oftentimes, considering our long-lasting cooperation, we do things for them that are a result of... simply commitment". On the other hand, according to Alpha's co-owner 2, both sides appropriate the same amount of value.

Impact of Digitalisation on Value Creation and Appropriation in the Alpha–Beta Network Relationship

Considering the fact that the relationship between Alpha and Beta concerns the provision of IT services, it is difficult to separate the value created and appropriated as a result of digitalisation from that related to the core exchange between both parties. However, some effects can still be identified.

Both companies' representatives stated that digitalisation makes contacts between parties easier. As previously stated, the communication often takes place via e-mail. Additionally, as per Alpha's account, digital technologies allow the company to oversee the progress made by Beta in the process of implementing new features and solutions. This system also makes it possible to post comments containing feedback regarding the current state of the tools in development, and for Beta to respond to them, which serves as a way of organising and streamlining the communication between both companies. As Alpha's co-owner 2 claimed, Alpha is capable of "monitoring, pretty much in real time, what is getting done, in what time, and to what effect".

Another way in which digital technologies factor into the value creation process within the relationship between Alpha and Beta pertains to their particular choices in the utilisation of these technologies. All the digital systems developed by Beta for Alpha are based on Java programming language. According to Beta's informant, this is a conscious choice on the part of the company, which would rather focus on a tried and tested technology rather than chase after the latest solutions and hence risk failure: "I know that some people use it and then get swept away, because it turns out that it isn't as effective as it was supposed to be. Instead, we focus on Java and try to improve in that field".

While the particular type of technology utilised within the relationship remains constant, as per Alpha's strategy, what changes as well with continuous digitalisation are the consumer needs and expectations. This leads to the necessity of being up to date with regard to the changing trends in fields such as user experience (UX). At the same time, according to Beta's informant, changes in such trends are usually accompanied by new tools being available within utilised technological ecosystem, which in turn creates new opportunities for dealing with customers.

An Analysis of the Alpha-Gamma Relationship

Value Creation in the Alpha-Gamma Network Relationship

The confectionery Gamma is an important customer for Alpha—it places in the top five partners that provide the highest turnover for Alpha. Initially, Gamma operated in a traditional way—it was selling confectionery in its own shop located in the city centre. Due to the parking problems, confectionery owners decided to create their own so-called Cake Post—via Gamma's own online shop, available on their webpage, customers were able to order confectionary goods, which were afterwards supplied to local customers. Shortly afterwards, in 2016, Gamma started cooperation with Alpha. The cooperation proposal came directly from Alpha, which was looking for a confectionery to carry out orders in this part of Poland. Gamma confectionery had a recognised position among customers and focused on the production of artistic cakes, which require a lot of time to be made (3–4 days). Alpha, in turn, required Gamma to make primarily cream cakes. Initially, the cooperation with Alpha was occasional, especially since Alpha was not so well-known at that time. Moreover, Gamma already had their own online confectionery shop that delivered artistic cakes and in effect, had know-how on the use of digital solutions in selling their product to final customers. That is why Alpha did not have to dedicate time to teaching Gamma from scratch how to sell via the internet.

One of the arguments presented by Gamma explaining the development of the cooperation was the fact that Alpha was investing a lot in marketing activities and the acquisition of final customers. This increased the number of subsequent orders. According to the manager of the confectionery, that meant that Gamma only had to focus on "making a cake implementing this product and delivering it to the customer. All marketing has already been taken over by this company [Alpha] because that is their job, that is what they get their money from".

As co-owner 1 from Alfa said, "in our cooperation it was a big challenge to reduce the lead time for our orders only to 24 hours". At the beginning there were misunderstandings due to this restriction, however, after a few months, Gamma met the time requirements. At the beginning of the cooperation, Gamma produced cream cakes only for the Alpha platform, which amounted to only several orders of this type per month. In 2020 it was already several hundred per month. Another problem in the initial cooperation and development of this network relationship, apart from the time needed for the production, was the delivery of the ordered goods. With the increased number of orders, Gamma was not able to carry them out in a timely manner. Therefore, representatives of Alpha connected Gamma with a courier company that supported the confectionery in these processes.

Alpha's manager appreciates that Gamma never refused to implement any orders. Alpha manager also places value on the fact that replies from the confectionery come almost immediately after sending a message. Telephone contact is only limited to emergencies. The relationship is formal, open, focused on cooperation and its development. Both companies admit that they value their cooperation even though they did not meet in person. The well-developing cooperation also means less contact between employees at both companies (Alpha and Gamma). As Gamma's manager adds: "the less time wasted on each order, the more time I have left. That is why it is important that the more efficiently everything is refined, without any problems, the more successful this cooperation is". Alpha appreciates Gamma's confectionery for its great excellence in making cakes and professional approach to cooperation.

Taking into consideration the opinions presented above, it is interesting that the cooperation with Alpha company is perceived by Gamma's manager as cooperation with a competitor, rather than with a supplier of services or an intermediary. That being said, in the opinion of Gamma's manager, cooperation with Alpha is profitable for both parties—the manager was unable to indicate who gains more from this cooperation, since these gains change over time. Rather, the informant sees both companies growing in parallel. Having a relationship with Alpha helped Gamma a lot in the early stages of their cooperation, when Gamma was short of orders. However, after a few years, the loss of Alpha would not cause major financial problems for Gamma confectionery. Thanks to the relationship with Alpha, Gamma confectionery can maintain employment and the fluidity of production. In turn manager 1 from Alpha believes that Gamma confectionery gains greater value from cooperation, because thanks to the purchases via Alpha's platform Gamma receives more orders. Alpha's co-owner 1 adds that due to the large number of orders to Gamma from Alpha's platform, the latter company may impose conditions on cooperation.

According to Alpha's co-owner 1, if the cooperation and network relationship were terminated, it would be possible to find another confectionery fulfilling the orders, but this would entail greater costs. As Alpha's co-owner 1 claims, for Gamma, ending cooperation with Alpha would result in a decrease in turnover, as Alpha believes they are an important partner for Gamma. However, according to Gamma, the turnover generated by the sales through the Alpha platform represents only a small amount of the total online sales of this confectionery (the majority is achieved mainly through Gamma's own online shop). In addition, Gamma is also working with three other online cake distributors that are Alpha's rival.

A point of contention in the cooperation between companies is the consideration of complaints, as they induce costs. Alpha co-owners admit that they are trying to be fair and determine who made a mistake during the processing of the order. If it is due to technical reasons, Alfa is to blame, but if the fault clearly results from the actions of the confectionery, the confectionery bears the costs.

Cooperation with Alpha, according to the Gamma manager, contributes to better recognition of the confectionery in their city—the cakes are delivered by a vehicle with a Gamma confectionery logo. The company sees this as a benefit—potential customers see the logo of the confectionery.

An important benefit achieved by both companies is the exchange of information. Alpha shares information on, for example, recipes or tax solutions with the Gamma confectionery. In turn, Gamma exchanges ideas for new assortments, the price level of the products offered on the platform, the predicted number of orders or delivery options particularly at times of increased interest in the delivery of cakes (such as Mother's Day). The Gamma confectionery also shares its observations on market trends.

The Impact of Digitalisation on Value Creation and Appropriation in the Alpha-Gamma Relationship

Digitalisation impacts value creation and value appropriation processes within the network relationship, and the use of digitalisation solutions, such as the digital platform, impacts the companies' outcomes. The development of the network relationship with Alpha, and taking orders through Alpha's digital platform, allowed the Gamma confectionery to increase its orders from the Alpha platform year by year. The confectionery notes that customers are getting more comfortable with looking for information and products on the internet. The growth of orders from the platform is also influenced by the development of online payments and convincing customers to pay with credit cards. According to the confectionery manager, ordering cakes online saves valuable time for customers. The confectionery saves time as well, because it does not have to ask the customer about the order details, especially now, when there is so much choice in terms of cakes offered. As the Gamma manager adds, the confectionery previously focused on local customers and word of mouth marketing (which accounted for 90% of all orders), but it has now been replaced by new technologies (social media, positioned websites or advertisements), which in 2020 accounted for the vast majority of all orders. In particular, this increase was visible during the start of the COVID-19 pandemic in spring 2020, when Gamma's orders through the Alpha platform soared from 10 to 40% of total orders. It was a godsend for the confectionery which had been carrying out a large part of orders for B2B customers and tourists. Thanks to many orders from Alpha platform, the confectionery was able to work with the entire crew during the formal countrywide lockdown, in March and April 2020.

Despite the growing importance of new technologies in sales and communication with final customers, Gamma's manager still believes in word-of-mouth marketing and customers recommending their products. He underlines that for this confectionery, profit is not the most important thing, as they want to create a company that, apart from profits, gives the employees satisfaction and the belief that their activity has some greater meaning. Gamma's manager believes that the danger of dealing solely by means of technology is the loss of personal contact with customers.

Thanks to the adopted digital solutions, the technology streamlines and automates Gamma's order fulfilment process, which was initially manual. As Alpha's co-owner 1 stresses, Alpha showed what the order fulfilment process via their platform could look like, which was associated with interference in the internal processes of the Gamma confectionery. According to the Gamma manager, the use of technology allows them to observe changes taking place on the market and foresee how these changes may impact the activities of the confectionery. Moreover, technology facilitates the management of the order fulfilment process, including its automatisation. As for the Alpha manager, the most important benefits of digitalisation of the cooperation were identified as: time-saving due to electronic order processing and facilitated communication.

The Gamma confectionary also has its own online shop that is operated independently from Alpha. This is important, as the Gamma manager believes that Alpha, being a nationwide brand, positions itself on social media and the internet more intensively. As a result, the confectionery shop loses potential customers who could order products in Gamma's own online shop. The confectionery does not want to use the e-confectionery solution (the online shop offered by Alpha). As Gamma's manager claims "I would rather promote my own website than Alpha", which is why Gamma is constantly developing its own, independent online store. In turn, a manager 1 from Alpha believes that the specificity of artistic cakes, which constitute the dominant area of Gamma's activity, may be a problem for Gamma in selling through the online store—these cakes are very individual and difficult to standardise, which makes it impossible to take full advantage of digitalised solutions.

Results and Managerial Implications

To answer the question of how the value is created in the network relationships and afterwards appropriated by small companies, we have analysed various small business entities in the supply chain—a focal company, its supplier (an IT solutions provider) and its customer (a confectionery). Thanks to this analysis, we were able to identify specific dimensions of value created and appropriated in network relationships characteristic for small companies.

The value indicated by all the companies and created in each relationship is the financial value (according to the four dimensions of value defined by Biggeman and Buttle (2012)). It manifests itself in the increased number of orders from the final customers and the better financial results achieved by all the actors involved. It does not come as a surprise, since the direct goal of the relationships established between the network actors was to run their businesses and generate profit.

The financial value also includes an aspect especially characteristic for small companies, namely development. All the analysed companies indicated that network relationships allowed them to develop in the past and that they foresee further possible development. In terms of the relationship with the supplier, the companies' representatives expect joint development, since if the focal company reaches new markets, this means the simultaneous development of the supplier. Gaining access to some new business opportunities or simply company's development was underlined by all the companies' representatives. It seems that, because of their size, small companies need to develop, and if this is the case then they especially value the development gained thanks to network relationships.

Another dimension of value created in the analysed network relationships is knowledge value, and this is particularly important for small companies. This is a value underlined by the focal company's representative and is gained by the online platform provider from both relationships (i.e. the network relationship with a customer—a confectionery—and with a supplier). This dimension of value was also indicated by the confectionery (a customer), but not the supplier (the IT company). Through network relationships, the focal company gains knowledge of technological and market trends, accepted price levels and the forecasted number of orders. The confectionery gains information on tax solutions and new recipes which may translate into product development. Small companies, having limited resources, cannot always afford to obtain such insightful and detailed information, which can be expensive. Hence, this type of value is particularly important for these companies.

When we look at the four dimensions of value proposed by Biggemann and Buttle (2012), that is, financial, knowledge, personal and strategic value, within our analysis we are also able to identify the creation of personal value, identified as customer-retention, recommendations and better recognition of the confectionery in their city. However, this was only underlined by confectionery that is directly serving final customers. And although we were not able to identify the creation of strategic value within analysed network relationships, the respondents emphasised the benefits which could all be named as operational value. Named by us operational value includes saving time, the reliability of business partners, willingness to solve problems and implement orders quickly, maintaining the fluidity of production. We can conclude that these benefits ultimately translate into financial results. However, their clear emphasis by all companies' representatives, and the indication of these benefits in the interviews regardless of the financial results, suggests the separation of operational value as an additional dimension of value. Operational value is also especially important for small companies, for whom, due to limited resources, even minor day-to-day problems may eventually translate into large-scale issues.

When analysing value by taking the network approach, we see that although two companies—Beta, the supplier and Gama, the confectionery do not directly cooperate together, they and their created value are indirectly linked. The focal company offers a platform solution because of the services and knowledge gained from the IT supplier. This in turn is the basis for the cooperation with the confectionery and the resulting financial, knowledge, personal and operational value.

The continuation of network relationships is affected not only by the value creation, but foremost by the "fair" appropriation of this value by different network actors (Baraldi & Lind, 2017). However, defining the right amount of value to be appropriated by each actor of the relationship in order to maintain the equilibrium and satisfaction is difficult (Corsaro, 2019). Our research shows that there is no one ready-made solution in this regard, especially since our analysis showed that not only is the assessment of created value subjective and based on the actor's evaluation, but so is the assessment of value appropriation. In the case of both network relationships, the companies' representatives disagreed as to who (they or the partner) "gains more", and usually indicated the other side of the relationship as the one that benefits more in terms of appropriated value. This results from them perceiving more clearly their own commitment and contribution to the relationship.

Despite the differences in the perception of appropriated value, there is an agreement between all companies' representatives in their willingness to continue or even strengthen the relationships. The reason for this, in our view, is the occurrence of only minor operational problems and tensions during the value appropriation process. The way these problems were approached is determined by the managerial recommendations regarding the approach towards network relationships and the value appropriated from them. In this regard, our research confirms the importance of communication and information exchange, which helps to create and appropriate superior value in network relationships

(Wagner et al., 2010). First and foremost, this concerns the importance of smooth communication and a similar approach to efficient everyday cooperation (quick response, commitment, no time wasting). The role of communication is even greater since the personal component also contributes to creating the value of the business relationship (Glińska-Neweś et al., 2018). It is also important to have an approach to problem solving that is as fair as possible, in the form of not burdening only one side of the relationship with costs. These results are in line with the research on the handling of conflict in relationships which stresses the importance of considering the costs involved for the positive conflict handling (Ratajczak-Mrozek et al., 2019).

Considering the fact that the network relationships between the analysed companies involve the provision of an online platform solution, it is difficult to separate the value created and appropriated as a result of digitalisation from the value related to the core exchange between the companies. It can be said that digitalisation is becoming so common and irreplaceable that it is difficult to treat its effects only in relation to the effects of the general activity of enterprises.

However, some specific effects of value creation and appropriation associated with digitalisation processes in small companies' network relationships can still be identified. Digitalisation particularly impacts the creation of operational value. The application of new technologies facilitates the automatisation of different processes, saves time and simplifies the management of the order fulfilment process. By providing communication infrastructure, digital technologies (like social media platforms and positioned websites) are an important source of personal value, enabling consumer retention and recommendations in the form of word-of mouth marketing. However, this dimension of value is only acknowledged by the companies that directly serve final customers (in our case the confectionary). One should also not forget about a possible negative aspect of this form of communication with consumers, as indicated by one of the respondents, namely the lack of personal contact and a personal touch in communication.

We must emphasise that our research shows that network relationships make it possible to overcome the barriers faced by small companies, in the form of a lack of resources to experiment with business models and implement new strategies in order to adopt operations to new technologies (Bouwman et al., 2019). Cooperation with a company that has very well-developed necessary digital competencies (in our case the focal company, the online platform provider) enables a small company to take advantage of the development and improvement of these competencies in a short and accessible way. This, in turn, significantly affects the process of value appropriation. Another way digitalisation influences value appropriation processes in network relationships is through its effect on communication (via online communicators and applications, e-mails). Digitalisation supports intelligence gathering (Quinton et al., 2018) and makes contacts between parties easier.

Beyond the scope of our analysis were the relationships and value created or co-created by final customers (i.e. individual people and organisations buying confectionery products). Meanwhile these are the changes of behaviour of final customers that have a key impact on the creation of value of all the analysed companies, regardless of their position in the supply chain. What changes with the continuous digitalisation are consumer needs and expectations, including searching for information and products on the internet and the popularity of online payments. These changes of customers' behaviour lead to the necessity of being up to date with regard to the changing trends in fields such as user experience. Digitalisation also provides small companies with a technological framework for product customisation, allowing them to immerse their consumers in a vast array of value co-creation experiences (Prahalad & Ramaswamy, 2004) and the creation of consumer communities that can be easily and cheaply appropriated (Cova & Dalli, 2009).

Conclusions

Digitalisation is becoming an immanent feature of companies' environment, regardless of their size or willingness to adopt new technologies. The analysis of our case study showed mainly a positive impact of digitalisation on relationships of small companies. Despite some drawbacks stemming from digital technologies, the analysed companies were able to create value. As the result of long-lasting network relationships and the adopted approach to these relationships, the amount of value appropriated by each side of the relationship was fair enough to continue the cooperation and the ongoing processes of new value creation and appropriation.

Our analysis sets the direction of further research. First, regardless of the companies' size, in-depth analysis of the indicated dependencies and elements impacting the amount of appropriated value is needed. Second, the analysis of value creation and appropriation requires taking broad wide network picture, and such research should take into consideration the impact of final customers on the indicated processes taking place in network relationships.

Acknowledgements The study has been financed within the Regional Initiative for Excellence programme of the Minister of Science and Higher Education of Poland, years 2019–2022, grant no. 004/RID/2018/19, financing 3,000,000 PLN.

References

Anderson, J. C. (1995). Relationships in business markets: Exchange episodes, value creation, and their empirical assessment. *Journal of the Academy of Marketing Science, 23*(4), 346–350.

Autio, E. (2017). Digitalisation, ecosystems, entrepreneurship and policy. *Perspectives into topical issues is society and ways to support political decision making. government's analysis, research and assessment activities policy brief*, 20/2017 (December):1–12.

Baraldi, E., & Lind, J. (2017). Value measuring and value appropriation in business networks. *No Business Is an Island* 47–66.

Behera, A., Nayak, N., & Das, H. (2015). Performance measurement due to IT adoption. *Business Process Management Journal, 21*(4), 888–907.

Biggemann, S., & Buttle, F. (2012). Intrinsic value of business-to-business relationships: An empirical taxonomy. *Journal of Business Research, 65*(8), 1132–1138.

Bouwman, H., Nikou, S., & Reuver, Mark de. (2019). Digitalization, business models, and SMEs: How do business model innovation practices improve performance of digitalizing SMEs? *Telecommunications Policy 43*(9), 101828.

Chou, H.-H., & Zolkiewski, J. (2018). Coopetition and value creation and appropriation: The role of interdependencies, tensions and harmony. *Industrial Marketing Management, 70*, 25–33.

Clauss, T., Bouncken, R. B., Laudien, S., & Kraus, S. (2019). Business model reconfiguration and innovation in Smes: A mixed-method analysis from the electronics industry. *International Journal of Innovation Management, 24*(02), 2050015.

Corsaro, D. (2014). The emergent role of value representation in managing business relationships. *Industrial Marketing Management, 43*(6), 985–995.

Corsaro, D. (2019). Capturing the broader picture of value co-creation management. *European Management Journal, 37*(1), 99–116.

Corsaro, D., & Snehota, I. (2010). Searching for relationship value in business markets: Are we missing something? *Industrial Marketing Management, 39*(6), 986–995.

Cova, B., & Dalli, D. (2009). Working consumers: The next step in marketing theory? *Marketing Theory, 9*, 315–339.

Dubois, A., & Gadde, L.-E. (2002). Systematic combining: An abductive approach to case research. *Journal of Business Reserach, 55*, 553–560.

Ellegaard, C., Medlin, C. J., & Geersbro, J. (2014). Value appropriation in business exchange—Literature review and future research opportunities. *Journal of Business and Industrial Marketing, 29*(3), 185–198.

Eller, R., Alford, P., Kallmünzer, A., & Peters, M. (2020). Antecedents, consequences, and challenges of small and medium-sized enterprise digitalization. *Journal of Business Research, 112*(2020), 119–127.

Ford, D., Mattsson, L.-G., & Snehota, I. (2017). Management in the interactive business world. In *No business is an Island* (pp. 27–45). Emerald Publishing Limited.

Gioia, D. A., Patvardhan, S. D., Hamilton, A. L., & Corley, K. G. (2013). Organizational identity formation and change. *Academy of Management Annals, 7*(1), 123–193.

Glińska-Neweś, A., Escher, I., Brzustewicz, P., Szostek, D., & Petrykowska, J. (2018). Relationship-focused or deal-focused? building interpersonal bonds within B2B relationships. *Baltic Journal of Management, 12*(4), 508–527.

Håkansson, H., & Snehota, I. (Eds.). (2017). *No business is an Island: Making sense of the interactive business world*. Emerald Publishing.

Halinen, A., & Törnroos, J. Å. (2005). Using case methods in the study of contemporary business networks. *Journal of Business Research, 58*(9 SPEC. ISS.), 1285–1297.

Heim, I., Kalyuzhnova, Y., Li, W., & Liu, K. (2019). Value co-creation between foreign firms and indigenous Small- and Medium-Sized Enterprises (SMEs) in Kazakhstan's oil and gas industry: The role of information technology spillovers. *Thunderbird International Business Review, 61*(6), 911–927.

Ingaldi, M., & Ulewicz, R. (2020). Problems with the implementation of industry 4.0 in enterprises from the SME sector. *Sustainability (Switzerland), 12*(1).

Jeansson, J., Nikou, S., Lundqvist, S., Marcusson, L., Sell, A., & Walden, P. (2017). SMEs' Online channel expansion: Value creating activities. *Electronic Markets, 27*(1), 49–66.

Joensuu-Salo, S., Sorama, K., Viljamaa, A., & Varamäki, E. (2018). Firm performance among internationalized SMEs: The interplay of market orientation, marketing capability and digitalization. *Administrative Sciences, 8*(3), 31.

Kähkönen, A.-K., Lintukangas, K., & Hallikas, J. (2015). Buyer's dependence in value creating supplier relationship. *Supply Chain Management, 20*(2), 151–162.

Lechman, E. (2017). *The diffusion of information and communication technologies*. Routledge.

Lee, S., Park, G., Yoon, B., & Park, J. (2010). Open innovation in SMEs—An intermediated network model. *Research Policy, 39*(2), 290–300.

Li, J., Merenda, M., & Venkatachalam, A. R. (2009). Business process digitalization and new product development. *International Journal of E-Business Research, 5*(1), 49–64.

Loborıţiu, G., & Loborıţiu, M. (2014). The owner-manager and the functional management of a small firm. *Procedia—Social and Behavioral Sciences, 124*, 552–561.

Miguel, P. L. S. S., Brito, L. A. L. L., Fernandes, A. R., Abio, F., Tescari, V. C. S., Martins, G. S., Tescari, F. V. C. S., & Martins, G. S. (2014). Relational value creation and appropriation in buyer-supplier relationships. *International Journal of Physical Distribution and Logistics Management, 44*(7), 559–576.

Nguyen, T. H., Newby, M., & Macaulay, M. J. (2015). Information technology adoption in small business: Confirmation of a proposed framework. *Journal of Small Business Management, 53*(1), 207–227.

Pagani, M., & Pardo, C. (2017). The impact of digital technology on relationships in a business network. *Industrial Marketing Management, 67*, 185–192.

Prahalad, C. K., & Ramaswamy, V. (2004). Co-creation experiences: The next practice in value creation. *Journal of Interactive Marketing, 18*(3), 5–14.

Quinton, S., Canhoto, A., Molinillo, S., Pera, R., & Budhathoki, T. (2018). Conceptualising a digital orientation: Antecedents of supporting SME performance in the digital economy. *Journal of Strategic Marketing, 26*(5), 427–439.

Ratajczak-Mrozek, Milena, Fonfara, K., & Hauke-Lopes, A. (2019). Conflict handling in small firms' foreign business relationships. *Journal of Business and Industrial Marketing, 34*(1), 240–252.

Ritala, P., & Tidström, A. (2014). Untangling the value-creation and value-appropriation elements of coopetition strategy: A longitudinal analysis on the firm and relational levels. *Scandinavian Journal of Management, 30*(4), 498–515.

Salo, J. (2012). The role of mobile technology in a buyer-supplier relationship: A case study from the steel industry. *Journal of Business & Industrial Marketing, 27*(7), 554–563.

Shi, X., Zhang, Q., & Zheng, Z. (2019). The double-edged sword of external search in collaboration networks: Embeddedness in knowledge networks as moderators. *Journal of Knowledge Management, 23*(10), 2135–2160.

Thomas, G. (2011). *How to do your case study. A guide for students & researchers*. Sage.

Ullrich, A., Vladova, G., Grum, M., & Marquart, D. (2018). Does size matter? The effects of enterprise size on the perception of benefits and risks of open innovation projects. *Journal of Innovation Management, 6*(2), 71–101.

Wagner, S. M., Eggert, A., & Lindemann, E. (2010). Creating and appropriating value in collaborative relationships. *Journal of Business Research, 63*(8), 840–848.

Woodside, A. G., & Wilson, E. J. (2003). Case study research methods for theory building. *Journal of Business and Industrial Marketing, 18*(6–7), 493–508.

Yadav, M. S., & Pavlou, P. A. (2014). Marketing in computer-mediated environments: Research synthesis and new directions. *Journal of Marketing, 78*(1), 20–40.

Yan, T., & Wagner, S. M. (2017). Do what and with Whom? value creation and appropriation in inter-organizational new product development projects tingting. *International Journal of Production Economics, 191*, 1–14.

Yin, R. K. (2009). *Case study research: Design and methods* (4th ed.). Sage.
Zhao, S., Haiqing, Y., Yancheng, X., & Bi, Z. (2014). Relationship-specific investment, value creation, and value appropriation in cooperative innovation. *Information Technology and Management, 15*(2), 119–130.

4

Digital-Driven Business Model Innovation: The Role of Data in Changing Companies' Value Logic

Chiara Ancillai, Luca Marinelli, and Federica Pascucci

Introduction

The increasing complexity of the business context means that business models (BMs) age faster than ever before. Hence, finding new ways of creating, delivering, and capturing value becomes of the utmost importance in maintaining a firm's competitiveness, alongside product and processes innovations (Müller, 2019; Sorescu, 2017). Therefore, academics and practitioners alike have been devoting increasing attention to companies' business model innovation (BMI) (Zott et al., 2011).

C. Ancillai · L. Marinelli · F. Pascucci (✉)
Department of Management, Università Politecnica Delle Marche, Ancona, Italy
e-mail: f.pascucci@univpm.it

C. Ancillai
e-mail: c.ancillai@univpm.it

L. Marinelli
e-mail: l.marinelli@univpm.it

M. Ratajczak-Mrozek and P. Marszałek (eds.), *Digitalization and Firm Performance*,
https://doi.org/10.1007/978-3-030-83360-2_4

The literature on business model innovation has long emphasized the pivotal role of technological change in triggering the discovery or the emergence of new business models (BMs) that can potentially alter companies' value creation and value capture mechanisms (Khanagha et al., 2014; Zott & Amit, 2013). Yet, the research has witnessed an increased interest due to the rise of new digital technologies (DTs), such as cyber-physical systems (CPS), additive manufacturing, augmented reality, virtual reality, robotics, remote monitoring, artificial intelligence, big data, cloud, and smart connected products, which are likely to offer many opportunities for business model innovation in different industries (e.g. Chasin et al., 2020; Kiel et al., 2017; Müller et al., 2018; Sestino et al., 2020). Notably, the growing spread of digital technologies does not only concern companies in the most innovative sectors, but also affects more traditional industries. When it comes to implementing digital technologies most traditional companies are "thrown into panic", as they believe that digital technologies and business models pose an existential threat to their way of doing business (McGrath & McManus, 2020). If manufacturing firms do not seize opportunities in digitalization and do not transform themselves to embrace the opportunities offered by new digital technologies, they might suffer due to competition from innovative firms able to solve customer problems in more creative and effective ways (Björkdahl, 2020).

This has entailed that DT-driven business model innovation has become the chief focus of manufacturing companies (e.g. automotive, electrical engineering, medical engineering industries), mostly due to the Industry 4.0 megatrend (e.g. Kiel et al., 2017; Müller et al., 2018; Paiola & Gebauer, 2020). Hence, the existing empirical evidence is mostly focused on companies' implementation of the Industrial Internet of Things (IIoT) in the manufacturing process and its consequences in terms of BMI, while less is known about how data-driven business model innovation unfolds in other industries. This is quite surprising as a positive relationship exists between big data analytics capabilities and business model innovation in different sectors (Alshawaaf & Lee, 2021; Ciampi et al., 2021). Furthermore, digitalization has the potential to affect many other functions beyond the manufacturing process (Björkdahl, 2020) and previous studies have argued that the degree of influence of digital technologies on BM components might depend greatly on the company's industry (see Arnold et al., 2016; Rachinger et al., 2019).

Therefore, this study aims at filling this gap by providing a thorough understanding of the opportunities and challenges entailed in digital-driven BMI of a product/service firm. Hence, we extend the current debate over the pervasive impact of digital technologies—especially big data—as supportive enablers of change and innovation in existing organizations. By doing so, this book chapter answers previous calls for further research to be conducted on data-driven business model innovation (e.g. Sorescu, 2017; Urbinati et al., 2019).

Business Model Innovation: A Challenging Path for Firms' Competitive Advantage

A substantial number of studies have addressed the business model concept, as the topic has drawn an increasing research interest across multiple disciplines and research fields, such as entrepreneurship, strategy, and innovation management (Foss & Saebi, 2017; Osterwalder et al., 2005; Schneider & Spieth, 2013). This has led to a general lack of conceptual clarity around the business model concept, with studies developing largely in silos (Foss & Saebi, 2017; Zott et al., 2011). Notwithstanding, a commonly agreed-upon definition is still lacking, the multitude of BM definitions seems to be centred on the notion of value and increasingly converge towards its conceptualization as the sum of at least three complementary elements, namely value proposition, value creation and value capture (e.g. Casadesus-Masanell & Ricart, 2010; Chesbrough & Rosenbloom, 2002; Teece, 2010; Zott et al., 2011). Value proposition primarily relates to the bundle of products and services a firm offers. Value creation refers to the operational activities, resources and competences needed to craft the value proposition; the segments of customers a company addresses, as well as the relationships and interactions with them; and the network of partners involved in the company's business model. Finally, the value capture component relates to the cost structure and the revenue model describing the way a company makes money through a variety of revenue flows.

The business model offers a holistic and systemic perspective of how companies "do business" (Osterwalder et al., 2005) by representing not only what business do (e.g. what products and services they produce to serve customers) but also on how they do it (Zott et al., 2011). The business model describes a conceptual model for explaining the corporate strategy, able to connect it to daily activities and processes, thus bridging the gap between strategy formulation and implementation (Richardson, 2008). However, the BM construct was initially employed to understand and classify the value drivers of (e-commerce) BMs and as an antecedent of heterogeneity in firm performance (see Foss & Saebi, 2017; Zott et al., 2011); more recently the literature has devoted attention to the business model as a potential unit of innovation (Zott et al., 2011). Hence, BMI is an extension of the BM, and as such its literature mirrors the lack of conceptual clarity characterizing business model research (Casadesus-Masanell & Zhu, 2013; Schneider & Spieth, 2013). At root, business model innovation might be defined as "the search for new logics of the firm and new ways to create and capture value for its stakeholders" (Casadesus-Masanell & Zhu, 2013, p. 464; see also Teece, 2010). Yet, although optimizing internal processes or merely implementing new technologies and activities in an organization do not represent BMI (Bouwman et al., 2018), the literature seems to agree that business model innovation does not manifest solely in a radically reconfigured BM (e.g. Li, 2020; Sorescu, 2017). Firms might innovate their BM when they take ideas from one domain and adapt them for another domain, as long as the innovation affects the core business logic of the firm and its value creation, value delivery and value capture mechanisms (Sorescu, 2017). This perspective adopts a transformational approach towards BM, emphasizing how managers can change firms' activities and value logics (e.g. Demil & Lecocq, 2010; Johnson et al., 2008). BMI is said to be a necessary response to "strategic discontinuities and disruptions, convergence and intense global competition" (Doz & Kosonen, 2010, p. 370) and a key to firm performance (Zott et al., 2011). Firms can effectively compete through their business models (Casadesus-Masanell & Ricart, 2010).

Yet, the process of BMI might be hindered by internal and external barriers. Existing configurations of assets and processes, which may be subject to inertia, as well as the cognitive inability of managers to understand the value potential of a new BM are important impeding factors (Chesbrough, 2010). As a matter of fact, BMI is a strategic decision-making process and managers might be influenced by perceived threats, perceived performance shortfall, and the lack of perceived opportunity (Osiyevskyy & Dewald, 2015). Interestingly, scholars have also investigated organizational configuration to deal with business model innovation by suggesting two contrasting approaches: separation or integration between the existing BM and the new BM (Kim & Min, 2015). Some studies recommend an organizational spin-off (i.e. separation) so that the dedicated organizational unit is focused on managing the innovation (e.g. Chesbrough, 2010; Chesbrough & Rosenbloom, 2002). In contrast, companies may decide to run multiple BMs concurrently (i.e. integration or business model portfolio) as running multiple business models at the same time enables the exploitation of synergies between them (e.g. Li, 2020). Moreover, Khanagha et al. (2014) show that organization might iterate between structural separation and the integration of new BMs to leverage the potential of experimenting with the new BM.

Digital-Driven Business Model Innovation: The Value of Data

It has been extensively argued that digital technologies drive or enable companies' business model innovation (see Khanagha et al., 2014; Zott & Amit, 2013). As a matter of fact, business models are fundamentally linked with technological innovation (Baden-Fuller & Haefliger, 2013). Some studies describe BMI as an attempt to seize new opportunities introduced by the advent of, for example, specific digital technologies (Foss & Saebi, 2017). For instance, researchers have focused on the influence of information and communications technologies on the emergence of new BMs in the context of e-commerce (e.g. Sabatier et al., 2012; Wirtz et al., 2010).

Notably, in recent years, the growing academic interest in how the 4th Industrial Revolution is taking place within companies has led to a steady annual increase in publications addressing the role of digital technologies in firms' BMI (e.g. Arnold et al., 2016; Frank et al., 2019; Kiel et al., 2017; Müller et al., 2018). In fact, the rapid spread of digital technologies has led to the introduction of new business models that have radically changed entire industries. Many traditional firms have been suffered due to the fast growth of innovative digital entrants, such as Alibaba and Amazon, which have profoundly challenged incumbents (Verhoef et al., 2021). Scholars have highlighted that digital technologies have the potential to affect each BM component, thus showing that implementing DTs within companies is effectively changing how companies "do business", as changes in value proposition, value creation and value capture mechanisms are strongly interdependent (Burström et al., 2021; Kiel et al., 2017; Ritter & Pedersen, 2020). For instance, digital technologies are playing a major role in driving service-led growth strategies of product firms which have shifted from manufacturing and selling products to innovating, selling, and delivering services (i.e. digital servitization) (e.g. Björkdahl, 2020; Frank et al., 2019; Kohtamäki et al., 2019; Paiola & Gebauer, 2020). In fact, such transformation is so deeply rooted in the product firms' value architecture that their BMs require innovation.

Indeed, the value proposition appears to be the most affected BM component (Arnold et al., 2016; Kiel et al., 2017). Companies show an improved ability in offering new and more complex products and services (Kiel et al., 2017; Müller et al., 2018; Rachinger et al., 2019; Urbinati et al., 2019). Hence, digital technologies are embedded not only in factories, but also in the products themselves. Manufacturing companies are increasingly integrating DTs in established products to make them more "intelligent" (Björkdahl, 2020). When innovating traditional manufacturing products by making them "intelligent", firms are able to move downstream and provide new operational and complementary services. Moreover, digital technologies have the potential to make manufacturing firms' product development more efficient (Björkdahl, 2020). It is noteworthy that the digitalization of product development decreases the need for physical artefacts and prototypes, thus streamlining and easing product design. Also, testing procedures, which are an important part of a firm's product development activities, can be accomplished quickly, by allowing various outcomes to be checked. In general, the literature has widely emphasized the pivotal role of data mining and analytics in innovating companies' value propositions. As a matter of fact, DTs provide access to valuable customer data, which allows the customer to be better understood, and product quality and product customization to be enhanced (Cheah & Wang, 2017; Kiel et al., 2017; Laudien & Daxböck, 2016; Müller et al., 2018). Having new data and insights about what customers would like to buy, how they want to pay for and use their products, companies are better equipped to create value for their customers. By using customer-generated data, firms might leverage user-centred innovation and develop co-creation initiatives. This information allows firms to come up with innovative value propositions to differentiate themselves from their competitors.

Moreover, digital technologies might contribute to innovating the value creation component of the BM. In particular, the implementation of new DTs is largely associated with enhanced production efficiency and optimization, in terms of resource and energy usage, time, and equipment effectiveness. Digital technologies allow companies to collect, process, and handle relevant data for production traceability purposes, such as monitoring production status-quo, including bottlenecks and production output (Björkdahl, 2020; Kiel et al., 2017; Müller et al., 2018). In some organizations, these activities are limited to the possibility of integrating machines, thereby obtaining new data, and linking different data sources to improve decision-making processes. In addition, leading firms also perform more advanced activities. For instance, computer visualization systems employing machine learning algorithms to identify defects and flaws in the manufacturing process reduce the need to take products or materials out of the production line and check them manually (Björkdahl, 2020). In this regard, manufacturing firms often employ the "digital twins" of a given product to reflect the entire manufacturing process, thereby allowing enhancements based on the performance of the product in a live environment.

New DTs also guarantee the information transparency of shop floor processes, through systems that show the tasks performed at each machine, task duration, given commands, and eventual failures. They can increase quality, decrease variance, and minimize the number of breakdowns and stoppages by making the manufacturing process more intelligent through the use of digital technologies and more and better data (Björkdahl, 2020). Overall, this improves managers' speed, reaction capability, and flexibility in responding to malfunctions and problems.

Furthermore, entirely new skills and competencies are required among employees (Arnold et al., 2016; Müller et al., 2018; Rachinger et al., 2019; Urbinati et al., 2019). Firms need to develop or acquire new competencies, such as data analysis or human intervention in the event of machine failures. For instance, a shift might occur from traditional marketing capabilities with the focus on advertising and brand awareness to one-to-one contextual marketing to support personalized offerings driven by data analytics and machine learning.

The actual implementation of DTs also influences companies' relationships with both customers and partners (Arnlod et al., 2016; Björkdahl, 2020; Rachinger et al., 2019; Urbinati et al., 2019). Hence, digital technologies bring about changes in the existing partner network configuration. For instance, IT suppliers and development partners play an important role for companies in all manufacturing companies (Arnold et al., 2016; Kiel et al., 2017). In this environment of data-driven innovation, customer relationships become more intensive: manufacturers increasingly establish longer term, communicative, and collaborative contacts with customers (Cheah & Wang, 2017; Kiel et al., 2017). Hence, customer relationship changes refer to a growing degree of intensity in terms of communicating with, understanding, and satisfying customers, transforming relationships into partnerships, and integrating customers early. For instance, Müller et al. (2018) highlight that automated online platforms enable wider customer reach, easier order placement, and facilitate customer co-design and co-engineering processes. Furthermore, companies leveraging new DTs show an increasing orientation towards direct sales as direct and close customer contact is necessary to meet the increased consultation requirements of complex digital-embedded products and solutions (Kiel et al., 2017; Laudien & Daxböck, 2016). Therefore, digital technologies seem to improve inter-company connectivity with customers. However, data exchange and information transparency concern the entire supply chain, as digital technologies might also ease suppliers' access to real-time information

(Müller et al., 2018). Despite that, firms might struggle to convince suppliers and partners that digitally linked processes are beneficial for both sides, as they fear to disclose sensitive information and incur high investment costs (Laudien & Daxböck, 2016).

Lastly, the implementation of digital technologies has the potential to affect value capture mechanisms as well. Basically, the data-driven core of DTs leads to changes in the cost structure. On the one hand, companies experience costs savings linked with increased productivity, on the other hand, they incur additional costs due to significant IT-related investments (Arnold et al., 2016). Moreover, digital technologies have the potential to enable the switching from payments per product to new revenue models, such as dynamic pricing, pay-per-feature, pay-per-use, or pay-per output models (Laudien & Daxböck, 2016; Müller et al., 2018). Importantly, although the data-driven nature of the DTs significantly facilitates the implementation of usage fees, these practices are highly related to the company's industry as more traditional companies, such as manufacturing ones, hardly experience revenue model changes (Kiel et al., 2017), unless they shift from being product manufacturers to being service or solution providers (Müller et al., 2018).

However, despite the increasing potential of recent technological developments, companies are still struggling with making successful digital transformation (McKinsey, 2018; Sund et al., 2021). This process seems to conceal several challenges. Companies are likely to incur high investment costs for the IT infrastructure, as well as costs for hiring and training employees (Müller et al., 2018), who need to possess specific IT and data analytics capabilities, as well as market competence and understanding of customers (Kiel et al., 2017). This might lead to high costs in the short term, while the benefits of implementing new DTs might only become apparent in the long run (Müller et al., 2018). An additional major issue regards data security and privacy concerns (Müller, 2019). Furthermore, companies investing in gathering information through digital technologies often face difficulties in putting the information to commercial use (Müller et al., 2018). There is indeed anecdotal evidence of companies facing a so-called digitalization paradox, which means that they invest in digital offerings, but struggle to achieve the expected revenue growth, despite the proven growth potential of digital technologies (Gebauer et al., 2020; Kohtamäki et al., 2019).

Overall, the effects of implementing new digital technologies can be traced primarily to better performing products with new functionalities and more efficient firm operations and manufacturing processes, thanks to improved production output, fewer breakdowns, enhanced maintenance, and more effective integration across value chains. "Front-end" and "back-end" data analytics allow the data to be transformed into valuable insights and actionable directives, which improves companies' decision-making processes. "Front-end" data about customers allows to better understand customers' value creating process, strengthening customers relationships and interactions, while the collection of "back-end" operational and production data through sensors enhanced production efficiency. Therefore, data collection and analysis are critical in allowing firms to access the full potential of digital-driven business model innovation (Laudien & Daxböck, 2016; Paiola & Gebauer, 2020; Parida et al., 2019; Sorescu, 2017).

Despite the growing interest in DT-driven business model innovation, the literature has thus far devoted greater attention to the manufacturing companies (e.g. automotive, electrical engineering, medical engineering industries), mostly due to the Industry 4.0 megatrend (e.g. Kiel et al., 2017; Müller et al., 2018; Paiola & Gebauer, 2020). The existing empirical evidence is mostly focused on companies' implementation of the Industrial Internet of Things (IIoT) in the manufacturing process and its consequences in terms of BMI, while less is known on how the data-driven business model innovation is impacting product/service firms.

Methodology

A single case study methodology was employed, as this method fits the purpose of the study by allowing for an explorative analysis of a contemporary phenomenon in its real-life contexts (Yin, 2003). Importantly, the main objective of a single case study is to understand and examine a single subject of analysis in a thorough way, instead of aiming at statistical generalization (Stake, 1995). In this regard, qualitative methodologies are largely used in business model and business model innovation literature (Foss & Saebi, 2017), as companies might experience different and unique paths to digital-driven business model innovation (e.g. Frank et al., 2019; Paiola & Gebauer, 2020; Verhoef et al., 2021). Thus, this methodology enhances the understanding of the dynamics and contextual complexities of data-driven business model innovation.

The company GrottiniLab, a technological solution provider which has been experiencing changes in the business model, was selected as the research setting and case study company. The company provides retailers with innovative technological solutions supported by artificial intelligence, deep learning, and machine learning, in order to monitor, analyse and optimize the shopping experience in stores, shopping centres, showrooms, supermarkets, stations, and other centres. Recently, the company developed a new solution named Shopper Science Lab, a retail shop fully equipped with permanent shopper analytics technologies to monitor and analyse shopping behaviours.

The study was conducted between March 2020 and March 2021. Data were collected primarily through semi-structured interviews. In this regard, all the knowledgeable company members who contributed to the design of the new solution as well as to the design of the innovative business model were involved. In particular, the following executives participated in the study: (i) the Chief Growth Officer, (ii) the Head of Data Science—Executive Consultant for Commercial Growth, and (iii) the Digital Communication Manager. Involving multiple key informants who perform different job roles allows stronger evidence to be provided (Eisenhardt, 1989; Yin, 2003). The interview track was based on open-ended questions trying to guarantee a good balance between guidance and consistency, as well as an adequate level of freedom in answering. Furthermore, this allows to identify recurrent themes among participants. The track was based on the current literature on digital-driven business model innovation. Data reduction and condensation procedures were used to remove non-relevant information. The authors also performed manual coding, aggregating data into categories to streamline the analysis (De Massis & Kotlar, 2014; Miles & Huberman, 1994).

Moreover, we used direct observation and archival data analysis as additional sources (Eisenhardt, 1989; Yin, 2003). This material provides additional information and makes it possible to verify findings and increase evidence. Since the aim of the study is to analyse the BMI process related to the Shopper Science Lab project, we believe it is useful to describe this process in a narrative way in order to identify and understand how the business model innovation process occurs.

The Business Model Innovation in GrottiniLab: The Shopper Science Lab Experience

The Company

GrottiniLab is an Italian company that was founded in 2011 and is strongly oriented towards technological innovation. The Company operates mainly in the retail sector and its core business is to provide innovative retail analytics solutions. In fact, the company designs and implements solutions aimed at monitoring, analysing, and improving the shopping experience of consumers within stores. The technological configurations are supported by proprietary algorithms. Over the years, GrottiniLab has established itself on the market thanks to a working methodology divided into three phases:

- Big Insights: this phase is aimed at generating a deep understanding of the consumer's behaviour, needs and decision-making process for purchasing.
- Big Data: this is the phase of data collection and analysis aimed at producing information and generating metrics.
- Big Actions: this is the phase in which data-driven answers are provided to specific business questions posed by client companies.

The New Solution: The Shopper Science Lab

At the beginning of 2020, the company decided to launch a new solution called the Shopper Science Lab, in partnership with an important Italian brand leader in the drugstore sector. According to the Executives, t Shopper Science Lab is configured as a real store equipped with the main technologies that GrottiniLab provides in the field of shopper behaviour analysis. The purpose of this solution is therefore to allow customers to test the performance of their retail and trade marketing activities, and to test the new products and packaging in a realistic shopping context. Thus, within the Shopper Science Lab it is possible to conduct the following types of analysis:

- Detection of store entrances.
- Tracking the paths taken by shoppers within the store.
- Detection of shopper interactions with products on the shelves.
- Calculation of purchase conversion rates thanks to integration with sell-out data.

Moreover, all this data may be integrated with sales data provided at the store level. The technological equipment available in the Shopper Science Lab is configured as follows:

- Tracking system: these are technologies based on Real-Time Locating System (RTLS) tags that are applied to both baskets and shopping carts in the store. The RTLS sensors allow the paths taken by shoppers to be detected, including stop times, and also provide a navigation map of the store.
- Stereoscopic sensors: the reference technologies are mini-personal computers (PCs) and 3D Optical Smart Sensors (OSS); the latter are applied to the false ceiling over the entire surface of the store; like the previous ones, they also contribute to enriching the analysis of the routes by mapping the navigation.
- Infrared Sensors: mini-PCs and 2D Optical Smart Sensors technologies are adopted; the latter are placed in correspondence with individual shelves or particular areas of interest such as promotional

areas. The adoption of these sensors allows the presence and nature of the shopper's interaction with the product category to be detected. Additionally, they provide a mapping of shopper navigation at the shelf level.

- Image recognition sensors: they are applied in specific areas of interest within the store; they allow aspects such as gender and age group in shoppers to be detected; these data help to elaborate a clustering of shoppers.

This technological configuration allows retailers to collect data in a non-intrusive way and to answer their most frequent questions, such as evaluating the effectiveness of promotional materials within the store, assortment and shelf layout choices, planograms, etc. As mentioned before, it is also possible to conduct tests aimed at monitoring the performance of new product launches or new packaging.

In this scenario, the introduction of the Shopper Science Lab as a new solution in the company portfolio required a new approach to the customers, both in terms of value proposition formulation and communication. It is worth noting that bricks-and-mortar retail stores generally adopt a "traditional" approach to the market. On the one hand, the practices aimed at improving the shopper experience in store are still limited, on the other hand, traditional retailers are still lagging behind when it comes to the "data culture". While in the online stores data represent a key element to inform decision-making processes, offline retailers largely rest on the sell-out data to make business decisions as well as plan marketing and promotion tactics. Furthermore, consumer knowledge is still acquired using traditional market research methods, such as surveys or direct observation.

As a matter of fact, data generated by the technologies installed within the Shopper Science Lab can be of interest to several customer segments, such as the manufacturers that sell their products through the retail channel, or any other company operating in the retail industry that is looking for valuable consumers' data on shopping behaviour for marketing research purposes.

This opening to a new pool of potential customers has led the company to design an innovative business model which, when compared to the previous one, has undergone some substantial changes in various aspects within the value proposition and value capture components of the business model. The following sections illustrate the main aspects of the business model innovation.

Business Model Innovation: Value Proposition

The introduction of the Shopper Science Lab led the company to formulate a new value proposition centred on the strengths of the lab's solution. It is important to point out that the Shopper Science Lab project contributed to consolidating one of the company's mission, that is, spreading a data-driven culture among retailers through its solutions. Real data to support retailers' decisions are therefore one of the core elements of the value proposition. With this in mind, the new value proposition is based on two main pillars.

A first element is related to the context: the Shopper Science Lab is not an artificial environment but a real store, already configured and ready for different types of analyses. According to the Chief Growth Officer: "by offering a permanent laboratory, GrottiniLab can guarantee to the user companies a series of advantages such as a data collection on an ongoing basis, the ability to launch multiple tests during the year and to independently manage their duration time as well. The real store, already fully equipped with technology, also allows the user companies to reduce or in some cases delete the kick-off times of the analysis projects".

The second pillar is related to the data: as previously stated, Shopper Science Lab is equipped with various shopper behaviour analytics technologies; the integrated use of multiple systems allows a very accurate analysis of shopping behaviour. Therefore, data is the core element of the new value proposition which materializes into a new service, consisting in the access to the Shopper Science Lab database to those companies that are not present in the store with their products. In this way, for the first time, GrottiniLab can sell retail insights without installing a complex technological solution on the retail shop floor, providing customers with the ability to access the Shopper Science Lab database containing the history of real data that is produced within it. According to GrottiniLab executives, this aspect represents one of the main new elements that characterize the current business model. In fact, the company is now able to expand its portfolio of solutions in the retail market by presenting itself not only as a technology/service provider, but also as a player competing in the marketing research industry.

Notably, the features of the technologies within the Shopper Science Lab have allowed the company to introduce into its business model not only new activities, but also new combinations of those already existing. From this standpoint, a first aspect concerns the possibility of offering in a single solution a combination of services that are normally offered separately; from the perspective of GrottiniLab Executives, the data generated are processed and transformed into actionable insights that can support the decision-making processes of the brands with regard to their marketing strategies and tactics. These insights are useful, for example, to understand the purchase conversion funnel of shoppers who, once logged into the store, are monitored until the purchase stage. For example, it is possible to analyse the impact of an advertising flyer on the shoppers' path in the store. By comparing the heatmaps that provide information on shoppers' behaviour within the store before, during and after they saw the flyer, it is possible to understand if and in which areas there was a greater flow of customers. The heatmaps analysis provides a more complete evaluation than the mere sell-out data evaluation, as it allows to understand how the variations of the paths determine different sell-out performances by answering questions such as: "how has the conversion path changed (purchases / steps in category) in relation to the flyer?" Or: which categories received the greatest benefit during and after the flyer launch?

This is possible thanks to the integration between various areas of analysis such as monitoring the level of attractiveness of the single product category which considers the time spent by each shopper in each single category, shelf, stock keeping unit and product. Data about the number of visitors who stop in front of that product category is combined into the "time spent" metric, and moreover, the average number of interactions per visitor is calculated.

It is also possible to identify the presence of clusters of shoppers that can be segmented by gender and age group, as well as to understand whether shoppers make purchases alone or in pairs/groups.

Business Model Innovation: Value Creation

Value creation is the second-most affected dimension of the business model. In this regard, one of the most important aspects relating to the business model innovation process of GrottiniLab's business model is its approach to customer segments. As stated by the Chief Growth Officer: "the Shopper Science Lab targets different types of customers: retailers - the traditional market segment of GrottiniLab – and manufacturers. The latter represents a new market segment for the company, and it includes both firms that sell their products through the stores and firms that do not distribute their products through the stores, but who are interested in obtaining shoppers' insights". In particular, for the latter type of customer, the value proposition is based on the ability to conduct market research based on real-world and real-time data that are constantly generated.

The introduction of a new solution on the market that is aimed partially at new customers has led GrottiniLab to innovate customer interactions. In particular, also due to the ongoing Covid-19 pandemic, the company intensified the use of social media channels to communicate with its potential customers and present the complexity of the Shopper Science Lab in a smart and engaging way.

In this regard, a social media strategy was developed, mainly based on the professional social network LinkedIn, with the aim of launching the Shopper Science Lab. The content published in the form of infographics, free guides and blog articles had a dual purpose: on the one hand, to increase the brand awareness of the GrottiniLab company as a European leader in the retail analytics sector, and on the other hand to present the Shopper Science Lab solutions in order to generate potential leads that might be interested in having more information.

As the Chief Growth Officer stated: "the content, produced in a clear language, were intended to answer typical questions that a potential customer might have asked to a company salesman, such as: "which type of customer is the Shopper Science Lab addressed to?" Or "what can I do inside a Shopper Science Lab?".

Each lead acquired was contacted by the company's sales managers for an in-depth interview and a proposal for a quote that could vary, depending on the characteristics of the customer and the options chosen. Particularly effective in terms of communication was the production and dissemination through the company website and the official LinkedIn profile of use cases through which the company was able to illustrate real examples of application of the Shopper Science Lab. Starting from the identification of the business question formulated by the customer, the use case was intended to present how, thanks to the analysis of the data acquired within the store, it was possible to generate useful insights to solve that particular business question.

The creation of the Shopper Science Lab was made possible thanks to a strategic partnership with the Italian brand leader in the drugstore sector. The leading company in Italy in the drugstore segment has in fact made its own store available, within which all the retail analytics technologies have been installed. In addition to providing the location, the partner supports GrottiniLab by helping to spread its promotional campaigns related to the Shopper Science Lab.

Conclusions

The current literature has shown considerable interest in digital-driven business model innovation (e.g. Khanagha et al., 2014; Sabatier et al., 2012). Recently, academics have been devoting increasing attention to those digital technologies which fall under the Industry 4.0 paradigm (Arnold et al., 2016; Frank et al., 2019; Kiel et al., 2017; Müller et al., 2018). In this regard, scholars have found that digital technologies profoundly affect the BM components, namely value proposition, value creation/delivery and value capture. However, while focusing on those technologies which drive the 4th Industrial Revolution, existing studies are largely focused on understanding digital-driven BMI in manufacturing companies. By doing so, they highlight the tremendous potential of digital technologies to enhance the manufacturing process and operational efficiency. Although the existing empirical evidence somewhat shows that, in manufacturing companies, the value of digital technologies largely lies in the data generated, which allows for uncovering production bottlenecks, products flaws and for a better understanding of customers' needs and dissatisfaction, less is known about how data-driven business model innovation is developing in other industries.

This chapter contributes to the ongoing debate on the topic by showing how a digital-driven business model innovation might occur in a product/service firm. The study findings confirm the existing empirical evidence in the manufacturing industry by showing that digital technologies might entail a data-driven business model in other industries as well. The study also highlights some differences regarding customer segments, customer relationships and revenue model.

First, the case study company experienced major changes in the value proposition. These findings are in line with previous studies showing that the value proposition appears to be the most affected BM component, among others (see Arnold et al., 2016; Kiel et al., 2017). Specifically, thanks to the Shopper Science Lab, the company can leverage its capabilities to offer a new integrated solution at its best, since the Shopper Science Lab represents a real store equipped with various shopper behaviour analytics technologies. More interestingly, the company is now able to sell retail insights, providing customers with the ability to access the Shopper Science Lab database containing the history of real data generated, without installing the technological solution in the retailer's store.

The study findings also highlight significant changes in the value creation dimension of the business model.

Importantly, the literature has shown that the implementation of new digital technologies is not directly linked with reaching out to new customers (see Arnold et al., 2016; Kiel et al., 2017), rather it strengthens existing customer relationships. In addition, the study shows that the Shopper Science Lab opens new opportunities in terms of customer acquisition. Two are the new customer categories for GrottiniLab. Firstly, the company that used to sell its technological solutions to retailers can now address manufacturing companies selling their products through the

Shopper Science Lab's retail partner, by offering a real testing environment and retail analytics. Secondly, GrottiniLab can also address both manufacturers which do not sell through the retail channel or are not interested in testing their products and other retailers that are instead interested in buying the retail insights. By doing so the company expands beyond the boundaries of a technology/service provider to become a player competing in the marketing research industry.

The study findings also emphasize changes in customer interactions due to the increased use of social media and digital channels. The company leverages digital communication to create relevant content, such as use cases, aimed at addressing their needs and answering customers' doubts. This confirms the existing empirical evidence on digital-driven business model innovation that highlights increased contact via digital platforms and eased interaction through digital communication (see Müller et al., 2018). Yet, in contrast to a previous study emphasizing that the use of new digital technologies in manufacturing companies leads to an intensification of existing customers relationships and a somewhat partner-like collaboration (see Kiel et al., 2017), the case study company seems not to have experienced significant changes in customer relationships. There might be a twofold reason explaining these dynamics. Firstly, this might be due to the product/service nature of GrottiniLab whose relationships with customers have always been rather intensive. The company has constantly tried to build long-term partnerships with customers to effectively implement the complex technological solutions offered for the retailers' shop floor. Secondly, the new value proposition mostly addresses new customer segments, hence new customer relationships are created. Therefore, rather than witnessing an intensification of such relationships, it is likely that the company might build close relationships with customers from the very beginning.

The study also confirms previous findings emphasizing changes in the firm's key partner network structure in data-driven business model innovation (see Björkdahl, 2020; Müller, 2019; Müller et al., 2018; Urbinati et al., 2019). Digital-driven business model innovation is not limited to the focal firm, rather it involves companies beyond the firm's boundaries, such as component manufacturers, system suppliers, system integrators, solution providers, operators, distributors, and customers (e.g. Grieger & Ludwig, 2019; Kohtamäki et al., 2019). It is noteworthy that the current literature on manufacturing companies highlights the pivotal role of partnerships outside the firms' boundaries to overcome a widespread lack of skills and expertise on the technology side. In this regard, we show that also companies other than manufacturing ones, which have already a large expertise in technology, benefit from key partnerships to innovate their business models.

Lastly, the study findings show that companies still experience difficulties in changing the value capture component of the business model. Therefore, although some studies highlight the potential for using data collected through new digital technologies to make changes in companies' value capture mechanisms by introducing new revenue models such as dynamic pricing and pay-per-use (see Müller et al., 2018), our findings are in line with previous studies showing that those changes are still difficult to observe (see Kiel et al., 2017; Rachinger et al., 2019). On the one hand, this might depend on customers' resistance in shifting towards unfamiliar billing models (see Kiel et al., 2017). On the other hand, it might be surprising, because companies addressing new customers might leverage data to implement new revenue models based on usage fees. In this regard, the product/service nature of the case company and its strong customer focus might open new opportunities for changes in the revenue model in the future (see Rachinger et al., 2019).

From a managerial perspective, the study confirms the disruptive role that digital technologies are playing even in those companies that cater to customers operating in the more traditional sectors. The work also highlights that the introduction of innovative solutions is effective if the company also pays attention to how they can impact business models. The study findings show that addressing digital transformation processes not only involves the adoption of new technologies within companies, but also the need to design consistent business models capable of making these technologies key elements for new value propositions.

The study is subject to limitations, which however offer fruitful opportunities for future research. A single case study does not allow for statistical generalization (Yin, 2003), yet this was beyond the scope of the present analysis. Of course, the literature would benefit from a multiple case study to enhance external validity (cf. De Massis & Kotlar, 2014; Eisenhardt, 1989) as multiple cases allow for comparisons between different organizations that clarify whether an emergent finding is consistently replicated by several cases. However, a single case study allows a complex phenomenon such as the BMI to be thoroughly represented. In this regard, conducting a longitudinal case study might be appropriate for analysing the BMI as a process which unfolds and changes over time, thereby offering new interesting insights.

Acknowledgements The present chapter was written thanks to the support of GrottinLab S.r.l. Company.

References

Alshawaaf, N., & Lee, S. H. (2021). Business model innovation through digitisation in social purpose organisations: A comparative analysis of Tate Modern and Pompidou Centre. *Journal of Business Research, 125*, 597–608.

Arnold, C., Kiel, D., & Voigt, K. I. (2016). How the industrial internet of things changes business models in different manufacturing industries. *International Journal of Innovation Management, 20*(08), 1640015.

Baden-Fuller, C., & Haefliger, S. (2013). Business models and technological innovation. *Long Range Panning, 46*(6), 419–426.

Björkdahl, J. (2020). Strategies for digitalization in manufacturing firms. *California Management Review, 62*(4), 17–36.

Bouwman, H., Nikou, S., Molina-Castillo, F. J., & de Reuver, M. (2018). The impact of digitalization on business models. *Digital Policy, Regulation and Governance, 20*(2), 105–124.

Burström, T., Parida, V., Lahti, T., & Wincent, J. (2021). AI-enabled business-model innovation and transformation in industrial ecosystems: A framework, model and outline for further research. *Journal of Business Research, 127*, 85–95.

Casadesus-Masanell, R., & Ricart, J. E. (2010). From strategy to business models and onto tactics. *Long Range Planning, 43*(2–3), 195–215.

Casadesus-Masanell, R., & Zhu, F. (2013). Business model innovation and competitive imitation: The case of sponsor-based business models. *Strategic Management Journal, 34*(4), 464–482.

Chasin, F., Paukstadt, U., Gollhardt, T., & Becker, J. (2020). Smart energy driven business model innovation: An analysis of existing business models and implications for business model change in the energy sector. *Journal of Cleaner Production,* 122083.

Cheah, S., & Wang, S. (2017). Big data-driven business model innovation by traditional industries in the Chinese economy. *Journal of Chinese Economic and Foreign Trade Studies.*

Chesbrough, H. (2010). Business model innovation: Opportunities and barriers. *Long Range Planning, 43*(2–3), 354–363.

Chesbrough, H., & Rosenbloom, R. S. (2002). The role of the business model in capturing value from innovation: Evidence from Xerox Corporation's technology spin-off companies. *Industrial and Corporate Change, 11*(3), 529–555.

Ciampi, F., Demi, S., Magrini, A., Marzi, G., & Papa, A. (2021). Exploring the impact of big data analytics capabilities on business model innovation: The mediating role of entrepreneurial orientation. *Journal of Business Research, 123,* 1–13.

De Massis, A., & Kotlar, J. (2014). The case study method in family business research: Guidelines for qualitative scholarship. *Journal of Family Business Strategy, 5*(1), 15–29.

Demil, B., & Lecocq, X. (2010). Business model evolution: In search of dynamic consistency. *Long Range Planning, 43*(2–3), 227–246.

Doz, Y. L., & Kosonen, M. (2010). Embedding strategic agility: A leadership agenda for accelerating business model renewal. *Long Range Planning, 43*(2–3), 370–382.

Eisenhardt, K. M. (1989). Building theories from case study research. *Academy of Management Review, 14*(4), 532–550.

Foss, N. J., & Saebi, T. (2017). Fifteen years of research on business model innovation: How far have we come, and where should we go? *Journal of Management, 43*(1), 200–227.

Frank, A. G., Mendes, G. H., Ayala, N. F., & Ghezzi, A. (2019). Servitization and Industry 4.0 convergence in the digital transformation of product firms: A business model innovation perspective. *Technological Forecasting and Social Change, 141,* 341–351.

Gebauer, H., Arzt, A., Kohtamäki, M., Lamprecht, C., Parida, V., Witell, L., & Wortmann, F. (2020). How to convert digital offerings into revenue

enhancement–Conceptualizing business model dynamics through explorative case studies. *Industrial Marketing Management, 91*, 429–441.
Grieger, M., & Ludwig, A. (2019). On the move towards customer-centric business models in the automotive industry-a conceptual reference framework of shared automotive service systems. *Electronic Markets, 29*(3), 473–500.
Johnson, M. W., Christensen, C. M., & Kagermann, H. (2008). Reinventing your business model. *Harvard Business Review, 86*(12), 57–68.
Khanagha, S., Volberda, H., & Oshri, I. (2014). Business model renewal and ambidexterity: Structural alteration and strategy formation process during transition to a Cloud business model. *R&D Management, 44*(3), 322–340.
Kiel, D., Arnold, C., & Voigt, K. I. (2017). The influence of the Industrial Internet of Things on business models of established manufacturing companies–A business level perspective. *Technovation, 68*, 4–19.
Kim, S. K., & Min, S. (2015). Business model innovation performance: When does adding a new business model benefit an incumbent? *Strategic Entrepreneurship Journal, 9*(1), 34–57.
Kohtamäki, M., Parida, V., Oghazi, P., Gebauer, H., & Baines, T. (2019). Digital servitization business models in ecosystems: A theory of the firm. *Journal of Business Research, 104*, 380–392.
Laudien, S. M., & Daxböck, B. (2016). The influence of the industrial internet of things on business model design: A qualitative-empirical analysis. *International Journal of Innovation Management, 20*(08), 1640014.
Li, F. (2020). The digital transformation of business models in the creative industries: A holistic framework and emerging trends. *Technovation*, 92, 102012.
McGrath, R., & McManus, R. (2020). Discovery-driven digital transformation. *Harvard Business Review*, 2–11.
McKinsey. (2018). *Unlocking success in digital transformations*. Accessed January 2020. https://www.mckinsey.com/business-functions/organization/our-insights/unlocking-success-in-digital-transformations
Miles, M. B., & Huberman, A. M. (1994). *Qualitative data analysis: An expanded sourcebook*. Sage.
Müller, J. M. (2019). Business model innovation in small-and medium-sized enterprises. *Journal of Manufacturing Technology Management, 30*(8), 1127–1142.
Müller, J. M., Buliga, O., & Voigt, K. I. (2018). Fortune favors the prepared: How SMEs approach business model innovations in Industry 4.0. *Technological Forecasting and Social Change, 132*, 2–17.

Osiyevskyy, O., & Dewald, J. (2015). Inducements, impediments, and immediacy: Exploring the cognitive drivers of small business managers' intentions to adopt business model change. *Journal of Small Business Management, 53*(4), 1011–1032.

Osterwalder, A., Pigneur, Y., & Tucci, C. L. (2005). Clarifying business models: Origins, present, and future of the concept. *Communications of the Association for Information Systems, 16*(1), 1.

Paiola, M., & Gebauer, H. (2020). Internet of things technologies, digital servitization and business model innovation in BtoB manufacturing firms. *Industrial Marketing Management.*

Parida, V., Sjödin, D., & Reim, W. (2019). Reviewing literature on digitalization, business model innovation, and sustainable industry: Past achievements and future promises. *Sustainability, 11*(2), 1–18.

Rachinger, M., Rauter, R., Müller, C., Vorraber, W., & Schirgi, E. (2019). Digitalization and its influence on business model innovation. *Journal of Manufacturing Technology Management, 30*(8), 1143–1160.

Richardson, J. E. (2008). The business model: An integrative framework for strategy execution. *Strategic Change, 17*(5/6), 133–144.

Ritter, T., & Pedersen, C. L. (2020). Digitization capability and the digitalization of business models in business-to-business firms: Past, present, and future. *Industrial Marketing Management, 86*, 180–190.

Sabatier, V., Craig-Kennard, A., & Mangematin, V. (2012). When technological discontinuities and disruptive business models challenge dominant industry logics: Insights from the drugs industry. *Technological Forecasting and Social Change, 79*(5), 949–962.

Schneider, S., & Spieth, P. (2013). Business model innovation: Towards an integrated future research agenda. *International Journal of Innovation Management, 17*(01), 1340001.

Sestino, A., Prete, M. I., Piper, L., & Guido, G. (2020). Internet of things and big data as enablers for business digitalization strategies. *Technovation*, 102173.

Sorescu, A. (2017). Data-driven business model innovation. *Journal of Product Innovation Management, 34*(5), 691–696.

Stake, R. E. (1995). *The art of case study research*. Sage.

Sund, K. J., Bogers, M. L., & Sahramaa, M. (2021). Managing business model exploration in incumbent firms: A case study of innovation labs in European banks. *Journal of Business Research, 128*, 11–19.

Teece, D. J. (2010). Business models, business strategy and innovation. *Long Range Planning, 43*(2–3), 172–194.

Urbinati, A., Bogers, M., Chiesa, V., & Frattini, F. (2019). Creating and capturing value from Big Data: A multiple-case study analysis of provider companies. *Technovation, 84*, 21–36.

Verhoef, P. C., Broekhuizen, T., Bart, Y., Bhattacharya, A., Dong, J. Q., Fabian, N., & Haenlein, M. (2021). Digital transformation: A multidisciplinary reflection and research agenda. *Journal of Business Research, 122*, 889–901.

Wirtz, B. W., Schilke, O., & Ullrich, S. (2010). Strategic development of business models: implications of the Web 2.0 for creating value on the internet. *Long Range Planning, 43*(2–3), 272–290.

Yin, R. K. (2003). *Case study research: Designs and methods* (3rd ed.). Sage.

Zott, C., & Amit, R. (2013). The business model: A theoretically anchored robust construct for strategic analysis. *Strategic Organization, 11*(4), 403–411.

Zott, C., Amit, R., & Massa, L. (2011). The business model: Recent developments and future research. *Journal of Management, 37*(4), 1019–1042.

5

Economic Structure, Globalisation, Governance, and Digitalisation: Global Evidence from Digital-Intensive ICT Trade

Mehmet Demiral and Özge Demiral

Introduction

Digitalisation has influenced all aspects of societies in many political, social, and economic arenas. Although this process was already widely known, the COVID-19 pandemic, caused by a novel coronavirus, has reminded us of the importance of digitalisation, which has allowed individuals, businesses, governments, and international organisations to tackle the challenges stemming from the pandemic-related social distancing and quarantine measures (Fu, 2020; Soto-Acosta, 2020; Vargo et al., 2021). With the increased spread of the pandemic since early

M. Demiral (✉)
Department of Economics, Niğde Ömer Halisdemir University, Niğde, Turkey
e-mail: mdemiral@ohu.edu.tr

Ö. Demiral
Department of International Trade and Logistics, Niğde Ömer Halisdemir University, Niğde, Turkey
e-mail: odemiral@ohu.edu.tr

M. Ratajczak-Mrozek and P. Marszałek (eds.), *Digitalization and Firm Performance*,
https://doi.org/10.1007/978-3-030-83360-2_5

2020, many people have stayed at home, employees have teleworked, educational institutions have turned to distance teaching/learning, and local businesses have started using online ordering and delivery apps, etc., due to the social distancing measures taken by most governments. Governments have also adopted e-government practices to sustain public services. Globally, this confinement has increased the demand for information and communications technology (ICT) products[1] and accelerated the digital transformation of societies.

Digitalisation is the increasing access, adoption, and use of computer-based digital opportunities through digital transformation, which is a structural change of economies, governments, institutions, and societies towards the integration of ever-advancing digital technologies at a system level (Rachinger et al., 2019; Ritter & Pedersen, 2020). Digitalisation is based on digitisation, which is widely referred to as the process of converting analogue into digital data sets (Rachinger et al., 2019). Digitisation is driven by the increasing use of digital technologies for connecting people, systems, companies, products, and services (Ritter & Pedersen, 2020).

Academic interest in the concept of digitalisation has increased over time, even though the empirical literature has been restricted by the limited availability of digitalisation data. Addressing the scarcity of internationally comparable and cross-country harmonised data, there are some initiatives measuring countries' digitalisation levels by considering some headline indicators, such as ICT development, digital innovation, future and change readiness, societal adoption of ICT technologies, production and export performance in high-tech products, the prevalent use of digital technologies, among many others (European Commission, 2020, 2021; IMD, 2020, 2021; OECD, 2021; Oxford Economics, 2021). Notwithstanding these internationally comparable proxy indicators for the digital economy and information society, the empirical literature on the causes and effects of digitalisation has remained limited because of the lack of directly comparable indicators and the substantial variation within the dimensions constituting composite measurements.

[1] In this chapter, the definition of ICT products covers both ICT goods and ICT services, while the description of ICT goods excludes ICT services unless otherwise specified.

As one of the common factors, ICT involvement is seen as the key driver of the digital capabilities of countries. Consistently, many ICT indicators are among the main components of digitalisation gauges and the digital economy definitions (IMD, 2021; OECD, 2021).

ICT goods are characterised by the higher intensity of knowledge, innovation and new technology, and they include computers and peripheral equipment, communication equipment, consumer electronic equipment, and electronic components. Thus, involvement in ICT sectors is also considered among the most important driving forces of the digital competitiveness of countries (Calvino et al., 2018). The vast multifaceted opportunities provided by ICT vary across countries, depending on their digitalisation performance measured by the capacity to explore and embrace new digital technologies. In the context of countries' ICT involvement, both the consumption-side indicators (use and adoption of ICT) and production-side indicators (investment, production, and export in ICT) are considered (IMD, 2021; OECD, 2021). The ICT involvement of countries is affected by many country-specific factors (subsidies and incentives, local programmes, training, infrastructure, etc.), economic factors (income level, industrialisation, economic complexity, economic integration, trade openness, etc.), and non-economic factors (demographics, institutions/governance, physical and regulatory infrastructure, education, human capital, population, urbanisation, social and political globalisation, etc.). Some of these variables are also widely included as the determinants of global digitalisation (Chinn & Fairlie, 2007; Huang & Chen, 2010; Serrano-Cinca et al., 2018; Tirado-Morueta et al., 2018).

For the income effect, digitalisation and its economic implications seem to be no longer limited to only high-income advanced economies, as middle-income and low-income developing countries are also increasingly engaging in the production and export of many digital goods. This spillover effect can be defined as digital globalisation which interacts mutually with all three dimensions (economic, social, and political) of overall globalisation, although a considerable digital gap persists between developed and developing countries[2] (De Marchi et al., 2018; Foster & Azmeh, 2020; Ngwenyama & Morawczynski, 2009). From the ICT exports approach to digitalisation, imports of ICT products also enable local producers to know how these products are produced, which is related to the imitation and learning effects (learning by importing). In addition, the ICT sector embodies key digital products with a wide range of global value chains in which both developed and developing countries participate (Banga, 2019; Mayer, 2018).

Digitalisation and industrialisation are closely related, especially in the era of the Fourth Industrial Revolution, which is formed and operated mostly by digital technologies that also facilitate global trade (WEF, 2020). Digitalisation can provide new opportunities for industrialisation, particularly in developing countries (Mayer, 2018). However, the digital contribution to industrialisation remains unclear and even becomes more complex with the development of industrial value chains and science-industry linkages, which also bring about structural challenges and make some national digital policies necessary (Foster & Azmeh, 2020). Economic complexity, which is an indicator of sophisticated, innovation-based, and knowledge-intensive production and export structures (Hausmann et al., 2013), may affect countries' digital readiness and ICT production/export capacities.

Digital transformation also has its institutional origins on a driver-barrier basis. Governance concepts, especially those that are measured by high-quality institutions, government effectiveness, regularity quality, and control of corruption, have different and unclear effects on business performance and other economic activities (Abed & Gupta, 2002). Weaker institutions and worse governance may produce varied channels, both encouraging and discouraging the ICT performance. Even though the impacts of ICT performance and digitalisation indicators on governance indicators have been widely examined (Agarwal & Maiti, 2020; Ali & Sassi, 2017; Asongu & Nwachukwu, 2019), the reverse direction, i.e. the influences of governance on ICT exports, needs to be explored as a missing link in the related literature.

[2] In this chapter, the designations of countries by development stage, income level, advancement, and digital competitiveness are intended for only statistical convenience. There is no intention to express any judgement about the stages and ranks of countries.

Given the digital directions in a global context, new cross-country studies examining the potential determinants of countries' digitalisation performance are needed. Starting from the higher digital intensity of many ICT goods and relying on the close link between ICT production (and consumption) and ICT exports, this chapter explores whether countries' export performance in digital-intensive ICT goods is affected by their industrialisation, economic complexity, globalisation, and governance levels, as well as domestic income and ICT imports. The empirical framework of the chapter builds on a panel data analysis over the 2000–2018 period of 54 countries distinguished between 27 relatively higher digitally-competitive countries (HDCCs) and 27 lower digitally-competitive countries (LDCCs) designated by the world digital competitiveness rankings (WDCR) of the Institute for Management Development (IMD, 2020, 2021).[3] In the rest of the chapter, the following section provides an outline of digital competitiveness, as well as its measurement with a specific reference to the role of ICT sectors. Next, the considered potential determinants of ICT exports are explained. The empirical framework describes variables, data, and the model, before presenting summary statistics and some diagnostics of the data. After the presentation of the results, the chapter concludes with a brief discussion of the findings.

Digital Competitiveness and ICT

Recently, several global initiatives have begun to score and rank countries in terms of digital competitiveness. The digital density index, provided by Oxford Economics, takes many digital technology indicators into account from both private and public sources of the major economies.

[3] Relatively higher digitally-competitive countries (HDCCs), in descending order of rank, are *Singapore, USA, Sweden, Denmark, Netherlands, Finland, Switzerland, Canada, Norway, UK, Israel, Australia, Republic of Korea, New Zealand, Germany, Austria, Ireland, Belgium, Japan, France, Malaysia, Estonia, Lithuania, China, Spain, Portugal,* and *Czechia*. Relatively lower digitally-competitive countries (LDCCs) include *Slovenia, Latvia, Poland, Saudi Arabia, Kazakhstan, Italy, Chile, Thailand, Russia, Hungary, Bulgaria, Slovakia, Croatia, South Africa, Romania, India, Jordan, Mexico, Greece, Philippines, Turkey, Brazil, Argentina, Colombia, Indonesia, Ukraine,* and *Peru*.

This initiative confirms the close link of the increased use of digital technologies with greater productivity, competitiveness, and economic growth (Oxford Economics, 2021). The digital economy and society index (DESI) is an initiative of the European Commission (2020, 2021). DESI is a composite index that uses the key digital indicators to gauge countries' digital performance and to track the evolution of countries in digital competitiveness. The DESI is calculated for a large sample of countries internationally and for European Union (EU) countries separately, which are defined as the international DESI (I-DESI) and EU-DESI, respectively. Since it was first calculated in 2014, the DESI project has extended and updated its constituent indicators to reflect new priorities and changing trends.

The overall DESI index is divided into five leading dimensions, which consider various digitalisation indicators (European Commission, 2020, 2021). (i) Connectivity dimension is about the deployment and quality of broadband infrastructure. It considers indicators of fixed broadband coverage, fixed broadband take-up, 4G coverage, mobile broadband take-up, fixed broadband speed, and fixed broadband price. (ii) Human capital dimension is related to the skills needed to take advantage of the possibilities offered by a digital society. It assesses basic skills, above basic skills, at least basic software skills, telecommunication terminal equipment, and ICT graduates. (iii) Use of internet services dimension is based on the variety of online activities performed by citizens. It considers internet users, fixed broadband traffic, video calls, social networks, online banking, and online shopping. (iv) Integration of digital technology dimension assesses the digitalisation of businesses and online sales channels by measuring the availability of latest technologies, firm-level technology absorption, small and medium-sized enterprises' online selling, and secure internet servers. Finally, (v) digital public services dimension is based on the e-government practices and the digitalisation of public services and it considers e-participation index, online service completion, and open data.

Table 5.1 shows the 2015–2018 average of EU and some non-EU countries' I-DESI scores (the highest score is 100). As can be seen from Table 5.1, on average, Poland has the lowest score and Finland and Denmark are the best performers in EU countries during the period.

Table 5.1 I-DESI scores of countries (2015–2018 avg.)

Country	Avg. score	Country	Avg. score	Country	Avg. score
Austria	50	Lithuania	42	China[a]	38
Belgium	48	Luxembourg	62	Iceland[a]	63
Bulgaria	39	Malta	49	Israel[a]	47
Croatia	41	Netherlands	62	Japan[a]	52
Cyprus	45	Poland	34	Korea[a]	51
Czechia	43	Portugal	41	Mexico[a]	36
Denmark	65	Romania	38	New Zealand[a]	55
Estonia	55	Slovakia	38	Norway[a]	62
Finland	65	Slovenia	44	Russia[a]	39
France	51	Spain	47	Serbia[a]	38
Germany	52	Sweden	61	Switzerland [a]	60
Greece	40	UK	58	Turkey[a]	30
Hungary	42	Australia[a]	57	USA[a]	62
Ireland	52	Brazil[a]	36	*EU-28 avg*	*48*
Italy	37	Canada[a]	54	*17 non-EU avg*	*48*
Latvia	42	Chile[a]	41	*45-country avg*	*48*

Note [a]Non-EU country. Even though the UK withdrew from the EU in early 2020, it is included since the period spans until 2018
Source European Commission (2020, 2021)

Turkey has the lowest score in all 45 countries, while Iceland is the best performer among non-EU countries. Despite considerable variations within groups, both the EU and non-EU averages are around the same (48).

Another initiative is the Institute for Management Development's (IMD) world digital competitiveness ranking (WDCR). Since 2017, which also covers the 2016 ranking, this project has analysed the digital transformation in government practices, business models, and society in general to rank the extent to which countries adopt and embrace digital technologies. The WDCR (IMD, 2020, 2021) assesses 52 criteria based on 32 hard data indicators (statistics obtained from a variety of local and global sources) and 20 survey data indicators (experts and executives opinion surveys), that are aggregated under three main factors, and each is also divided into three sub-factors, as shown in Table 5.2.

Given the above-mentioned multidimensions of digitalisation, it is a challenge to measure digital transformation directly with a one-data indicator in empirical studies, especially in cross-country settings, since

Table 5.2 Dimensions and indicators comprising the IMD's WDCR

Factors	Explanations	Sub-factors	Considered indicators[a]
(I) Knowledge	Know-how necessary to discover, understand and build new technologies	Talent	(i) PISA-math score, (ii) international experience[a], (iii) foreign highly-skilled personnel[a], (iv) management of cities[a], (v) digital/technological skills[a], (vi) flows of international students
		Training and education	(i) Employee training[a], (ii) public expenditure on education, (iii) higher education achievement, (iv) pupil-teacher ratio (tertiary education), (v) graduates in sciences, (vi) women with degrees
		Scientific concentration	(i) Research and development (R&D) expenditures, (ii) R&D personnel, (iii) female researchers, (iv) R&D productivity by publication, (v) scientific and technical employment, (vi) high-tech patents, (vii) robots in education and R&D
(II) Technology	Overall context that enables the development of digital technologies	Regulatory framework	(i) Starting a business, (ii) enforcing contracts, (iii) immigration laws[a], (iv) development-application of technology[a], (v) scientific research legislation[a], (vi) intellectual property rights[a]

(continued)

Table 5.2 (continued)

Factors	Explanations	Sub-factors	Considered indicators[a]
		Capital	(i) Information technology (IT) & media stock market capitalisation, (ii) funding for technological development[a], (iii) banking-financial services[a], (iv) country credit rating, (v) venture capital[a], (vi) investment in telecommunications
		Technological framework	(i) Communications technology[a], (ii) mobile broadband subscribers, (iii) wireless broadband, (iv) internet users, (v) internet bandwidth speed, (vi) high-tech exports
(III) Future readiness	Level of country preparedness to exploit digital transformation	Adaptive attitudes	(i) E-participation, (ii) internet retailing, (iii) tablet possession, (iv) smartphone possession, (v) attitudes toward globalisation[a]
		Business agility	(i) Opportunities and threats[a], (ii) world distribution of robots, (iii) agility of companies[a], (iv) use of big data and analytics[a], (v) knowledge transfer[a], (vi) entrepreneurial fear of failure

(continued)

Table 5.2 (continued)

Factors	Explanations	Sub-factors	Considered indicators[a]
		IT integration	(i) E-government, (ii) public–private partnerships[a], (iii) cyber security[a], (iv) software piracy

Note IMD obtains multidimensional indicators from hard data and survey data[a] sources
Source IMD (2020, 2021)

internationally comparable data is lacking. However, digital capabilities and better access to modern ICT are closely and reciprocally associated with ICT exports in both developed and developing countries (WEF, 2020; Xing, 2018). Digitalisation, from the ICT perspective, is a dynamic transformation process driven by varied areas ranging from education and innovation to trade and socio-economic structures (OECD, 2011, 2019a). The nexus between digitalisation and ICT sectors comes from the high digital intensity of most ICT sectors. For example, in a taxonomy of digital-intensive sectors grouped and ranked by Calvino et al. (2018), ICT sectors are mostly defined under the label of medium–high and high digital-intensive sectors. In relation to digital transformation, several indicators are used to measure the ICT involvement of countries: (i) international trade in ICT sectors, (ii) household expenditure on ICT products, (iii) business and government expenditures on ICT products, and (iv) domestic production of ICT products (OECD, 2011). In the chapter, the international trade dimension of ICT involvement has been considered for also capturing the domestic ICT production.

Potential Determinants of ICT Exports

In line with the existence of multifaceted determinants of digital transformation, the ICT exports of a country are affected by a wide range of factors including both internal and external determinants, as well as economic and non-economic ones. In this chapter, the potential impacts of domestic income, ICT imports, industrialisation, globalisation, economic complexity, and governance have been considered within a cross-country empirical setting. Domestic income measured by gross domestic product (GDP) per capita is one of the widely identified determinants of cross-country disparities in the use and acceptance of digital technologies (Chinn & Fairlie, 2007; Serrano-Cinca et al., 2018; Tirado-Morueta et al., 2018). Similarly, heterogeneity in ICT export performances across countries may be explained by income level. Therefore, in some cases, countries are also grouped by domestic income to have more homogeneous country groups in terms of income level and/or development stage (Kozma & Vota, 2014; Lwoga & Sangeda, 2019).

Digital transformation evolves as new digital technologies are invented. Over the past two decades, digitalisation trends have been determined by the widespread diffusion of the internet, mobile telephony, and broadband networks. More recently, however, many new digital technologies are related to artificial intelligence, which entails machines performing human-like learning, understanding, reasoning, and interacting functions (OECD, 2019a). Unlike the other high-tech investments, digital-intensive ICT investments require more knowledge, research, and multidisciplinary scientific efforts related to human capital besides physical investment. The process of technological diffusion is so complex and expensive, and thus developing countries, which lack financial, technical, and managerial/human resources, may fall behind the capital-rich and knowledge-abundant advanced economies (Pianta, 2019; UNIDO, 2019). Consequently, digital firms and digital-intensive ICT production remain concentrated in advanced economies (Foster & Azmeh, 2020). Consistently, despite considerable cross-country variations, ICT investments and outputs such as ICT patents and inventions are more common in high-income advanced countries in spite of some increasing improvement in certain developing countries, especially in emerging economies including China and India (EPO, 2021; WIPO, 2021). Therefore, digitally-competitive advanced economies seem to be taking some digital advantages of better initial conditions (education, industrial development, income level, digital experience, societal readiness, etc.) and making a greater investment in ICT sectors. Nevertheless, in the context of ICT consumption, ICT products have become much cheaper over time, thanks to sustained technological progress globally (OECD, 2019a). From the ICT production viewpoint, many middle-income emerging economies have been increasingly involved in the global value chains of ICT products, although most developing countries continue to suffer from a lack of local technological resources and capabilities, and rely mainly on the transfer of technologies created in high-income developed countries (De Marchi et al., 2018; Ngwenyama & Morawczynski, 2009; UNIDO, 2019). Since the income-ICT nexus tends to weaken over time, countries have been classified by digital competitiveness instead of income or development stages.

International trade provides a varied set of technologies and innovations, which are referred to as trade-tech (WEF, 2020), through which local businesses, regardless of their size, and countries, regardless of their development and income levels, may efficiently learn the production and adoption of digital-intensive ICT products. More specifically, importing ICT products enables local producers to know how these products are produced, which is related to the imitation and learning effects (learning by importing). Furthermore, many ICT products are involved in a wide range of global value chains in which many countries participate (Mayer, 2018). Thus, both the learning effect and global value chain involvement indicate a positive relationship between the imports and exports of ICT goods.

The exploration of the potential relation between digitalisation and industrialisation is an ongoing endeavour. Digitalisation can provide new opportunities for industrialisation, particularly in developing countries (Mayer, 2018). However, the digital contribution to industrialisation remains unclear and even becomes more complex with the development of industrial value chains and science-industry linkages, which also bring about structural challenges and make some national digital policies necessary (Foster & Azmeh, 2020). Although some are of the view that services promote new digital technologies more than industrial sectors, manufacturing industries dynamically provide efficient channels through which both new ICT technologies may be developed and/or received from technologically advanced economies (López-Pueyo et al., 2009; Mayer, 2018). In the context of digital industrialisation, the

Fourth Industrial Revolution, which is characterised by the combination of industrial activities and digital technologies, including robotics and automation, blockchain, the internet of things, artificial intelligence, 3D printing, etc., need digitalisation-oriented industrialisation (Foster & Azmeh, 2020; WEF, 2020; Yang & Gu, 2021). The digital contribution of industrial development needs to be explored empirically by cross-country studies.

Globalisation, which is defined as the integration of the world's societies through economic, political, and social interactions, may affect the digital transformation of countries from different channels. Broadly, globalisation means cross-border flows of goods and services, technologies, investments, people, and information. Globalisation has been accelerated by the decreasing costs of communication and transactions thanks to ICT developments and digital advances. In the ever-globalising world, digital flows have been increasingly transmitting information, ideas, and innovation around the world, and enhancing the multi-country participation in the production of digital-intensive goods in global value chains (Banga, 2019; De Marchi et al., 2018; Fu, 2020; McKinsey Global Institute, 2016). Given the data evidence showing that cross-border transactions increasingly involve digital components, globalisation is expected to facilitate the spread of ICT products. However, the validity of this premise tends to vary across countries since they have different knowledge, skills, and competencies to adopt and develop new ICT products. Thus, the globalisation-ICT exports nexus remains blurry and requires more research (Akpan, 2003).

ICT goods contain complex and sophisticated digital technologies that underpin digital transformation. Economic complexity, which entails that knowledge is a core production factor, is an indicator of sophisticated and innovation-based production structures. Economic complexity is closely related to product diversification in both the domestic production and export bundle. Another feature of complex economies is having dynamic markets where knowledge is distributed rapidly among economic agents (Hausmann et al., 2013). The present chapter argues that complexity variations may explain the digitalisation gap and ICT performance differences across countries, since many ICT goods are also characterised by complex and diversified components.

The concepts of governance and/or institutional quality have been increasingly linked to many aspects of economic performance (Abed & Gupta, 2002). Governance has implications for government policies (decision-making, transparency, and accountability) and business operations (bureaucratic structures, corporate ethics, corporate responsibility, ethical behaviours, and interactions with public officials, politicians, and other businesses). One of the driving forces of the digitalisation of a country is governmental digitalisation, particularly e-government practices (Schou & Hjelholt, 2018), which also provide new motivations for private businesses to invest in digital technologies (Brown et al., 2014). The digital world demands governance mechanisms that foster democratic and inclusive multilateral cooperation at both the national and international levels. Nationally, a well-governed market-oriented business environment requires support from good governance practices from governmental institutions to benefit all of society by promoting the use of ICT products (Filgueiras & Almeida, 2021). ICT use in the digital age, however, may have some adverse effects on governance, since there are technology-enabled and digitalisation-driven problems including cyber-bullying, disinformation, cyber-hacking, social media violence, and online attacks on governmental institutions, democratic elections, and some specific groups, etc. (Bannister & Connolly, 2018; OECD, 2019b). From the ICT perspective, it is commonly evidenced that better governance practices and export performance in ICT goods, as well as in other goods, are associated especially in developing countries that are suffering from relatively weaker institutions, which generate insecure and difficult international transactions (Asongu & Nwachukwu, 2019; Martínez-Zarzoso & Márquez-Ramos, 2019). In contrast to the widespread interest in the impacts of ICT on governance, this chapter provides an empirical analysis of the governance influences on ICT exports.

Empirical Framework

Variables, Data, and Model

In the empirical section, a panel data analysis is conducted using a 19-year annual (2000–2018) balanced panel data set of 54 countries (all sampled countries-ASCs). These countries have been also divided into 27 relatively higher digitally-competitive countries (HDCCs) and 27 relatively lower digitally-competitive countries (LDCCs), based on the 2016–2019 average of the IMD's WDCR (IMD, 2020, 2021). The relevant model in Eq. 5.1 links ICT exports to a set of potential determinants consisting of domestic income (income effect), imports of ICT goods (learning effect), manufacturing share in GDP (industrialisation effect), globalisation (openness effect), economic complexity (knowledge and diversification effect), and governance (institutional effect).

$$\begin{aligned}(ICTex_{c,t}) = {} & \beta_0 + \beta_1(GDPpc_{c,t}) + \beta_2(ICTim_{c,t}) \\ & + \beta_3(MVAsh_{c,t}) + \beta_4(Glob_{c,t}) + \beta_5(ECI_{c,t}) \\ & + \beta_6(Gov_{c,t}) + e_c f_t + u_{c,t} \qquad (5.1)\end{aligned}$$

The dependent variable (*ICTex*) is countries' exports in ICT goods as a percentage of total merchandise exports. Domestic income is gross domestic product (GDP) per capita (*GDPpc*) as thousand United States dollar (USD) at constant (2015) prices, while *ICTim* is imports of ICT goods as a percentage of total merchandise imports. Industrialisation is proxied by the percentage share of manufacturing value-added (*MVAsh*) in total GDP. The data sets for *ICTex*, *GDPpc*, and *ICTim* variables were taken from the digital economy and income database of UNCTAD (2021), while the *MVAsh* data set was taken from competitive industrial performance calculations of UNIDO (2021). Globalisation (*Glob*) is the overall (economic, social, and political) KOF globalisation index (2021) of Gygli et al. (2019), and economic complexity is the economic complexity index of the Atlas of Economic Complexity (2021). Finally, governance (*Gov*) is the average score of control of corruption, government effectiveness, regulatory quality, and rule of law metrics of the World Bank's worldwide governance indicators (WB WGI, 2021). In the model, c ($c = 1,\ldots,54 = C$) shows all sampled (ASCs) individual countries (cross-sectional units) classified into two sub-panels of HDCCs and LDCCs, for each the model is estimated separately. The time units are denoted by t ($t = 2000,\ldots,2018 = T = 19$), while β_0 is the regression constant and f is the unobserved common factors with e individual impacts. Finally, β_k ($k = 1,2,\ldots,6$) parameters are the coefficients to be estimated and u is a composite error term.

Defining a certain list for ICT goods is a challenge because ICT productions take place in many related industries (OECD, 2011). Notwithstanding this difficulty, it is well known that ICT goods broadly include office machines, data processing machines, telecommunication, and advance electrical machinery. In the case of this chapter, ICT goods consist of 94 goods defined at the 6-digit level of the 2017 version of the Harmonized System (UNCTAD, 2017). These ICT goods are characterised by high digital intensity (Calvino et al., 2018) and are defined under five broad categories: (i) computers and peripheral equipment, (ii) radio, television, and communication equipment, (iii) consumer electronic equipment, (iv) electronic components, and (v) miscellaneous ICT goods. In relation to digital transformation, international trade, household expenditure, business and government expenditures, and domestic production indicators related to ICT products can be used to measure the ICT involvement of countries (OECD, 2011). This chapter's empirical setting builds on the international trade dimension of ICT involvement for also capturing domestic ICT production. ICT services have been excluded from the analysis.

A wide range of economic and non-economic factors may affect the ICT export performance of countries. Therefore, it is another challenge to reflect all the factors in a cross-country setting. To overcome this challenge, composite indices of globalisation, complexity, and governance variables have been used. Industrial development is also an important determinant of ICT exports with both positive and negative effects, depending on the stage and structure of industrialisation. Manufacturing value-added share in total GDP is an efficient indicator of industrialisation, since the value-added approach, compared to gross value terms, provides an ideal way to eliminate possible biases caused by double-counting. Manufacturing sectors correspond to divisions 10–33 under section C in the fourth revision of the international standard industrial classification of all economic activities-ISIC (UN, 2008). Because the considered dimensions of governance are strongly and positively correlated for all the panels of country samples (greater than 0.92 for ASCs, greater than 0.84 for HDCCs, and greater than 0.83 for LDCCs), the average score is used as a proxy of the overall governance. The missing governance scores from 2001 have been linearly interpolated.

Key Statistics and Correlations

Summary descriptive statistics and Pearson correlation coefficients (r) are reported in Table 5.3. For the ASCs panel, the mean value of *ICTex* is *8.168*, with a maximum value of *54.974* (in the year 2000 of Singapore) and a minimum value of *0.003* (in the year 2000 of Kazakhstan). For the *GDPpc* variable, the highest per capita income (*85,267 USD*) is that of Switzerland in 2018, while India has the lowest per capita income (*773 USD*) in 2000. Regarding globalisation, Switzerland had the highest (*90.984*) globalisation index in 2016 whereas India had the lowest index (*46.356*) in 2000. In the context of economic complexity, Japan had the most complex economic structure, with the highest ECI score (*2.895*) in 2000, while Kazakhstan had the lowest score (*−0.947*) in 2011. Similarly, governance varies considerably across countries. Overall governance index changes between *2.185* (2007 value of Denmark) and *−0.970* (2002 value of Kazakhstan). The independent-groups t-test statistics reveal the heterogeneity of the sub-samples in terms of the variables except for *ICTim* and *MVAsh*, in which the differences between the mean values of HDCCs' and LDCCs' sub-samples are not statistically significant at the level of 10%. Overall, it can be inferred from the comparison of means that the HDCCs group, on average, has a higher ICT exports share, a higher income level, and better governance practices; in addition, they are also more complex and more globalised compared to LDCCs.

The pairwise correlation matrix of Pearson coefficients in Table 5.3 shows that *ICTex* is strongly (>*0.70*) correlated with only *ICTim* for all panels. The high correlations between the imports and exports of ICT goods indicate a prevalent two-way (i.e. intra-industry trade) ICT

Table 5.3 Descriptive statistics and correlation (r) matrix

	ICTex	*GDPpc*	*ICTim*	*MVAsh*	*Glob*	*ECI*	*Gov*
	All sampled countries-ASCs (Obs.:1026)						
Mean	8.168	23.506	10.383	15.766	75.691	0.896	0.776
Max.	54.974	85.267	51.477	35.240	90.984	2.895	2.185
Min.	0.003	0.773	0.007	5.412	46.356	−0.947	−0.970
ICTex(r)	1						
GPPpc(r)	−0.045	1					
ICTim(r)	0.905*	−0.037	1				
MVAsh(r)	0.579*	−0.207*	0.455*	1			
Glob(r)	0.019	0.731*	−0.053	−0.131*	1		
ECI(r)	0.369*	0.514*	0.209*	0.349*	0.593*	1	
Gov(r)	0.070	0.846*	0.051	−0.172*	0.813*	0.564*	1
	Higher digitally-competitive countries-HDCCs (Obs.:513)						
Mean	10.638**	37.258**	11.684	15.896	81.659**	1.290**	1.437**
Max	54.974	85.267	42.827	35.240	90.984	2.895	2.185
Min	0.794	2.147	2.687	5.412	52.018	−0.628	−0.397
ICTex(r)	1						
GPPpc(r)	−0.395*	1					
ICTim(r)	0.932*	−0.285*	1				
MVAsh(r)	0.609*	−0.358*	0.513*	1			
Glob(r)	−0.426*	0.619*	−0.365*	−0.395*	1		
ECI(r)	0.227*	0.198*	0.119*	0.413*	0.247*	1	
Gov(r)	−0.392*	0.791*	−0.267*	−0.492*	0.726*	0.155*	1
	Lower digitally-competitive countries-LDCCs (Obs.:513)						
Mean	5.699**	9.753**	9.081	15.636	69.722**	0.502**	0.115**
Max	47.761	33.888	51.477	29.964	85.361	1.721	1.444
Min	0.003	0.773	0.007	8.658	46.356	−0.947	−0.970
ICTex(r)	1						
GPPpc(r)	−0.164*	1					
ICTim(r)	0.866*	−0.202*	1				
MVAsh(r)	0.564*	−0.247*	0.385*	1			
Glob(r)	0.071	0.548*	−0.091	0.037	1		
ECI(r)	0.376*	0.369*	0.149*	0.376*	0.533*	1	
Gov(r)	0.055	0.499*	−0.016	−0.039	0.623*	0.427*	1

Note * denotes statistical significance of correlation coefficient at the level of 1%. ** denotes statistical significance of the difference between mean values of HDCCs' and LDCCs' sub-samples at the level of 1%

trade, and multi-country participation in global value chains of many ICT sectors. Among the potential predictors, *GDPpc* is highly correlated with *Glob* and *Gov* variables for the ASCs' panel and with only *Gov* for HDCCs' sub-sample panel. Additionally, *Glob* and *Gov* variables are strongly correlated in the cases of the ASCs' panel and HDCCs' sub-sample panel.

Cross-Sectional Dependence and Stationarity Controls

The stationarity (the absence of a unit root) and non-stationarity (the presence of a unit root) of variables matter for the selection of an appropriate methodology, as well as for the efficiency of estimations. Stationarity can be controlled through a variety of panel root tests which are grouped into two generations. The first-generation panel unit root tests assume cross-sectional independence while the second-generation tests consider cross-sectional dependence (CD) (Baltagi & Pesaran, 2007). Therefore, it is necessary to check the series for CD to determine an appropriate unit root test. In this chapter, variables are controlled for CD through the scaled Lagrange Multiplier (*LM*) test (Pesaran, 2021) and bias-corrected scaled LM test (Baltagi et al., 2012), which are based on a null hypothesis of the absence of CD. The test results reported in Table 5.4 strongly indicate the existence of CD. Thus, the second-generation tests are more appropriate. One of the widely used second-generation panel root tests is the cross-sectionally augmented Dickey–Fuller (CADF) test (Pesaran, 2007) based on the null hypothesis of non-stationarity. The CADF test results in Table 5.4 show that the series of variables do not contain any unit root for either the trended or detrended cases of all three panels.

Estimation of the Predictors of ICT Exports

The level-stationary variables have enabled the estimation of the linear model in Eq. 5.1 within the traditional least squares (LS) framework,

Table 5.4 Results of cross-sectional dependence and stationarity tests

	ASCs		HDCCs		LDCCs	
	Cross-sectional dependence (CD) tests					
	Pesaran scaled LM	*Bias-corrected scaled LM*	*Pesaran scaled LM*	*Bias-corrected scaled LM*	*Pesaran scaled LM*	*Bias-corrected scaled LM*
ICTex	170.09***	168.59***	135.41***	134.66***	45.44***	44.693***
GPPpc	328.11***	326.61***	179.75***	179.00***	153.60***	152.85***
ICTim	156.24***	154.74***	122.47***	121.72***	42.099***	41.349***
MVAsh	178.35***	176.85***	78.658***	77.90***	95.928***	95.178***
Glob	357.51***	356.01***	179.93***	179.18***	176.77***	176.02***
ECI	158.72***	157.22***	96.889***	96.139***	62.833***	62.083***
Gov	94.836***	93.336***	39.980***	39.230***	51.651***	50.901***
	CADF panel stationarity test (at level)					
	Detrended	*Trended*	*Detrended*	*Trended*	*Detrended*	*Trended*
ICTex	−3.200***	−3.271***	−2.846***	−2.651***	−2.474***	−2.412***
GPPpc	−1.975**	−25.91***	−2.017**	−2.131**	−3.847**	−3.689***
ICTim	−2.964***	−3.106***	−3.270***	−3.272***	−2.413***	−2.812***
MVAsh	−1.820**	−2.105**	−2.066**	−2.803***	−1.651**	−2.630***
Glob	−1.885**	−4.997***	−2.305***	−1.942**	−4.747***	−5.462***
ECI	−2.078**	−3.446***	−2.177**	−2.675***	−2.108***	−2.757***
Gov	−1.663**	−2.605***	−1.539*	−3.159***	−1.432*	−7.370***

Note ***, **, and * denote statistical significance at the levels of 1%, 5%, and 10%, respectively

which can be conducted using the pooled LS, fixed-effects, and random-effects regression models. Estimating a common constant term for all countries, the pooled LS estimator omits individual country effects. Since the pooled LS model ignores the panel structure of the data, the fixed-effects and random-effects models are two key approaches when the panels are heterogeneous, as in the case of this chapter.

The fixed-effects model assumes that variations across countries and years can be captured in differences in the constant term. The fixed-effects model allows the unobserved country effects to be correlated with the predictors. The fixed-effects estimates fit better when all the relevant countries are included in the sample. In the random-effects model, however, the country-specific effects are uncorrelated with the regressors. Thus, this model is appropriate when a small sample of countries is drawn randomly from a large population (Greene, 2008). Notwithstanding these antecedents, several tests may help in selecting appropriate estimators. In this chapter, the Hausman (1978) test is applied for the final inference.

The results from the estimation of the ICT exports model are reported in Table 5.5. The results produced by the one-way fixed-effects estimation in the case of the ASCs' panel show that GDP per capita is negatively associated with ICT export performance, whereas the increased ICT imports and manufacturing value-added (industrialisation) lead to increases in ICT exports. Economic complexity is positively associated with ICT export performance.

The results from the two-way random-effects estimation for the HDCCs' sub-sample reveal a positive relationship between ICT imports and ICT exports, which confirms the validity of the presumed learning effect. On the other hand, globalisation is ascertained as a barrier to ICT exports. The increased economic complexity, which is one of the common characteristics of digitally-competitive countries, is found to be an important driver of ICT exports, while governance has a negative impact in the case of HDCCs.

In general, the results for the HDCCs' sub-sample considerably differ from those found from one-way fixed-effects estimation for the LDCCs' sub-sample. The insignificant positive impact of manufacturing value-added share on the HDCCs' ICT exports becomes significant, while the

Table 5.5 Estimates of the predictors of ICT export performance

Samples → ↓ Predictors	ASCs	HDCCs	LDCCs
GPPpc: β_1	−0.164*** (0.037)	0.014 (0.027)	−0.036 (0.100)
ICTim: β_2	0.875*** (0.026)	1.179*** (0.029)	0.436*** (0.037)
MVAsh: β_3	0.135** (0.057)	0.043 (0.054)	0.358*** (0.079)
Glob: β_4	−0.003 (0.027)	−0.167*** (0.044)	0.023 (0.037)
ECI: β_5	1.806*** (0.477)	1.603*** (0.547)	−0.576 (0.596)
Gov: β_6	0.101 (0.679)	−2.490*** (0.815)	2.989*** (0.785)
Constant: β_0	−0.641 (1.952)	10.804*** (3.246)	−5.153** (2.474)
Weighted statistics			
R^2; Adjusted R^2	0.951; 0.948	0.843; 0.841	0.947; 0.943
F-stat	320.510***	451.528***	265.403***
Model specification (Hausman test)			
Cross-section	48.738***	8.155	72.058***
Period	4.744	6.976	2.748
Estimated model	Fixed-effects	Random-effects	Fixed-effects

Note ***, **, and * denote statistical significance at the levels of 1%, 5%, and 10%, respectively. Standard errors are in parentheses

estimated negative influence of globalisation turns out to be positive but insignificant for LDCCs. Again, the positive and significant impact of economic complexity becomes negative and insignificant for LDCCs. The positive association between ICT exports and the governance of LDCCs also contradicts the negative nexus between governance and ICT exports of HDCCs. The only result that remains significant and with similar impacts for both sub-samples is that of ICT imports, despite a large reduction in magnitude for the LDCCs' sub-sample. Overall, there is no evidence found to support the presence of possible income effects for both sub-samples.

Panel Causalities

The export performance in ICT sectors may interact reciprocally with its predictors. Therefore, the empirical analysis of the chapter is concluded with an investigation of bidirectional causalities between ICT exports and its examined predictors. The Granger non-causality procedure of Dumitrescu and Hurlin (2012) is followed in connection with the level-stationary properties of the variables. Based on the null hypothesis of homogeneous non-causality, this test produces standard Zbar statistics which are robust to the presence of cross-sectional dependence. The results reported in Table 5.6 ascertain bidirectional causalities between ICT exports and most of its examined predictors in all three panels. For the ASCs' panel, the causalities between ICT exports and its predictors (except for that unidirectional causality from ICT exports to governance) are statistically significant. For the HDCCs' sub-sample panel, causalities (except for that unidirectional causality from ICT exports to ICT imports and bidirectional causalities between governance and ICT exports) are statistically significant. Finally, in the case of the LDCCs'

Table 5.6 Results of the Dumitrescu-Hurlin panel causality test

Null hypothesis	ASCs		HDCCs		LDCCs	
	Zbar-stat	Prob. (p)	Zbar-stat	Prob. (p)	Zbar-stat	Prob. (p)
GPPpc↛ICTex	4.387	0.000***	3.868	0.000***	2.337	0.019**
ICTex↛GPPpc	2.676	0.008***	2.964	0.003***	0.820	0.412
ICTim↛ICTex	4.607	0.000***	2.053	0.040**	4.462	0.000***
ICTex↛ICTim	3.298	0.001***	0.893	0.372	3.771	0.000***
MVAsh↛ICTex	3.676	0.000***	1.877	0.061*	3.321	0.001***
ICTex↛MVAsh	7.997	0.000***	5.657	0.000***	5.653	0.000***
Glob↛ICTex	7.009	0.000***	3.826	0.000***	6.086	0.000***
ICTex↛Glob	6.678	0.000***	8.236	0.000***	1.208	0.227
ECI↛ICTex	3.814	0.000***	2.130	0.033**	3.263	0.001***
ICTex↛ECI	4.403	0.000***	2.393	0.017**	3.833	0.000***
Gov↛ICTex	2.532	0.011**	1.582	0.114	2.000	0.046**
ICTex↛Gov	1.083	0.279	0.406	0.685	1.126	0.260

Note ***, **, and * denote statistical significance at the levels of 1%, 5%, and 10%, respectively. Lag length is 2

sub-sample panel, significant causalities could not be established from only ICT exports to per capita GDP, globalisation, and governance.

Concluding Remarks

The digital transformation and information revolution have changed societies in many ways, from how they learn and communicate to how they produce and consume. Recently, governments, businesses, institutions, and individuals in every country have been busy responding to social and economic challenges related to the coronavirus pandemic, which is one of the most formidable and unforgettable human crises in recent history. Now, it is well understood that digitalisation is contributing to dealing with the pandemic and it will empower governments, businesses, and societies to stay agile and resilient after recovery. The vast multifaceted opportunities provided by digital transformation motivate many countries to design new digitalisation strategies in which the access, adoption, use, and production of ICT technologies have a curial role. Accordingly, notwithstanding the important lack of internationally comparable and reliable statistics, flourishing multidimensional literature has tried to explore the causes and effects of digitalisation and the digital gap across countries.

In the empirical literature, while one strand has quite intensively examined the contribution of digitalisation on a wide range of socio-economic indicators, the other strand has focused on exploring the determinants of digitalisation performance. One of the components of the digitalisation performance of countries is their involvement in the ICT sectors that are characterised by higher digital intensity. The ICT involvement of countries can be proxied by several indicators including ICT infrastructure, the prevalence of ICT use, ICT production and exports as well as ICT investment and consumption. Measuring these indicators is a challenge in cross-country analyses, though. Relying on the strong link between digitalisation and digital-intensive high-tech ICT goods and the close relationships between the export and production of ICT goods, this chapter used ICT exports to measure the involvement of countries in ICT. In the empirical part, how industrial development, globalisation, economic complexity, and governance, as well as income per capita and ICT imports, affect ICT exports were analysed by utilising a 19-year (2000–2018) balanced panel data set of 54 countries. Furthermore, in order to have more homogenous country groups in terms of digitalisation performance, all the sampled countries (ASCs) were grouped by digital competitiveness as 27 relatively higher digitally-competitive countries (HDCCs) and 27 lower digitally-competitive countries (LDCCs). In the analysis, after confirming the presence of cross-sectional dependency and level-stationarity features of the variables, the model was estimated using fixed- and random-effects estimators, followed by an inspection of bidirectional causalities running between the ICT exports and the examined predictors.

The results provided some noteworthy findings: economic growth measured by an increase in GDP per capita was found to reduce ICT exports in ASCs, while the income effect was statistically insignificant for the sub-samples. This evidence is in line with the premise that the income-ICT nexus is a dynamic process in which higher (lower) income does not necessarily bring about higher (lower) performance in ICT exports. Thus, LDCCs need to design and implement digital plans to improve ICT export performance. The HDCCs, which have significantly a higher average income level, may invest more in the production of digital-intensive ICT goods, which require relatively more investments compared to other mid-tech and high-tech products.

The positive and significant relationships between ICT exports and ICT imports for all panel groups confirm the existence of the mutual learning effect and underline the increased global value chains in ICT goods, to which many countries contribute, regardless of digital competitiveness or income level. This trade-in-task pattern gives new directions, including investments in education, research-development programmes, and infrastructures in ICT sectors for countries that aim to stimulate their ICT exports and digital competitiveness or increase their domestic digital contribution in global value chains of ICT goods.

During digital transformation, both LDCCs and HDCCs may adopt digital industrialisation from the ICT exports perspective, as it was found that industrial development proxied by the growth in manufacturing value-added share had consistently positive effects on ICT exports for both groups of countries. However, the statistically insignificant impact of industrialisation for HDCCs, which have been typically experiencing a declining share of manufacturing in GDP (deindustrialisation), implies that the improved digital services and service infrastructures may support the digital transformation of digitally-competitive and deindustrialising economies. Furthermore, industrial capabilities may be used to foster the digitalisation functions of the Fourth Industrial Revolution for these countries. These premises also provide new motivations for future studies to consider modelling the potential impacts of digital services and deindustrialisation.

Globalisation was ascertained with a varying impact across country samples. Even though the positive coefficient is statistically insignificant, LDCCs have the potential to take advantage of the globalisation-driven export performance whereas globalisation significantly means lower exports in ICT sectors for HDCCs. The estimated impacts of globalisation are in line with the ever-changing feature and dynamic structure of digital transformation from the ICT perspective. The possibility of digital relocation across countries and the potential catch-up trajectory between digitally-advanced countries and less advanced ones require more research.

Economic complexity was verified as one of the drivers of ICT exports for HDCCs. This finding implies that the dynamics of economic complexity tend to raise the capacity of the ICT exports of digitally-competitive economies, although this impact is negative and statistically insignificant for lesser digital economies. Previous research has revealed that the empirical link between governance and digitalisation is unclear and changes across countries with different characteristics. Better governance was found as a drawback to the ICT export performance of HDCCs, while it is one of the driving forces of ICT exports for LDCCs. This evidence indicates that worse governance may either grease or sand the wheels of digital transformation of countries, depending on their current digital capacities. Therefore, digitally-competitive countries need to formulate digital governance strategies to tackle the barriers to trade efficiency to facilitate ICT exports. Overall, from the digital transformation perspective, the ICT performance of countries may be affected by some initial conditions related to both policy and practices as well as a set of social, economic, and political antecedents. This potential existence of latent factors and/or omitted variables was also pointed by the higher regression constants. Hence, future studies may provide supportive evidence from country-specific factors such as subsidies and incentives, local programmes, training, and infrastructure. Additionally, significant bidirectional causalities were found among variables. Therefore, further studies are recommended to also examine the impacts of ICT exports on the examined predictors.

The empirical findings provided in this chapter have some shortcomings and thus require some caution in their interpretation. ICT export performance is only one of many components of digitalisation and thus a weak proxy indicator. Future studies may take other headline indicators of digitalisation, such as consumption, investment, and infrastructure dimensions, into account while analysing the causes and effects of digitalisation. As digitalisation is a dynamic transformation and its definitions and sectoral contents vary over time, systematic research is continuously needed. Furthermore, the excluded ICT services may also affect the digitalisation of countries. Finally, the present chapter used macro-data, thus the evidence will be enriched by future studies using micro-data on individuals, firms, employees, and consumers.

References

Abed, G. T., & Gupta, S. (2002). The economics of corruption: An overview. In G. T. Abed & S. Gupta (Eds.), *Governance, corruption, and economic performance* (pp. 1–16). IMF.

Agarwal, A., & Maiti, D. (2020). ICTs and effectiveness of governance: A cross-country study. In D. Maiti, F. Castellacci, & A. Melchior (Eds.), *Digitalisation and development* (pp. 321–343). Springer. https://doi.org/10.1007/978-981-13-9996-1_12

Akpan, P. I. (2003). Basic-needs to globalisation: Are ICTs the missing link? *Information Technology for Development, 10*(4), 261–274. https://doi.org/10.1002/itdj.1590100405

Ali, M. S. B., & Sassi, S. (2017). The role of ICT adoption in curbing corruption in developing countries. In H. Kaur, E. Lechman, & A. Marszk (Eds.), *Catalyzing development through ICT adoption* (pp. 37–50). Springer. https://doi.org/10.1007/978-3-319-56523-1_4

Asongu, S. A., & Nwachukwu, J. C. (2019). The role of openness in the effect of ICT on governance. *Information Technology for Development, 25*(3), 503–531. https://doi.org/10.1080/02681102.2017.1412292

Atlas of Economic Complexity. (2021). *Data*. http://atlas.cid.harvard.edu/

Baltagi, B. H., Feng, Q., & Kao, C. (2012). A Lagrange Multiplier test for cross-sectional dependence in a fixed effects panel data model. *Journal of Econometrics, 170*(1), 164–177. https://doi.org/10.1016/j.jeconom.2012.04.004

Baltagi, B. H., & Pesaran, M. H. (2007). Heterogeneity and cross section dependence in panel data models: Theory and applications. *Journal of Applied Econometrics, 22*, 229–232. https://doi.org/10.1002/jae.955

Banga, K. (2019). *Digital technologies and "value" capture in global value chains: Empirical evidence from Indian manufacturing firms* (WIDER Working Papers, 2019/43). https://doi.org/10.35188/UNU-WIDER/2019/677-7

Bannister, F., & Connolly, R. (2018). The fourth power: ICT and the role of the administrative state in protecting democracy. *Information Polity, 23*(3), 307–323. https://doi.org/10.3233/IP-180072

Brown, A., Fishenden, J., & Thompson, M. (2014). *Digitizing government—Understanding and implementing new digital business models*. Palgrave Macmillan.

Calvino, F., Criscuolo, C., Marcolin, L., & Squicciarini, M. (2018). *A taxonomy of digital intensive sectors* (OECD Science, Technology, and Industry Working Papers, 2018/14). OECD Publishing. https://doi.org/10.1787/f404736a-en

Chinn, M. D., & Fairlie, R. W. (2007). The determinants of the global digital divide: A cross-country analysis of computer and internet penetration. *Oxford Economic Papers, 59*(1), 16–44. https://doi.org/10.1093/oep/gpl024

De Marchi, V., Giuliani, E., & Rabellotti, R. (2018). Do global value chains offer developing countries learning and innovation opportunities? *The European Journal of Development Research, 30*, 389–407. https://doi.org/10.1057/s41287-017-0126-z

Dumitrescu, E. I., & Hurlin, C. (2012). Testing for Granger non-causality in heterogeneous panels. *Economic Modelling, 29*(4), 1450–1460. https://doi.org/10.1016/j.econmod.2012.02.014

EPO. (2021). *Patent data*. https://www.epo.org/searching-for-patents/data.html

European Commission. (2020). *2020 International Digital Economy and Society Index (I-DESI)*. Publications Office of the European Union.

European Commission. (2021). *The Digital Economy and Society Index (DESI)*. https://ec.europa.eu/digital-single-market/en/digital-economy-and-society-index-desi

Filgueiras, F., & Almeida, V. (2021). *Governance for the digital world: Neither more state nor more market*. Palgrave Macmillan.

Foster, C., & Azmeh, S. (2020). Latecomer economies and national digital policy: An industrial policy perspective. *The Journal of Development Studies, 56*(7), 1247–1262. https://doi.org/10.1080/00220388.2019.1677886

Fu, X. (2020). Digital transformation of global value chains and sustainable post-pandemic recovery. *Transnational Corporations, 27*(2), 157–166. https://doi.org/10.18356/d30d9088-en

Greene, W. H. (2008). *Econometric analysis* (6th ed.). Pearson/Prentice Hall.

Gygli, S., Haelg, F., Potrafke, N., & Sturm, J. E. (2019). The KOF Globalisation Index—Revisited. *The Review of International Organizations, 14*, 543–574. https://doi.org/10.1007/s11558-019-09344-2

Hausman, J. (1978). Specification tests in econometrics. *Econometrica, 46*(6), 1251–1271. https://doi.org/10.2307/1913827

Hausmann, R., Hidalgo, C. A., Bustos, S., Coscia, M., Chung, S., Jimenez, J., Simoes, A., & Yildirim, M. A. (2013). *The atlas of economic complexity: Mapping paths to prosperity* (2nd ed.). MIT Press.

Huang, C. Y., & Chen, H. N. (2010). Global digital divide: A dynamic analysis based on the bass model. *Journal of Public Policy & Marketing, 29*(2), 248–264. https://doi.org/10.1509/jppm.29.2.248

IMD. (2020). *The IMD World Digital Competitiveness Ranking (WDCR) 2020*. IMD World Competitiveness Center.

IMD. (2021). *IMD World Competitiveness Center*. https://www.imd.org/wcc/world-competitiveness-center/

KOF Globalisation Index. (2021). https://kof.ethz.ch/en/forecasts-and-indicators/indicators/kof-globalisation-index.html

Kozma, R. B., & Vota, W. S. (2014). ICT in developing countries: Policies, implementation, and impact. In J. Spector, M. Merrill, J. Elen, & M. Bishop (Eds.), *Handbook of research on educational communications and technology* (pp. 885–894). Springer.

López-Pueyo, C., Sanaú, J., & Barcenilla, S. (2009). International technological spillovers from ICT-producing manufacturing industries: A panel data analysis. *International Review of Applied Economics, 23*(2), 215–231. https://doi.org/10.1080/02692170802700583

Lwoga, E. T., & Sangeda, R. Z. (2019). ICTs and development in developing countries: A systematic review of reviews. *The Electronic Journal of Information Systems in Developing Countries, 85*(1), e12060. https://doi.org/10.1002/isd2.12060

Martínez-Zarzoso, I., & Márquez-Ramos, L. (2019). Exports and governance: Is the Middle East and North Africa region different? *The World Economy, 42*(1), 143–174. https://doi.org/10.1111/twec.12633

Mayer, J. (2018). *Digitalisation and industrialization: Friends or foes?* (UNCTAD Research Papers, 25). https://unctad.org/system/files/official-document/ser-rp-2018d7_en.pdf

McKinsey Global Institute. (2016). *Digital globalisation: The new era of global flows*. https://www.mckinsey.com/business-functions/mckinsey-digital/our-insights/digital-globalisation-the-new-era-of-global-flows

Ngwenyama, O., & Morawczynski, O. (2009). Factors affecting ICT expansion in emerging economies: An analysis of ICT infrastructure expansion in five Latin American countries. *Information Technology for Development, 15*(4), 237–258. https://doi.org/10.1002/itdj.20128

OECD. (2011). *OECD guide to measuring the information society 2011*. OECD Publishing. https://doi.org/10.1787/9789264113541-en

OECD. (2019a). *Measuring the digital transformation: A roadmap for the future*. OECD Publishing. https://doi.org/10.1787/9789264311992-en

OECD. (2019b). *How's life in the digital age? Opportunities and risks of the digital transformation for people's well-being*. OECD Publishing. https://doi.org/10.1787/9789264311800-en

OECD. (2021). *Digital economy*. https://www.oecd.org/sti/ieconomy/

Oxford Economics. (2021). *The digital density index: Guiding digital transformation*. https://www.oxfordeconomics.com/recent-releases/the-digital-density-index-guiding-digital-transformation

Pesaran, M. H. (2007). A simple panel unit root test in the presence of cross-section dependence. *Journal of Applied Econometrics, 22*(2), 265–312. https://doi.org/10.1002/jae.951

Pesaran, M. H. (2021). General diagnostic tests for cross-sectional dependence in panels. *Empirical Economics, 60*, 13–50. https://doi.org/10.1007/s00181-020-01875-7

Pianta, M. (2019). *The challenge of digitalization for firms in developing countries* (UNIDO Working Papers, 18/2019). UNIDO.

Rachinger, M., Rauter, R., Müller, C., Vorraber, W., & Schirgi, E. (2019). Digitalization and its influence on business model innovation. *Journal of Manufacturing Technology Management, 30*(8), 1143–1160. https://doi.org/10.1108/JMTM-01-2018-0020

Ritter, T., & Pedersen, C. L. (2020). Digitization capability and the digitalization of business models in business-to-business firms: Past, present, and future. *Industrial Marketing Management, 86*, 180–190. https://doi.org/10.1016/j.indmarman.2019.11.019

Schou, J., & Hjelholt, M. (2018). *Digitalisation and public sector transformations*. Palgrave Macmillan.

Serrano-Cinca, C., Muñoz-Soro, J. F., & Brusca, I. (2018). A multivariate study of internet use and the digital divide. *Social Science Quarterly, 99*(4), 1409–1425. https://doi.org/10.1111/ssqu.12504

Soto-Acosta, P. (2020). COVID-19 pandemic: Shifting digital transformation to a high-speed gear. *Information Systems Management, 37*(4), 260–266. https://doi.org/10.1080/10580530.2020.1814461

Tirado-Morueta, R., Aguaded-Gómez, J. I., & Hernando-Gómez, Á. (2018). The socio-demographic divide in internet usage moderated by digital literacy support. *Technology in Society, 55*, 47–55. https://doi.org/10.1016/j.techsoc.2018.06.001

UN. (2008). *International Standard Industrial Classification of All Economic Activities (ISIC), Revision 4*. UN. https://unstats.un.org/unsd/publication/seriesm/seriesm_4rev4e.pdf

UNCTAD. (2017). *ICT goods categories and composition (HS 2017)*. https://unctadstat.unctad.org/en/Classifications/DimHS2017Products_Ict_Hierarchy.pdf

UNCTAD. (2021). *UNCTADstat data center*. https://unctadstat.unctad.org/wds/ReportFolders/reportFolders.aspx?sCS_ChosenLang=en

UNIDO. (2019). *Industrial Development Report 2020: Industrializing in the digital age*. UNIDO.

UNIDO. (2021). *Competitive Industrial Performance (CIP) Index Database*. https://stat.unido.org/cip/

Vargo, D., Zhu, L., Benwell, B., & Yan, Z. (2021). Digital technology use during COVID-19 pandemic: A rapid review. *Human Behavior and Emerging Technologies, 3*(1), 13–24. https://doi.org/10.1002/hbe2.242

WB WGI. (2021). The *Worldwide Governance Indicators (WGI) project*. https://info.worldbank.org/governance/wgi/

WEF. (2020). *Mapping TradeTech: Trade in the Fourth Industrial Revolution* (Insight Report). https://www.weforum.org/reports/mapping-tradetech-trade-in-the-fourth-industrial-revolution

WIPO. (2021). *The PATENTSCOPE database*. https://www.wipo.int/patentscope/en/

Xing, Z. (2018). The impacts of Information and Communications Technology (ICT) and E-commerce on bilateral trade flows. *International Economics and Economic Policy, 15*, 565–586. https://doi.org/10.1007/s10368-017-0375-5

Yang, F., & Gu, S. (2021). Industry 4.0, a revolution that requires technology and national strategies. *Complex & Intelligent Systems*. https://doi.org/10.1007/s40747-020-00267-9

6

The Digitalization of Contracts in International Trade and Finance: Comparative Law Perspectives on Smart Contracts

Cristina Poncibò

Introduction

The term "digital economy" has been extensively used to describe the functioning of the economy and, in particular, that part of the economy which is linked to information and communication technologies (ICT). The digital economy is characterised by three main factors, including network effects, change of business cycles and new business methods (OECD, 2000). Briefly, "digitalisation" represents a new way of doing business that uses information and technology as facilitators of communication, data transfer and commercial transactions. In particular, the chapter examines the case of digitalisation of commercial transactions by considering, specifically, the case of smart contracts. Notwithstanding the vast amount of literature on blockchains (Seebacher & Schüritz, 2017), the legal framework remains uncertain, particularly, in relation to the

C. Poncibò (✉)
Department of Law, University of Turin, Turin, Italy
e-mail: cristina.poncibo@unito.it

M. Ratajczak-Mrozek and P. Marszałek (eds.), *Digitalization and Firm Performance*, https://doi.org/10.1007/978-3-030-83360-2_6

legal meaning of smart contracts (Di Matteo et al., 2019; Hacker et al., 2019). Thus, the chapter contains a legal analysis of this phenomenon. It analyses the legal framework for smart contracts by considering European private international law and employing a comparative law approach. It also questions the role of technology and industry self-regulation to develop smart contract models and standardise them. For example, the latter approach is central in the case of smart Incoterms® rules and smart derivative contracts. To deal with these issues, section "Smart Contracts: Main Characteristics and Applications" introduces the main economic applications of smart contracts and their relationship with blockchain technology. Section "Smart Contracts: EU Private International Law" deals with smart contracts according to European private international law. Section "Smart Contracts: Comparative Perspectives" contains a comparative analysis of common law and civil law approaches to the legal meaning of smart contracts. Section "Self-Regulation and Technology" examines the role of programmers and industries in self-regulating and standardising smart contracts. Section "Conclusions" contains our preliminary conclusions.

Smart Contracts: Main Characteristics and Applications

Blockchain as a Basis for Smart Contracts

The expression "blockchain technology" is often used to refer to the wider concept of distributed ledger technology (DLT) (a decentralised ledger) in which there is no central authority that controls, verifies and validates these transactions, as it consists of a peer-to-peer system which shares these records with all nodes. These records are unchangeable and continuous and are merged into blocks that are chained to each other to produce the blockchain (Buterin, 2015; Finck, 2018; Wright & De Filippi, 2015). Specifically, it has been said that "Blockchain is a peer-to-peer, distributed ledger that is cryptographically-secure, append-only, immutable (extremely hard to change), and updateable only via consensus or agreement among peers" (Bashir, 2018).

Thus, when we talk about decentralisation in blockchain, we refer to a fundamental feature of blockchain: the platform works without the need for intermediators and it functions by consensus mechanism.[1] For instance, the economic relations within the blockchain are defined as decentralised and disintermediated. An author notes "When value is transferred through blockchain networks, the traditional intermediaries responsible for verifying and validating transactions – human-based institutions – may become obsolete" (Finck, 2018). Regarding decentralisation, it is difficult to identify the participants on the platform or their location, and that makes determining the applicable law and jurisdiction increasingly difficult when disputes arise.

With respect to our understanding of such technology, it is necessary to make a preliminary distinction between public and private blockchains. In public (permissionless) blockchains, there is no single authority or entity which controls or manages the chain of nodes and the transactions are open to the public, with the anonymity of the nodes preserved and without any privileges being given. Generally, this type of blockchain is criticised due to the absence of a reliable authority for validating or/and verifying the transactions, although it requires a consensus by the nodes. In contrast, in private (permissioned) blockchains, the permission to join is given by an authority and the nodes are well known to the entity. However, such a model assigns certain privileges to the authority and/or certain nodes in order to verifying the data, thus it is highly efficient. Usually, private blockchains might use their own standards and, consequently, this practice creates an endless number of standards for blockchain and smart contracts. The problem of interoperability specifically concerns the difficulties of connecting various private blockchains.

Blockchain technology is facing many obstacles that would adversely affect its adoption. Therefore, it is necessary to point out that one of the main challenges affecting blockchain adoption by businesses is the current absence of a clear legal framework. Historically, the law always finds a path to regulate the technology, hence, the law will find an

[1] Adopting the consensus pattern makes the decentralisation of blockchain possible without the necessity of a central authority or entity, it should be borne in mind that not having a unique liable authority creates legal concerns related to defining the jurisdiction.

appropriate model for regulating blockchains and smart contracts (EU Blockchain Observatory, 2019).

Smart Contracts: The Main Characteristics

According to Nick Szabo (1996), the computer scientist who coined the term, a "smart contract is a computerised transaction protocol that executes the terms of a contract". Thus, smart contracts are applicable in the blockchain arena and the latter qualifies the smart contract by building on its distributed ledger. To be more precise, it has been stressed that "A block is a software-generated container that bundles together the messages relating to a particular smart contract. Those messages may act as inputs or outputs of the smart contract programming logic and may themselves point to other computer code" (Chamber of Digital Commerce, 2016, p. 10). Another definition of a smart contract based upon a blockchain could be "a self-executing piece of code situated on the shared ledger and maintaining its own state and that is theoretically immutable" (de Caria, 2017; Poncibò, 2020b).

When discussing smart contracts, one should consider their different aspects and features. Firstly, smart contracts are programmes that can be executed automatically under certain conditions or requirements. This idea met with unprecedented popularity, as they have the feature of being unchangeable once they are stored on the blockchain(Perugini & Dal Checco, 2015). Thus, they rely on software language and are automatically executed without the human element (de Caria, 2017).

On such basis, the legal meaning of smart contracts is disputed in the legal scholarship, and the binding nature of smart contracts (i.e. smart legal contracts) can only be ascertained on a case-by-case analysis, by considering certain factors, such as parties' consent, consideration, and legality, according to the applicable law. Thus, it is necessary to clarify that this chapter considers only smart (legal) contracts that generally contain the essential elements of a valid and binding contract according to the common standards of domestic contract laws. In fact, it is true to say that "(…) under certain circumstances and if so decided by the parties, smart contracts can fulfil the elements of a legally binding contract under common law and civil law systems, such as the United States and Spain" (US Chamber of Digital Commerce, 2018 at 15).

Secondly, it is also important to clarify that there are many different models: contracts entirely in code; contracts in code with a separate natural language version; natural language contracts with encoded performance; and/or natural language contracts with encoded payment mechanisms (Chamber of Digital Commerce, 2016, p. 9). In any event, here the point is that traditional contracts are drafted by lawyers using natural language, while smart contracts are written in programming language, hence, this will be an enormous challenge to contract law. In the future, lawyers will have to learn how to code contracts instead of drafting contracts, and this entails uncertainties and complexities regarding the interpretation of smart contracts before the courts (Wilkinson & Giuffre, 2021). Additionally, parties may face difficulties with a contract written in programming language, because this language in not as flexible as the natural language of a traditional contract, and it is not able to express many significant legal terms, e.g. good faith or force majeure (de Caria, 2017; Poncibò, 2020b).

Thirdly, smart contracts are self-executing once specific conditions and requirements have been verified. The self-executing is due to the simple mechanism of executing that characterises the course of smart contracts, which is based on identifying all the terms and conditions of the contract, following which the computer will implement the contract in a very precise and fair way. We can also add another positive effect of the self-executing feature: automation will lead to a reduction in the cost of commercial transactions. Unfortunately, self-executing deprives the parties of what is considered one of the most important features of traditional contracts, namely the possibility to amend or terminate the contract. In other words, in traditional contracts one party can ignore a partial breach of the contract by the other party if the commercial relation is highly valuable and parties have agreed upon a solution to that breach. In fact, in smart contracts this option is not available, due to the automatic execution with no ability to make amendments. Additionally, self-executing implies that undesired transactions cannot be undone. This problem manifests itself when there is a lack of legal capacity, particularly in regard to signatures, where in smart contracts there is only a digital signature instead of manual signatures, and this could open the door to unlawful activities.

Fourthly, the legal system guarantees that the rights of a party will be realised, as well as providing duties or remedies following any kind of breach of contract. This is based on the element of predictability that contract law provides. The distinction between digital enforcing and self-enforcing is relevant in the case examined here: digital enforcing is generally based on a third party, whereas a smart contract is self-enforcing and—ideally—it does not require a third party to enforce it (i.e. judges, arbitrators). Self-enforcement allows parties to a smart contract to secure mutual obligations without relying on third parties (de Caria, 2017; Poncibò, 2020b). Nevertheless, this mechanism of enforcement is criticised in many aspects. Some claim that smart contracts are automated and performed by computers without any external intervention, and they cannot be stopped by parties, courts, or any third party; however, these are considered as weaknesses of self-enforcement. Smart contracts are not flexible and not able to adapt to new situations or circumstances, and current legal systems and contract law are not able to adopt such a mechanism of enforcement. In this respect, unpredictability is also one of the challenges that have arisen with smart contracts.

Smart Contracts: Some Economic Applications

Turning to the relevance of smart contracts for business, the US Chamber of Digital Commerce has explored twelve use cases of smart contracts, including digital identity, records, securities, trade finance, derivatives, financial data recording mortgages, land title recording, supply chain, insurance, and the health sector (Chamber of Digital Commerce, 2016, pp. 15–37). Ream et al. (2016) also offer a detailed picture of the range of applications of smart contracts for business.

In particular, scholars are contributing by analysing the most promising applications of blockchain for business by discussing its impact on the following: (a) financial services, (b) manufacturing and industrial processes, (c) consumer goods and retail, (d) the food industry;

and (e) cybersecurity and Internet of Things (IoTs) (Christidis & Devetsikiotis, 2016). In the light of the above, they have looked at applications of blockchain in different industries and highlighted the great impact of this innovation for business in improving efficiencies and reducing costs (Attaran & Gunasekaran, 2019). For example, it seems that blockchain may play a significant role in fostering emerging markets and economies including smart cities, value-based healthcare, the decentralised sharing economy, machine to machine transactions, and the data-sharing marketplace.

From a legal perspective, smart contracts may represent good vehicles for the implementation and automation of business processes, particularly as regards those processes that, by involving multiple parties (e.g. global supply chains), need to be governed efficiently, through automation and digital trust. Interestingly, the parties need to trust each other fully in a contract system; they may also trust the State and, specifically, the judicial system to enforce the contract. In contrast, smart contracts eliminate the need for trust and intermediaries; therefore, self-enforcement will replace the legal system, and the parties will then be able to shape agreements without relying on the State. The mechanism of digital trust enabled by the blockchain, coupled with the flexible design and easy implementation made possible by smart contracts, can support existing business processes and pave the way for business relationships on a global scale hitherto impracticable due to costs and complications inherent to traditional methods of trust management (Huang & Carlsson, 2016; Werbach, 2018). We are therefore witnessing a metamorphosis of the concept of trust of economic operators: from that of the Hobbesian type—characterised by State authority which guarantees the fairness and execution of the contractual relationship—to blockchain trust, in which the parties involved ignore the existence of any authority, replacing it with the use of a specific technological medium (Cole, 2019; Werbach, 2018). Each user can in fact use blockchain technology while remaining almost anonymous or even, at least potentially, completely anonymous (De Filippi & Wright, 2018).

Smart Contracts: EU Private International Law

Legal Uncertainty

Having considered the above, it should be noted that the smart contract is particularly suitable for managing cross-border transactions, due to its digital nature as an agreement and computer programme running on blockchains. By relying on digitalisation and automation, such an instrument promises to be very efficient: it will contribute to cost reduction and trade facilitation. On the other hand, when the smart contract contains (and codes) cross-border commercial transactions, namely in the vast majority of cases, it presents serious legal risks with respect to the identification of the appropriate law and jurisdiction in the event that any dispute arises among the parties (Omlor, 2020; UNCITRAL/UNIDROIT, 2019).

In this respect, it should be stressed that the European legal framework for cross-border smart contracts remains unclear, according to legal scholars and, thus, this chapter attempts to address this gap (Lehmann, 2019; Pretelli, 2018; Rühl, 2019, 2020). In particular, the solutions offered under EU private international law are residual, in the sense that it intervenes only when the smart contract has not been able to execute itself or to find an internal remedy (in the code), thus inducing the alleged injured party to take recourse before the courts.[2] It should be noted that the scarcity and lack of homogeneity in the regulatory solutions adopted, particularly at the European level, gives rise to further legal doubts (Pretelli, 2018). Similar coordination problems had actually already arisen following the advent of the Internet and, in general, of ICT and, now, DLTs. In particular, doubts about the applicable law and the choice of jurisdiction have long affected cross-border contracts concluded online that ought to have been governed by the laws of cyberspace and

[2] Article 1.2 of the regulation excludes arbitration from the matters of application of the Brussels I-bis Regulation but specifies in recital 12 that "This regulation should not apply to arbitration. Nothing in this Regulation should prevent the courts of a Member State having an action in a matter for which the parties have entered into an arbitration agreement, from referring the parties to arbitration or from suspending the proceedings or declaring inadmissible. request and to examine the possible nullity, inoperability or inapplicability of the arbitration agreement, in accordance with its national law".

not by the sources identified by private international law. Over time, the image of the Internet as the seventh continent—necessarily without borders and endowed with autonomous discipline—has, however, been overcome. It has been found that the Internet consists of servers or, in any case, indirectly, of centres of interests and actions, and, thus, of responsibility. Furthermore, DLTs also present some centres of interests in the physical world (Finck, 2018).

Choice of Jurisdiction

In this section we discuss the issue of identifying the jurisdiction, leaving the question of the applicable law to the next section. Having said this, Brussels I Regulation (recast) could only be applied in the presence of certain requirements.[3] As a preliminary comment, the Regulation applies if the smart contract at issue contains a valid and binding agreement: as such, in accordance with the autonomous definition of the Court of Justice of the EU (CJEU), the smart contract must include an obligation that is freely assumed between the parties.[4]

With regard to the material field of application, the aforementioned Regulation applies to disputes in civil and commercial matters. In this regard, the CJEU has rejected the notion that these matters can be identified by looking at the law of one or the other State concerned.[5]

[3] Regulation (EU) 1215/2012 of the European Parliament and of the Council of 12 December 2012 on jurisdiction and the recognition and enforcement of judgements in civil and commercial matters (recast).

[4] The Court of Justice referred to a precedent in which it stated that the notion of "contractual matter" pursuant to Article 5 point 1 of the then 1968 Brussels Convention, "could not include the case in which there is no obligation freely assumed by one party towards another" (Réunion européenne SA and Others v Spliethoff's Bevrachtingskantoor BV and the Master of the vessel Alblasgracht V002, 27 October 1998, C-51/97, European Court Reports 1998 I-06511, point 17).

[5] Court of Justice, 14 October 1976, in case C-29/79, Verbaeys-Biondi v. Unpublished commission; cf. also Court of Justice, 18 October 2011, in case C-406/08, Realchemie v. Bayer Crop Science AG, ECLI: EU: C: 2011: 666.

Conversely, it is necessary to have regard to the legal nature of the relationship brought before the court, excluding those concerning one of the matters expressly listed in Article 1.2 of the Regulation.[6]

Moreover, the said Regulation is applicable provided that the defendant is domiciled in a member state of the EU. If this is not the case, the internal rules on jurisdiction in each member state become effective again. As regards the rules on jurisdiction, the EU has established that the general principle of the Brussels I Regulation (recast) is precisely that of the defendant's domicile. Operationally, it seems that, if the subject of the dispute is a case governed by a smart contract, the domicile of the defendant, whether a natural or legal person, is difficult to identify. In fact, it seems unreasonable to think that the parties may decide to indicate this expressly in the contract: one of the added values of the use of DLTs is precisely that of sharing as little personal data as possible.

In the absence of an express (and correct indication) of the domicile, as already occurs for analogue and/or digital contracts, even for a smart contract a court could establish its jurisdiction if the defendant—if a natural person—is actually domiciled in the same state in which he was sued (Article 62.1). If not, the court would have to assess whether the defendant is domiciled in another member state, having regard to the definition of domicile given by the latter's national law.

The same uncertainties apply to the legal person considering that, as prescribed in Article 63 of the Regulation, one could alternatively refer to the statutory domicile, to the place where the legal person is established as well as to the place where the main business centre is located. The statutory domicile is the only legal criterion and it is easily available, as it is public; however, this is unsafe, as there is no European qualification of statutory domicile. In fact, particularly for companies with significant turnover, the headquarters are often located in favourable jurisdictions in

---

[6] Article 1.2 Regulation: "The following are excluded from the scope of application of this regulation: a) the status and capacity of natural persons, the property regime between spouses or arising from relationships that according to the law applicable to the latter they have effects comparable to marriage; b) bankruptcies, procedures relating to the liquidation of companies or other legal persons that are in a state of insolvency, arrangements with creditors and similar procedures; c) social security; d) arbitration; e) maintenance obligations deriving from family, kinship, marriage or affinity relationships; f) wills and succession, including mortis causa maintenance obligations".

which they do not actually operate. Conversely, the other criteria, being geographically localised, are difficult to find in the hypothesis where the legal person in question conducts activity using blockchains, which are, as such, decentralised in many nodes that may be anonymous and located in a number of jurisdictions.

Finally, a similar application difficulty arises, then, in the hypothesis of the sale of goods, for which the legislator has established ad hoc rules in Article 7.1 (b). With regard to the sale, the place of performance of the obligation in question shall be: "i) in the case of the sale of goods, the place in a Member State where, under the contract, the goods were delivered or should have been delivered; ii) in the case of the provision of services, the place in a Member State where, under the contract, the services were provided or should have been provided; iii) where the asset was or should have been delivered" (Article 7.1 b).

Case law confirms that the place must be determined on the basis of the provisions of the contract and, if there are no such provisions, the commercial terms and clauses that contain an explicit indication of the place of delivery may be considered. In their absence, the place is that of the material delivery of the goods by which the buyer has obtained or should have obtained the power actually to dispose of those goods.[7] However, in our case, the digital contract is concluded on the blockchain so that, even in the hypothesis of the purchase and sale of a tokenised asset, i.e. the purchase and sale of the digital representation of the consideration for the physical or intangible asset, the contract is considered to be concluded with the provision of consent or with the transfer to the buyer's virtual wallet of the token representing that given asset. In both cases, the certainty of the place in which the buyer actually obtains the availability of the asset is absent.

The analysis conducted so far leads to the exclusion of the application of the Brussels I Regulation (recast) if the subject of the dispute is a smart contract. Finally, the parties may appeal to the national judge only after having carried out the alternative dispute resolution remedies if they are

[7] Court of Justice, 25 February 209, in case C-381/08 Car Trim, ECLI: EU: C: 2010: 90, paragraph 44. Court of Justice, 9 June 2011, in case C-87/10, Electrosteel Europe SA v. Edil Centro SpA, ECLI: EU: C: 2011: 375, point 18.

stated as being mandatory in the smart contract itself (from settlement to so-called ADR procedures).[8]

Applicable Law

The smart contract also poses problems with regard to the applicable law, the identification of which is governed by the Rome I Regulation.[9] The arguments already made in the previous section regarding the Brussels I Regulation (recast) apply. Here, the chapter therefore examines the application of the connecting criteria of the Regulation to cases involving a smart contract.

With regard to the main connecting factor, the principle of the autonomy of will of the parties, the cornerstone of the Regulation in question (see premise 11), recognises the freedom of the parties to decide upon the law that applies to the relationship (Article 3.1). Operationally, however, it seems difficult to translate the will of the parties into an algorithm (Rühl, 2019; Chandler, 2019).

The main issue remains as to whether the choice is attributable to the party and not to the algorithm or to the person who designed it. For the provision of consent to the choice of law, a separate agreement is therefore required, negotiated and stipulated in traditional forms and in natural language (ISDA White Paper, 2020). The same limit applies in the case of an implicit choice in the sense that, although admitted by the Regulation in question, it must be clear from the provisions of the agreement or the circumstances. Both items of evidence are difficult to find in a legal instrument built with algorithms, such as software. Certainly, the law chosen by the parties is an essential prerequisite for verifying that the consent of the parties has been legally expressed.

[8] Article 1.2 of the regulation excludes arbitration from the matters of application of the Brussels I bis Regulation but specifies in recital 12 that the judge: "This regulation should not apply to arbitration. Nothing in this Regulation should prevent the courts of a Member State having an action in a matter for which the parties have entered into an arbitration agreement, from referring the parties to arbitration or from suspending the proceedings or declaring the request and to examine the possible nullity, inoperability or inapplicability of the arbitration agreement, in accordance with its national law".

[9] Regulation (EC) 593/2008 of the European Parliament and of the Council of 17 June 2008 on the law applicable to contractual obligations (Rome I), OJ L 177, 4.7.2008, pp. 6–16.

The residual criterion is referred to in Article 4.1, which states that the law is that of the place where the lender of the characteristic obligation has his habitual residence—for example, the seller in the case of a sale (Article 4.1 a). The criterion of habitual residence then returns for other types of contracts (transport, consumers, insurance, and employment). In all cases, however, this concept requires precise legal identification, which is still lacking in European law. In fact, Article 19 merely specifies the notion of habitual residence for legal persons and for natural persons who operate as professionals; therefore, natural persons who are not professionals are excluded. Furthermore, as these are activities carried out by professionals, or entities operating on DLTs, it is difficult to identify the places that should be indicated as the habitual residence. The second paragraph of Article 19 then introduces for the branches a geographical criterion defined ex ante, in the sense that it sees the habitual residence as coinciding with the place where the branch is located. However, it is a specification that, as in all cases where it refers to a physical place, risks being of little use in smart contracts.

If it is impossible to identify the habitual residence, the criterion referred to in Article 4.4 could be applied, thus seeking the closest connection, namely, the place with which the case is most connected. For one (habitual residence) and for the other (closest connection) case, the use of blockchain technology makes the search complicated and the criteria difficult to apply (Rühl, 2019).

Smart Contracts: Comparative Perspectives

Civil Law

From the foregoing, it appears that EU private international law cannot immediately be used for identifying the jurisdiction and law applicable to disputes in civil and commercial matters concerning a smart contract. It is therefore necessary to see whether national courts, when called to settle a dispute, will legitimise the practice of entering into smart contracts to manage cross-border transactions, for example, by considering an extensive interpretation of the existing rules to these digital contracts. Clearly, if the law of the forum applicable to the case excludes the legal validity of a smart contract, the use of EU private international law is precluded in itself.

In practice, the parties will probably agree on a national law to govern the digital contract by inserting a clause into the smart contract. Thus, the clause is translated into programming language. Nevertheless, in a comparative perspective, the state of play as to the validity and enforceability of smart contracts remains unclear (Procopie, 2021).

Over the last two years, civil law jurisdictions in the EU have begun to question the possibility of legitimising blockchain applications, and the new legal instruments that derive from them, particularly smart contracts (Poncibò, 2020b). There are many current initiatives and they therefore offer a promising field of exploration for comparative law scholars.

This subsection considers the law passed in Italy on smart contracts as a very good example of the cautious approach towards blockchain regulation that generally characterises civil law jurisdictions, especially in the EU. Since 2019, Italian law has defined DLTs and, interestingly, smart contracts.[10] It states that "(…) 2. A 'smart contract is defined as a computer programme that operates on technologies based on distributed registers and whose execution automatically binds two or more parties on the basis of predefined effects". Smart contracts may also meet the written form requirement following the computerised identification of the interested parties through the technical process designed by the public authority.

In the light of the above, a smart contract is therefore identified as a computer programme which, when executed, binds the parties. This assertion raises numerous legal questions concerning the protection of software, the role of blockchain (or platforms), to mention just a couple. More importantly, the paragraph in question then specifies that the effects produced by the smart contract are legally binding; one limitation of the provision is that it focuses on the effects, and not on the validity, of the constraint signed between the parties, namely on the smart contract

[10] See Article 8-ter in Law 12/2019, Conversion into law with amendments to the decree law 14 December 2018, n. 135, containing urgent provisions on support and simplification for businesses and the public administration (so-called Simplification Decree), in the OJ, General Series no. 36 of 02/12/2016.

itself. It is, therefore, still unclear whether the data formally entered in the smart contract has legal validity.

Similarly, French and German legal scholars seem to be very cautious in admitting that such a contract and programme may include binding obligations between the parties. They usually agree with their Italian colleagues in arguing in favour of limiting smart contracts to computer programmes for the automatic execution of contracts (Poncibò, 2020a, 2020b).

Common Law

With respect to the common law, it is interesting to note that a UK Jurisdiction Taskforce (UKJT) has been established to examine the legal meaning of smart contracts. On 9 May 2019, it launched a consultation to define and make public the Government's orientation in the field of new technologies and smart contracts.[11] In particular, the UKJT noted that a smart contract may, or may not, have binding effects between the parties depending on the circumstances of the case and in the light of English contract law. Thus, the concepts of offer, acceptance and consideration are likely to be relevant in this context. In particular, the UKJT intends to clarify whether, and in which circumstances, a smart contract may contain binding obligations for the parties.

Additionally, in the United States, some states, such as California, Delaware, Vermont, Nevada, Arizona, Hawaii, New Hampshire, and Illinois, have proposed the introduction of (and partly introduced) legislation aimed at legitimising the use of digital (smart) contracts (Verstraete, 2019). Legal scholars appear to favour such clarification by formal law while the legal meaning of a smart contract mainly depends on the circumstances of the case. The US Digital Chamber of Commerce

[11] UKJT, *Legal Statement on cryptoassets and smart contracts*, 2019, https://35z8e83m1ih83drye280o9d1-wpengine.netdna-ssl.com/wp-content/uploads/2019/11/6.6056_JO_Cryptocurrencies_Statement_FINAL_WEB_111119-1.pdf (accessed June 1, 2021).

specifies: "[t]he term "smart contract" is itself imperfect. A smart contract is neither smart, nor is it necessarily a contract".[12]

In such a context, California has, for example, expressly confirmed that a smart contract falls under domestic contract law. Notably, in September 2018 the California Assembly passed Bill no. 2658 amending the California Civil Code. Section 1633.2 states that Contract "means the total legal obligation resulting from the parties' agreement as affected by this title and other applicable law. "Contract" includes a smart contract. (p) "Smart contract" means an event-driven programme that runs on a distributed, decentralised, shared, and replicated ledger that can take custody over, and instruct transfer of, assets on that ledger".[13] Basically, the Californian Civil Code has assimilated smart contracts and traditional contracts, clarifying that the former are distinguished only by their particular form, based on coding (Verstraete, 2019).

Comparative Analysis

In a comparative analysis, it seems that both EU member states and non-EU states have been reluctant to regulate this innovation (Finck, 2018). The approach may be explained by the fact that the DLTs at the basis of the smart contract are still in a phase of development. This technology is not mature and it should not be held back by the introduction of excessively rigid and binding regulatory definitions. Moreover, it should also be underlined that case law on the legal nature of smart contracts is definitely scarce and is therefore not particularly useful in answering such an important research question. Accordingly, Lord Sales confirms in a recent speech that "The fundamental issue which smart contracts pose for the judiciary is that contract law, to date, has not developed in response to

[12] Chamber of Digital Commerce (US), *Smart contracts legal primer—Why smart contracts are valid under existing law and do not require additional authorization to be enforceable*, 2018, https://digitalchamber.org/wpcontent/uploads/2018/02/Smart-Contracts-Legal-Primer-02.01.2018.pdf (accessed June 1, 2021).

[13] The Civil Code of California is a collection of statutes for the State of California. The code is made up of statutes which govern the general obligations and rights of persons within the jurisdiction of California. The full text of the Bill no. 2658 is available at https://legiscan.com/CA/text/AB2658/id/1732549.

contracts generated and monitored automatically by machines. The legal doctrines and concepts which we apply to the cases that come before us are not necessarily equipped to deal with the questions that these contracts will generate. The Law Commission, an independent statutory body set up to keep national law under review and to recommend reforms, is currently considering smart contracts" (Lord Sales, 2021).

Turning to legal scholars, there is extensive literature on the definition of smart contracts and, at this stage, the general view in England and in common law countries, including the US, is that smart contracts are contracts where some terms are capable of being automatically performed; they meet the requirements for an enforceable contract under English law by which two or more parties intend to create a legal relationship and have each given something of benefit; they should not be treated as being different in principle from conventional contracts (ISDA White Paper, 2020, p. 5). In contrast to the common law position, civil law scholars have emphasised that technology is the essential part of smart contracts and for this reason there are clear instances in which smart contracts have been considered as computer programmes to execute contracts.

Self-Regulation and Technology

Smart Contracts Standardisation

Notwithstanding the lack of a clear international legal framework, the practice of relying on smart contracts is particularly widespread in international trade (Ream et al., 2016). Most important, this occurs in the absence of a clear legal framework at the international and domestic levels. It therefore seems that security in operational processes, as well as reliability in the operation of technology, are the characteristics that now induce parties to commit themselves by entering into a smart contract.

Therefore, digital trust (even in relation to technology) takes on a primary role in inducing economic operators to enter into a contractual relationship in international trade and finance (Werbach, 2018). In fact, regardless of the uncertain regulatory framework, economic operators are increasingly ready to accept digital contracts for cross-border trade due to their characteristics, which include cost reduction, automation and standardisation. Additionally, smart contracts do not require trust as previously noted. In the case of smart contracts, economic operators (i.e. private entities) are substantially contributing to drafting, coding, managing and executing smart contracts for international trade and finance. This occurs primarily through the process of the international standardisation of smart contracts: a process that is mainly driven by industries themselves rather than public institutions.

Indeed, contract standardisation has a long history, which begins with the emergence of standard form contracts (SFC) for consumers and businesses. Technology and globalisation have fostered the practice of developing standard models of contracts in certain industries. Specifically, the chapter emphasises that cross-border contracts in the fields of banking and finance, energy, and construction, to mention just a few, have been the subject of an international standardisation process through the efforts of the relevant industry and economic operators. Furthermore, many of these contracts have become almost identical internationally (e.g. the standard contracts of the International Federation of Consulting Engineers, FIDIC; see Bari et al., 2019).

Here, the point is that, due to the lack of legal certainty, smart contracts are currently undergoing an international standardisation process and are being regulated accordingly. The drivers of this process aimed at overcoming the shortcomings of the law are: coders and programmers, and economic operators and their associations (e.g. ICC, ISDA). They provide smart contract models and standardise them in the relevant industry.

Indeed, the divergence of smart contract protocols depending on the blockchain at issue (i.e. the problem of lack of interoperability between blockchains) can be an additional motivation for identifying some standards that economic operators could adopt internationally, thereby avoiding chaos in terms of the huge number of different models of smart contracts.

Programmers

Programmers are cooperating with each other in order to design standards for digital contracts on the blockchain. One of the main examples is Ethereum ERC-20 (ERC—Ethereum Request for Comments) standard smart contract (Ansari & Kulkarni, 2020). Using the ERC-20 standard makes it possible to create a token exchange system on Ethereum: the "transfer function" is the key feature, as it ensures direct fund transfers according to the receiver's address and the number of tokens being sent. The transfer return value is supplied as a report on receipt of the tokens. All the functions are executed by the Ethereum Virtual Machine, powered by the computational power of every Ethereum node. This gives ERC-20 tokens the ability to be involved in the automation of complex business processes and tasks in cloud-like virtual machines. It is interesting to note that, in its current form, ERC-20 is based upon cooperation between programmers and nodes—physically located in any jurisdiction—who continuously share views, comments and suggestions for the best drafting and management on-chain of smart contracts on Ethereum.

Smart Incoterms®

Economic operators are also significantly contributing to regulatory design through international standardisation. This section considers some leading cases at the international level (ICC and ISDA).

In September 2019, the International Chamber of Commerce (ICC) published Incoterms 2020, in force from 1 January 2020. In that regard, it should be noted that the International Chamber of Commerce initially signed an agreement with Perlin, one of the most influential blockchain certification platforms, only then to develop "a customisable, self-executing digital sales agreement, incorporating the new Incoterms rules. The incorporation of smart Incoterms® rules, or Smart INCOs, will help facilitate trade by reducing costs and barriers faced by importers and exporters worldwide, notably, small and medium enterprises" (ICC,

2019). The ICC has recognised that blockchain technology can facilitate trade, making it more secure and thus engendering trust in traders. This technology in fact highlights all the steps in the production chain, thus simplifying cross-border imports and exports. This new "trust" in the chain should also facilitate exchanges between small or medium-sized economic operators (Werbach, 2018). The latter can in fact rely upon the fact that a contract signed in the smart form is self-executing, thus being more likely to be executed, irrespective of any recourse to the judicial authority (Dimitrieva & Schmidt-Kessen, 2019). This final step often involves particularly high costs.

Smart Derivative Contracts

In this section, we also note that the case of smart derivative contracts is worthy of particular attention as, notwithstanding the peculiarities of finance, it offers a promising example of the possible role that may be played by private entities and self-regulation (i.e. soft-law) in this respect. In finance, the need for regulatory reporting, portfolio reconciliation and a large number of transactions is pushing a trend towards transaction automation which could save money and time. Furthermore, derivative contracts are highly technical in nature, with the parties' primary obligations being payments to one another, which can be accomplished by debiting accounts (money or securities), making them especially well-suited to automation (OECD, 2020; Guo & Liang, 2016; Auer, 2015).

Thus, the International Swap Derivatives Association (ISDA) is leading the field in terms of contract digitalisation and standardisation. In fact, the ISDA has promoted the standardisation of contractual documents on derivatives with the aim of increasing efficiency and avoiding unnecessary complexity in cross-border transactions. In practical terms, the ISDA has released a set of legal guidelines for smart derivatives contracts which are intended to explain the core principles of ISDA documentation and raise awareness of important legal terms that should be maintained when a technology solution is used in derivatives trading.

It should also be noted that these guidelines define the terms of a smart derivatives contract (ISDA White Paper, 2020, p. 5).

More specifically, in January 2020, the ISDA published a White Paper entitled "Private International Law Aspects of Smart Derivatives Contracts Utilising Distributed Ledger Technology" ("ISDA White Paper"). Co-authored with Clifford Chance, R3 and Singapore Academy of Law, the ISDA White Paper discusses the private international law, or conflict-of-law, aspects of derivatives contracts governed by the laws of Singapore, and of England and Wales, involving distributed ledger technology. Indeed, DLT systems are frequently borderless, allowing multiple users or participants to exchange records in a shared database that may be based in multiple jurisdictions. The ISDA has also published three additional papers covering French law, Japanese law, Irish, and New York law.[14]

Conclusions

In the light of the above, it is possible to draw some preliminary conclusions.

Firstly, smart contracts may facilitate cross-border transactions, but they also pose serious challenges to contract law. For instance, decentralisation makes it difficult to identify the parties or their location, and it implies a fundamental change towards a new understanding of trust in business. Additionally, self-execution offers a great opportunity for implementing any duties included into the contract, but this attribute may also place many obstacles before the parties.

Secondly, legal scholars struggle to reach an agreement on the legal meaning of smart contracts, and they also question whether smart contracts can be integrated within both European private international law and national contract laws. With respect to digital (smart) contracts, the state of play of EU law appears to be unclear and fragmented. Moreover, the chapter questions whether, and to what extent, smart contracts

[14] ISDA publications are available at https://www.isda.org/2019/10/16/isda-smart-contracts (accessed May 14, 2021).

can be assimilated to traditional contracts and thus be governed by the contract law of a given legal system.

Thirdly, in the absence of a clear legal framework, in the chapter we noted that economic operators and programmers are significantly contributing to drafting, managing and executing digital (smart) contracts. Basically, they are relying on technology and industry self-regulation in setting standard smart contracts for specific sectors of the industry, as in the leading cases of smart Incoterms® rules and smart derivative contracts.

Finally, in the chapter, we have observed the development of this *lex mercatoria ex machina* where merchants are fostering cross-border trade by relying primarily on technology and digital trust. Future directions in research should investigate this fundamental change of the law of merchants in the digital age.

References

Ansari, K.H., & Kulkarni, U. (2020, April 8). *Implementation of Ethereum Request for Comment (ERC20) Token.* Proceedings of the 3rd International Conference on Advances in Science & Technology (ICAST) 2020. https://doi.org/10.2139/ssrn.3561395

Attaran, M., & Gunasekaran, A. (2019). *Applications of blockchain technology in business.* Springer.

Auer, R. (2015, September). *Embedded supervision: How to build regulation into blockchain finance* (Monetary and Economic Department [BIS] Working Papers, No. 811). The Bank for International Settlements. https://www.bis.org/publ/work811.htm. Accessed April 28, 2021.

Bari, P., Bhatt, V., & Sawant, P. (2019, January 25). *Techno legal aspect of FIDIC contract.* Proceedings of Sustainable Infrastructure Development & Management (SIDM) 2019. https://doi.org/10.2139/ssrn.3376108

Bashir, I. (2018). *Mastering blockchain: Distributed ledger technology, decentralization, and smart contracts explained*. Packt Publishing.

Buterin, V. (2015). *On public and private blockchains.* https://blog.ethereum.org/2015/08/07/on-public-and-private-blockchains/. Accessed April 28, 2021.

Chandler, S. (2019). *Smart contracts are no problem for the world's legal systems, so long as they behave like legal contracts.* https://cointelegraph.com/news/smart-contracts-are-no-problem-for-theworlds-legal-systems-so-long-as-they-behave-like-legal-contracts. Accessed April 28, 2021.

Christidis, K., & Devetsikiotis, M. (2016). Blockchains and smart contracts for the internet of things. *IEEE Access, 4*, 2292–2303.

Cole, G. M. (2019). The long convergence: Smart contracts and the customization of commercial law. *Southern California Law Review, 92*, 851.

de Caria, R. (2017, July 4–6). *A digital revolution in international trade? The international legal framework for blockchain technologies, virtual currencies and smart contracts: Challenges and opportunities.* Modernizing International Trade Law to Support Innovation and Sustainable Development Proceedings of the Congress of the United Nations Commission on International Trade Law Vienna. Volume 4: Papers presented at the Congress.

Di Matteo, L. A., Cannarsa, M., & Poncibò, C. (2019). *The Cambridge handbook of smart contracts, blockchain technology and digital platforms.* Cambridge University Press.

Dimitrieva, H. E., & Schmidt-Kessen, M. (2019). Smart contracts: Reducing risks in economic exchange with no-party trust. *European Journal of Risks Regulation, 10*, 245–262.

De Filippi, P., & Wright, A. (2018). *Blockchain and the law.* Harvard University Press.

European Union Blockchain Observatory & Forum. (2019). *Legal and regulatory framework of blockchains and smart contracts.*

Finck, M. (2018). *Blockchain regulation and governance in Europe.* Cambridge University Press.

Guo, Y., & Liang, C. (2016). Blockchain application and outlook in the banking industry. *Financial Innovation, 2*, 24. https://doi.org/10.1186/s40854-016-0034-9

Hacker, P., Lianos, I., Dimitropoulos, G., & Eich, S., (2019). *Regulating blockchain. Techno-social and legal challenges.* Oxford University Press.

Huang, S., & Carlsson, J. (2016). *Blockchain technology in the Swedish fund market: A study on the trust relationships between actors in a blockchain-based fund market.* KTH, School of Computer Science and Communication (CSC).

ICC. (2019, June 28). *ICC Blockchains solutions developed by ICC and Perlin now have direct access to MENA.* Press release. https://iccwbo.org/media-wall/news-speeches/blockchain-solutions-developed-icc-perlin-now-direct-access-mena. Accessed April 28, 2021.

ISDA (2020). *White paper, private international law aspects of smart derivatives contracts utilising distributed ledger technology*. https://www.isda.org/2020/01/13/private-international-law-aspects-of-smart-derivatives-contracts-utilizing-distributed-ledger-technology. Accessed April 28, 2021.

Lehmann, M. (2019). Who owns bitcoin? Private law facing the blockchain *Minnesota Journal of Law, Science & Technology, 21*, 93 European Banking Institute Working Paper Series no. 42, https://ssrn.com/abstract=3402678. Accessed April 28, 2021.

Lord Sales, UK Supreme Court, Law in the Digital World, Cour de Cassation seminar: Being a Supreme Court Justice in 2030. https://www.supremecourt.uk/speeches/cour-de-cassation-seminar.html#fn5. Accessed April 28, 2021.

OECD. (2000). *A new economy? The changing role of innovation and information technology in growth* (p. 17). OECD.

OECD. (2020, January 17). *The tokenisation of assets and potential implications for financial markets*. https://www.oecd.org/finance/The-Tokenisation-of-Assets-and-Potential-Implications-for-Financial-Markets.htm. Accessed April 28, 2021.

Omlor, S. (2020). The CISG and Libra: A monetary revolution for international commercial transactions. *Stanford Journal of Blockchain Law & Policy, 81* fs.

Perugini, M. L., & Dal Checco, P. (2015). *Smart contracts: A preliminary evaluation*. https://ssrn.com/abstract=2729548. Accessed April 28, 2021.

Poncibò, C. (2020a). Blockchain and comparative law. In B. Cappiello & G. Carullo (Eds.), *Blockchain, law and governance* (pp. 137–156). Springer.

Poncibò, C. (2020b). *Il diritto comparato e la blockchain* (Chapter VII). Memorie del dipartimento di giurisprudenza dell'Università di Torino, Edizioni Scientifiche Italiane.

Pretelli, I. (2018). *Conflict of laws in the maze of digital platforms*. Le droit International Privé dans le labyrinthe des platformes digitales, Acte de la 30ejournée de droit international privé du 28 Juin 2018, Geneva

Procopie, L. (2021). Are smart contracts actually contracts? How smart contracts can work globally. *Journal of International Banking Law and Regulation, 36*(1), 25–30.

Ream, J. Chu, Y., & Schatsky, D. (2016, June 8). *Upgrading blockchains: Smart contract use cases in industry*. Deloitte University Press. https://www2.deloitte.com/us/en/insights/focus/signals-for-strategists/using-blockchain-for-smart-contracts.html. Accessed May 14, 2021.

Rühl, G. (2019). *The law applicable to smart contracts, or much ado about nothing*. Oxford Business Law Blog. https://www.law.ox.ac.uk/business-law-blog/blog/2019/01/law-applicable-smart-contracts-or-much-ado-about-nothing. Accessed April 28, 2021.

Rühl, G. (2020). Smart (legal) contracts, or: Which (contract) law for smart contracts? In B. Cappiello & G. Carullo (Eds.), *Blockchain, law and governance*. Springer.

Seebacher, S., & Schüritz, R. (2017). Blockchain technology as an enabler of service systems: A structured literature review, In *Proceedings of the International Conference on Exploring Services Science* (pp. 12–23). Springer. https://doi.org/10.1007/978-3-319-56925-3_2

Szabo, N. (1996). *Smart contracts: Building blocks for digital markets*. www.fon.hum.uva.nl/rob/Courses/InformationInSpeech/CDROM/Literature/LOTwinterschool2006/szabo.best.vwh.net/smart_contracts_2.html. Accessed April 28, 2021.

UNCITRAL/UNIDROIT. (2019, May 6–7). *Workshop on smart contracts, artificial intelligence and distributed ledger technology*. Rome. https://www.unidroit.org/89-news-and-events/2609-uncitral-unidroit-workshop-on-smart-contracts-artificial-intelligence-and-distributed-ledger-technology. Accessed April 28, 2021.

US Chamber of Digital Commerce. (2016). *Smart contracts: 12 use cases for business & beyond. A technology, legal & regulatory introduction*. http://digitalchamber.org/assets/smart-contracts-12-use-cases-for-business-and-beyond.pdf. Accessed May 14, 2021.

US Chamber of Digital Commerce. (2018). *Smart contracts. Is the law ready?* https://digitalchamber.s3.amazonaws.com/Smart-Contracts-Whitepaper-WEB.pdf. Accessed May 23, 2021.

Verstraete, M. (2019). The stakes of smart contracts (May 14, 2018). *Loyola University Chicago Law Journal, 50*, 743. Arizona Legal Studies Discussion Paper No. 18-20. https://ssrn.com/abstract=3178393. Accessed April 28, 2021.

Werbach, K. (2018). *The blockchain and the new architecture of trust*. Cambridge, Mass.

Wilkinson, S., & Giuffre, J. (2021). *Six levels of contract automation: The evolution to smart legal contracts—Further analysis*. https://doi.org/10.2139/ssrn.3815445

Wright, A., & De Filippi, P. (2015). *Decentralized blockchain technology and the rise of lex cryptographia*. https://ssrn.com/abstract=2580664. Accessed June 1, 2021.

7

Industry 4.0 in the Messages Published by Employers and Trade Unions in France, Germany, Poland, and the UK

Michał Pilc, Beata Woźniak-Jęchorek, Katarzyna Woźniak, and Dawid Piątek

Introduction

Political power can be defined as the ability to achieve certain ends through the process of creating and enforcing social regulations (Mueller, 2003, p. 360; Scruton, 2007, p. 544). Based on Mueller (2003, pp. 360–361) two main sources of the agents' political power can be identified: social regulations established in the past, which entitle some agents to possess that power; and information possessed by some agents that others

M. Pilc (✉) · B. Woźniak-Jęchorek · K. Woźniak · D. Piątek
Poznań University of Economics and Business, Poznań, Poland
e-mail: michal.pilc@ue.poznan.pl

B. Woźniak-Jęchorek
e-mail: beata.wozniak-jechorek@ue.poznan.pl

K. Woźniak
e-mail: katarzyna.wozniak@ue.poznan.pl

D. Piątek
e-mail: dawid.piatek@ue.poznan.pl

M. Ratajczak-Mrozek and P. Marszałek (eds.), *Digitalization and Firm Performance*,
https://doi.org/10.1007/978-3-030-83360-2_7

do not have access to. The first source gives procedural power and is exercised by coercion or by the distribution of goods; the second is exerted using education and propaganda in the world of uncertainty (Mueller, 2003, p. 360).

The latter channel is especially important for leaders of interest groups, such as employer associations or trade unions. The cost of leaving such groups is usually relatively small (members can easily 'vote with their feet'). Thus, leaders of such groups are not granted large procedural power and the decision process in these groups requires reaching a consensus among a large share of its members. For this reason, distributing information becomes a relatively cheap way for group leaders to persuade other members to act according to the leaders' will. Moreover, distributing information can also attract new members to the group, provide more support for the group among non-members, and convince the imperfectly informed policymakers to adopt policies that are beneficial for the interest group (Lohmann, 1995).

The greater the uncertainty concerning the particular issue is, the greater political power can be exercised by group leaders who distribute information on that issue. In this context, a potentially fruitful topic to study is the distribution of information concerning Fourth Industrial Revolution (or Industry 4.0), the consequences of which still remain uncertain for the labour market. As such, this policy area is prone to welfare-reducing manipulation by agents who possess private information about the consequences of Industry 4.0 (Schnakenberg, 2017).

Thus, the study aims to identify economic motives in the public messages formulated by employer associations and trade unions concerning the challenges posed by the recent advances in manufacturing (Industry 4.0). The analysis is conducted for Germany, France, Poland, and the UK, which are diversified in terms of the role played by the manufacturing sector in their economies, its technological advancement, the way collective bargaining is organised, and the role that employer associations and trade unions play in the political process. The study was conducted over the period 2011–2019 and is based on a newly collected set of 1325 messages derived from the webpages of the 25 largest organisations representing employees or employers in the analysed countries.

This set of messages, collected specifically for this study, ensures the novelty of our analysis. Moreover, to our knowledge, from all the studies that have analysed the discussion concerning Industry 4.0, the present study is the largest. Other analyses that were interested in the opinions of social partners concerning Industry 4.0 were either conducted for one country (Haipeter, 2020; Schoreder et al., 2017) or were based on secondary data, such as interviews with experts who did not belong to trade unions or employer associations, or reports published by think tanks and research units (Kagermann et al., 2016; Ślusarczyk, 2018). There are also studies concentrated on a comparative analysis of governments' strategies to implement Industry 4.0 (Bongomin et al., 2020; Santos et al., 2017). However, due to their subject, they covered a much smaller number of documents.

The conducted analysis indicates that even though employer associations and trade unions differ substantially in their expectations concerning the state policy, and not only between themselves, but also between particular analysed countries, in the case of Industry 4.0 there is one message with regard to which all the social partners are in agreement. It transpires that all these interest groups in all the analysed countries agree with the following message: in order to help the manufacturing sector benefit from Industry 4.0, the government should invest much more in workers' skills. Moreover, employer associations also frequently present Industry 4.0 as an inevitable step that needs to be undertaken in order to remain competitive, while trade unions frequently underline that any policy reform related to Industry 4.0 must be consulted with and accepted by employee representatives.

The chapter is organised as follows. The second section discusses how employees and employer organisations may react to the recent technological advances in manufacturing (the so-called Industry 4.0) and proposes seven research hypotheses. The third section describes the method of collecting and analysing the employees' and employers' messages, presents the heterogeneity of the number and length of these messages in both space and time, and discusses whether the content of these messages is consistent with the proposed hypotheses. The last section concludes.

Theory and Hypotheses

The term Industry 4.0 was coined in 2011, when the German government started to prepare a new high-tech strategy (Federal Ministry of Education and Research, 2020). It became widespread when the World Economic Forum made Industry 4.0 the main topic of its annual meeting in 2016 (World Economic Forum, 2016). The term is used to describe the ongoing advances in such fields as artificial intelligence, robotics, the Internet of Things, autonomous vehicles, 3D printing, nanotechnology, biotechnology, materials science, energy storage, and quantum computing, all of which are expected to transform the way the manufacturing sector operates (Schwab, 2015). It affects these operations on different levels: from the process level (by reducing manual steps thanks to adopting new digital tools), via the organisation level (offering new services and existing services in new ways, and discarding obsolete practices), to the business domain level (changing value chains and the roles inside ecosystems) (Belli et al., 2019; Parviainen et al., 2017; Zimmermann et al., 2016). Thus, it is sometimes claimed that the pace, scope, and potential impact of these changes is so substantial that it is not justified to treat them only as a prolongation of the Third Industrial Revolution, but rather as a distinct stage of development (Schwab, 2015). Although such a claim is controversial (cf. Huberty, 2015), there is little doubt that the ongoing technological advances will have an impact on the structure of labour demand in the manufacturing sector (Carbonero et al., 2018; OECD, 2019, p. 40).

Generally, the impact of digitalisation and the robotisation on the world of work can take different forms, ranging from the destruction of jobs, through changing their tasks content, to the creation of new jobs, often in vocations that previously had not existed (Degryse, 2016). The growing number of tasks that can be automated may potentially lead to a polarised labour market, dominated by highly skilled specialists performing non-routine tasks and the low-skilled workers performing the simplest tasks that are not worth automating (Acemoglu & Restrepo, 2018; OECD, 2019, pp. 64–65). Middle-skilled jobs concentrated on performing routine tasks are the most likely to be crowded out by Industry 4.0.

Acemoglu and Restrepo (2020) estimate that one more robot per thousand workers reduces the employment-to-population ratio in the US labour market by 0.2 percentage points and wages by 0.42%. The frequently cited work of Frey and Osborne (2017) even predicts that around 47% of total US employment is at high risk of computerisation in the next decade or two. However, the OECD presents[1] much lower values for its member states, estimating that 14% of jobs are at risk of complete automation, while 32% of jobs may be automated to a large extent (OECD, 2019, pp. 64–65). The OECD study (2019, p. 49) also shows the geographic differentiation of this phenomenon. It is estimated that in France 16.4% of jobs are at high risk of automation, while 32.8% at significant risk. In Germany, these values are slightly higher and are equal to 18.4 and 35.8%, respectively. Similar values are estimated for Poland: 19.8% of jobs are at high risk of automation and 30.6% at significant risk. Interestingly, these estimates are the lowest for the UK, where they are equal to 11.7 and 26%, respectively.

These estimates indicate that the impact of the so-called Industry 4.0 on all participants of the labour market may be substantial. Thus, we conjecture that both employer and employee organisations are willing to devote their resources to taking an active role in the process of formulating every state policy related to Industry 4.0. We expect that this willingness will be reflected in the messages published by employers and trade unions, which allows us to propose the first hypothesis common to both these groups.

H1: Employer associations and trade unions expect that the government will consult them on the introduction of every policy related to Industry 4.0.

---

[1] In contrast to the OECD, Frey and Osborne (2017) assumed that all jobs within an occupation are identical and the professions as a whole would be automated. Their estimates are much higher as a result.

The next three hypotheses concentrate on employer associations. It may be argued that from the employer perspective Industry 4.0 is another step in the long-term process of moving from labour-intensive to the capital-intensive production methods (Autor et al., 2017; Barkai, 2020; IMF, 2017). Following this process allows companies to remain competitive in the globalised market, however implementing Industry 4.0 will first generate substantial costs before any benefits may be experienced. These costs involve not only implementing new technologies and the necessity of hiring new employees or retrain the already employed, but also include a large degree of uncertainty regarding rights and obligations connected with customer protection, or new forms of non-standard employment, such as employee sharing or platform work (Butt, 2020; de Freitas Júnior & da Silva, 2017; Degryse, 2016; Nerinckx, 2016). As a result, employers may expect that the government will help them to bear these costs (e.g. by helping to improve workers' skills or introducing tax reductions). Additionally, they may also expect a reduction in the costs of hiring employees to give them the possibility to postpone the substitution of labour by new technologies. These conjectures are reflected in the following hypotheses:

H2: Employer associations present Industry 4.0 as a challenge that, without substantial investment, will cause their businesses and the whole economy to lose international competitiveness.
H3: Employer associations expect the state to help them to adapt their businesses to the demands of Industry 4.0, in terms of improving the skills of the workforce.
H4: Employer associations indicate that decreasing the costs of hiring employees will help them in adjusting their businesses to the demands of Industry 4.0.

The next hypotheses concentrate on trade unions. Industry 4.0 affects predominantly middle-skilled industry workers which constitute a large share of trade unions members. This impact can be mitigated by improving the skills of employees and moving them to posts that consists predominantly of non-routine tasks. Instead of increasing the costs of layoffs (e.g. by strengthening the employment protection legislation) such a solution is much easier to accept by employers (especially when the government will at least partially finance the retraining) and in fact helps to implement Industry 4.0, because new technologies create the demand for new tasks in which labour still has a comparative advantage (Acemoglu & Restrepo, 2018). Thus, our next hypothesis is as follows:

> **H5**: Trade unions present Industry 4.0 as a challenge that can be mitigated by encouraging the employers or the state to invest in improving the skills of employees.

Even though retraining will be helpful for some employees, many middle-skilled workers will probably be made redundant. Bearing in mind that the pressure applied by trade unions is considered as the major determinant of the labour market policy generosity (Gordon, 2015), we expect that trade unions will try to put pressure on the government to provide a safety net for these workers. Thus, our next hypothesis is as follows:

> **H6**: Trade unions expect that expenditure on the labour market policy will be kept at a high level, to limit the potential social costs caused by Industry 4.0.

Finally, one of the consequences of digitalisation is blurring the boundary between working time and leisure. It makes easier for employers to force employees to work longer hours or, in any case, makes it difficult for workers to predict when and for how long they will work (Degryse, 2016). Thus, it not only may decrease employee work satisfaction, but also increase the risk of working overtime without proper renumeration. However, assuming that the wave of digitalisation comes with an increase in productivity, there is also a possibility that the average working time can be reduced without any reduction in GDP (de Spiegelaere & Piasna, 2017, p. 43; TUC, 2017). Thus, the impact of digitalisation on working time is not straightforward and depends on the bargaining power of employees versus employers. Therefore, in our last hypothesis we expect that the topic of working time will be also presented in the trade unions' messages:

H7: Trade unions expect that the employees' working time will not be increased because of Industry 4.0.

The Analysis of Published Messages

Methodological Issues

The messages published by employer associations and trade unions were derived from their webpages. Bearing in mind that the term Industry 4.0 can be understood in different ways by various agents we have created a list of almost thirty keywords related to Industry 4.0. Whenever a document published by employer associations or trade unions included at least one word from the list, it was analysed in detail. The list of these keywords (in English) is as follows: Industry 4.0, the fourth industrial revolution, new economy, robotics, robotisation, automation, artificial intelligence, smart, 3D printing, big data, Internet of Things, nanotechnology, biotechnology, blockchain, driverless car, quantum computing, platform work, telecommuting, telework, digitalisation, digital market, digital competences, digital exclusion, new technology, new technological solution, technological change, innovation, innovative business model.

The result of this process is the set of 1325 messages[2] published over the period 2011–2019 by the 25 largest organisations representing employers or employees in France, Germany, Poland, and the UK. Table 7.1 presents the list of all of them, together with the number of their messages included in the analysis. Unfortunately, in the case of some organisations, it was not possible to collect messages that were published in the earliest years of the analysed time scope. Thus, Table 7.1 also provides information about the period of message availability for each organisation. If it is less than 9 years, within the period 2011–2019, it is written in italics.

We decided to include in the analysis only the organisations that operate at the national level and represent more than a single industry.

[2] A detailed list of references to all these documents is available upon request.

Table 7.1 The number of analysed messages published by employer associations and trade unions included in the study, together with a time period of messages' availability

France		
Organisation	Number of messages	Time period
Employer associations:		
Mouvement des entreprises de France	82	2011–2019
Union des entreprises de proximité	36	2011–2019
Confédération des petites et moyennes entreprises	12	*2017–2019*
Trade unions:		
Confédération française démocratique du travail	214	*2012–2019*
Force Ouvrière	140	*2012–2019*
Confédération Générale du Travail	83	2011–2019
Germany		
Organisation	Number of messages	Time period
Employer associations:		
Der Bundesverband der Deutschen Industrie	82	*2012–2019*
Die Bundesvereinigung der Deutschen Arbeitgeberverbände	52	2011–2019
Deutsche Industrie- und Handelskammertag	18	*2017–2019*
Trade unions:		
DBB Beamtenbund und Tarifunion	198	*2013–2019*
Deutscher Gewerk-schaftsbund	170	2011–2019
Christliche Gewerk-schaftsbund Deutschlands	27	2011–2019
Poland		
Organisation	Number of messages	Time period
Employer associations:		
Lewiatan	53	2011–2019
Pracodawcy RP	26	*2017–2019*
Związek Rzemiosła Polskiego	11	2011–2019
Związek Przedsiębiorców i Pracodawców	6	*2012–2019*
Business Centre Club	4	*2015–2019*

(continued)

Table 7.1 (continued)

Poland		
Organisation	Number of messages	Time period
Trade unions:		
Ogólnopolskie Porozumienie Związków Zawodowych	23	*2014–2019*
Solidarność	19	2011–2019
Forum Związków Zawodowych	4	2011–2019
Tripartite commission[a]	7	*2016–2019*

United Kingdom		
Organisation	Number of messages	Time period
Employer associations:		
The Confederation of British Industry	16	*2017–2019*
The Federation of Small Businesses	4	*2013–2019*
Trade unions:		
The Trades Union Congress	32	2011–2019
The Scottish Trades Union Congress	6	2011–2019
The General Federation of Trade Unions	0	2011–2019

[a] These documents were signed by all the employer and employee organisations that participated in the works of the Tripartite commission. Therefore, these documents were categorised both as messages published by employers and by trade unions (i.e. they are included in the statistics for employers and unions)

In the case of France and Germany, we chose the three largest employer associations and trade unions. In the case of Poland, we decided to focus on five employer associations and three trade unions that are members of the Social Dialogue Council (in Polish: *Rada Dialogu Społecznego*), which is the tripartite commission operating at the national level. Moreover, the documents published by this council, which were signed by all its members were also included in the analysis. It may be added that the three chosen French unions represent almost 77% of trade union members in France (Ministry of Labour, Employment and Economic Inclusion, 2018), the three chosen German unions represent almost 95% of all members (Dribbusch & Birke, 2019, pp. 6–7), while in Poland this indicator exceeds 80% (CBOS, 2017). In the case of the UK, we focused on the messages published by the two biggest employer organisations and three principal national trade union centres.

The collected set of documents was analysed in two different ways. Firstly, to assess how the intensity and length of messages concerning Industry 4.0 evolved over time we recorded the year of publication and the number of words constituting a particular message. If the document covered a variety of topics, only the paragraphs related to Industry 4.0 were included in the word count.

Secondly, all the collected messages were read and assessed in terms of whether they were consistent, contradictory, or unrelated to the hypotheses. It should be noted that according to the social reader-response approach (Fish, 1980), which is one of the methods used to analyse literary work (Tyson, 2006, pp. 169–207), particular readers may attach different meaning to the same text, depending on the interpretative strategies used by the communities they belong to. However, knowledge about the socio-economic background of the reader allows the researcher to predict how the intended reader could interpret the text and, as a result, limit the potential bias of his or her analysis. Thus, in the presented study, we assumed that messages are read from the perspective of the hypothetical reader who, in the case of the employer associations' messages, is expected to be an entrepreneur in the manufacturing sector, whereas in the case of trade unions' messages it is an employee working in that sector. We assumed that both these hypothetical readers did not have knowledge about Industry 4.0 and treated the messages published by the members of their community (entrepreneurs or employees) as reliable.

The Heterogeneity of Messages in Time and Space

The conducted analysis revealed visible differences between France and Germany on the one hand, and Poland on the other hand, as far as the number of messages concerning Industry 4.0 that were published by the employer associations and trade unions. As Fig. 7.1 (and Table 7.1 presented in the previous section) indicates, with the former group the number of such documents amounted to several hundred, while in Poland it was around 150. Moreover, the typical length of these messages is also different. In the case of Poland, the average length of these messages was around 415 words, while in France and Germany

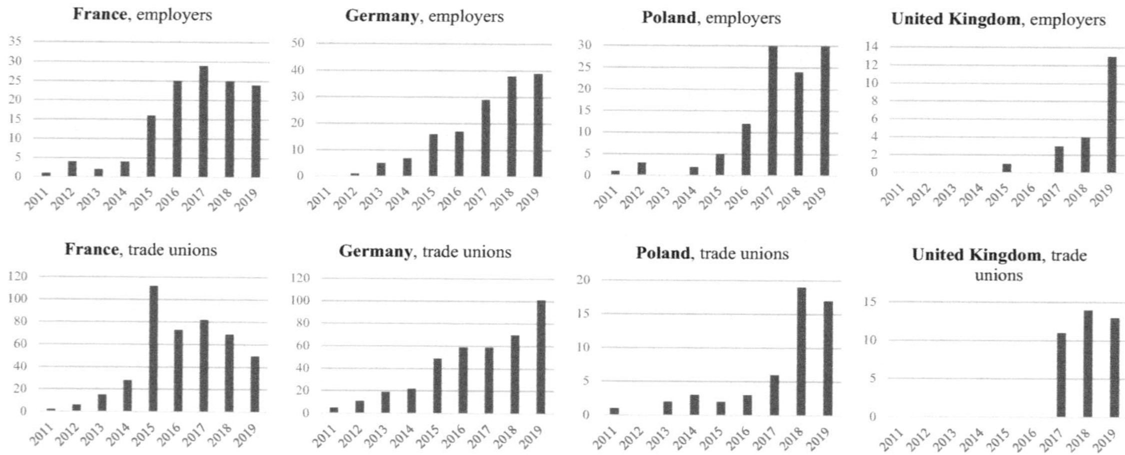

Fig. 7.1 The number of messages concerning Industry 4.0 published by the analysed employer organisations and trade unions in the years 2011–2019

it was more than two times longer. This reflects the fact that in France and Germany there are many publications that are entirely devoted to the topic of Industry 4.0 and its consequences. In Poland, the consequences of the technological advancement for the manufacturing sector are predominantly mentioned on the margins of more general documents concerning education, industrial policy, or social dialogue. These discrepancies not only result from the fact that employer and employee organisations are larger and richer in France and Germany than in Poland (Czarzasty et al., 2014), but it is also a consequence of a lag that characterises the Polish manufacturing sector in implementing the technologies associated with Industry 4.0 in comparison with France and Germany (European Commission, 2018, 2020). As a result, the topic of Industry 4.0 is less important for social partners in Poland than in Western European countries.

Of interest is the fact that the collected set of documents indicates that the UK shares a similarity with France and Germany, as far as the length of messages about Industry 4.0 is concerned, but must be placed after Poland with respect to the number of these messages, because we were able to identify only a few dozen of them. This is not only a consequence of the fact that in the UK there is no institutionalised cooperation between trade unions, employer organisations, and the government (Emmenegger, 2014, pp. 200–210; Howell, 2005, p. 132), but also probably results from the lowest level of job automation risk among the analysed countries (OECD, 2019, p. 49). Consequently, the employer and employee organisations in the UK are less inclined to publish messages on Industry 4.0 and prefer to focus their communication strategies on such topics as zero-hour contracts (TUC, 2016), increasing workplace surveillance (TUC, 2018b), or the conditions and consequences of leaving the European Union.

As far as the heterogeneity over time is concerned, Fig. 7.2 presents the distribution (in per cent) of the length of the published messages measured in words. As may be noticed, there is not a uniform increase in the amount of text published about Industry 4.0 over time for all organisations. This is especially evident with French trade unions, which published more than 30% of the collected texts in 2015 and less than 10% in 2019. A similar pattern can be noticed for the French and

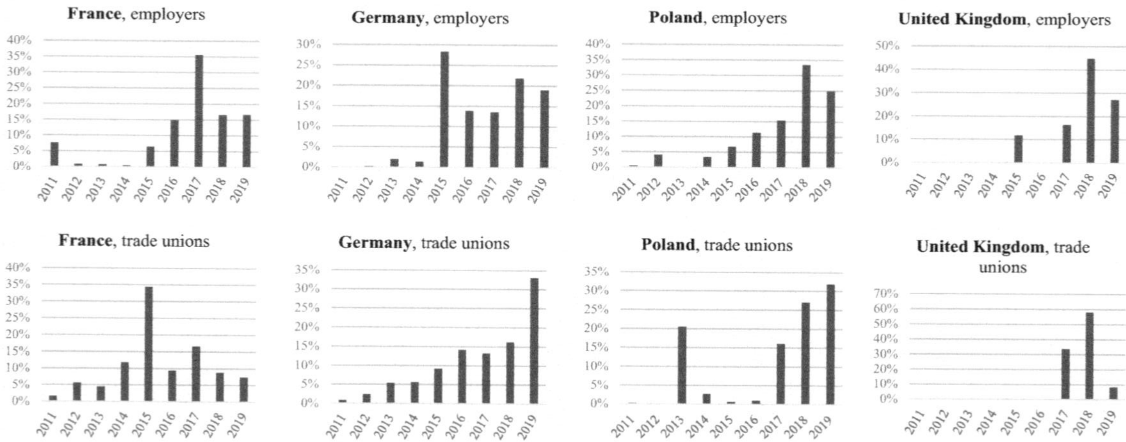

Fig. 7.2 The distribution of the length (in words) of messages concerning Industry 4.0 published by the analysed employer organisations and trade unions in the years 2011–2019

German employers and for the Polish trade unions (however, the latter case should be treated with caution, because the 2013 outlier is caused by a very long, single document). Probably this situation simply reflects the need to reduce the costs of preparing messages: after writing long reports about the consequences of technological advancements, the subsequent messages could be shorter and include only references to these long reports. However, it also suggests that as early as 2015 some organisations in France, Germany, and even Poland, predicted that the just-initiated technological changes may have such a substantial impact on the manufacturing sector in the future, that members of these organisations must be already informed and prepared for these changes. Even though in 2015 that impact for most of them was still just a potential threat, difficult to notice on the horizon, rather than something that forced them to respond immediately (OECD, 2019, pp. 40–41).

Do the Messages Support the Hypotheses?

Our first hypothesis concerned both employer associations and trade unions and predicted that these groups would express in their messages the expectation that the government would consult them on the introduction of every policy related to Industry 4.0. Table 7.2, which summarises the results, indicates that our conjecture finds stronger confirmation among the messages published by trade unions than by employers. Even though in the case of Germany the difference between these groups is small (30.38% of unions' messages is consistent with H1, while for employers it is 28.18%), in other countries the difference is substantial and exceeds 60 percentage points in the case of the UK. The smaller confirmation of H1 by employers' messages may be explained by the fact that governments in the analysed countries generally proposed policies that helped the companies to substitute labour with capital (European Commission, 2018, pp. 10–17). This resulted in employer associations being less inclined to express their expectation to be consulted.

This explanation is especially justified for Poland, where the lowest fraction of employer messages supports H1 (only 8.41%). It is well

Table 7.2 The number of documents that support, contradict, or are unrelated to H1

	The number of documents that:			The percentage of documents that:		
	Support	Contradict	Are unrelated	Support (%)	Contradict (%)	Are unrelated (%)
France—employers	10	0	72	12.20	0.00	87.80
Germany—employers	51	0	130	28.18	0.00	71.82
Poland—employers	9	0	98	8.41	0.00	91.59
UK—employers	3	0	17	15.00	0.00	85.00
France—unions	186	0	251	42.56	0.00	57.44
Germany—unions	120	0	275	30.38	0.00	69.62
Poland—unions	17	0	36	32.08	0.00	67.92
UK—unions	29	0	9	76.32	0.00	23.68

exemplified by the following quotation from the president of one of the employer associations[3] (Pracodawcy RP, 2017):

> (…) I took part in the ceremony of signing the so-called Second Innovativeness Act by the Polish President Andrzej Duda. This act is really something! (…) Not only the act itself should be praised. Also, the way it was created. The consultations with social partners were treated seriously. (…) The Ministry of Science and Higher Education has accepted the best suggestions, including those made by experts from our association. Thus, almost an optimal legal act has been created. Bearing in mind that the standards of preparing the legal acts these days are not the highest – it is an example that should be followed.

This suggests that even though employers in Poland are not fully satisfied with the way the social dialogue is functioning, on the topic of regulations aimed to promote new technological advancements they do not find much reason to blame the government.

At the same time, the European Commission (2018, p. 13) indicates that the cooperation between industry representatives and the government in the process of formulating the strategy to implement Industry 4.0 was not so close in Germany as it was in France, Poland, and the UK. This may explain why the highest fraction of employer messages supporting H1 was recorded for Germany. This explanation is well exemplified by the fragment of one of the employer associations' messages (BDA, 2017, p. 10):

> Although ICT infrastructure is an essential requirement, it alone is not enough to increase social participation and growth for the benefit of all. To better prepare businesses and people for the digital economy, governments have to work with the private sector. In this way, a better understanding of the current and future skills required can be developed.

In a similar fashion the president of this association observes (Kramer, 2017, p. 3):

---

[3] All quotations of French, German and Polish organisations were translated by the authors of the study and were not approved by these organisations.

> The changes in the digital revolution are so profound that I would like to initiate a fundamental debate about the opportunities and possibilities of digitization.

These examples suggest that the support provided for H1 differs among countries not because the employer associations have different expectations, but because they express them with a different intensity, which depends on the countries' economic and political context.

Our second hypothesis predicted that employer associations present Industry 4.0 as a challenge that, without substantial investment, will cause their businesses and the whole economy to lose international competitiveness. This claim is strongly supported by the employer messages in Germany, Poland, and the UK, while it is supported to a smaller extent in France (see Table 7.3). This is a result of the fact that French associations rather focused on presenting specific plans on how to implement Industry 4.0 than on publishing general statements on the challenge. A good example of this approach is the document published by MEDEF, the largest employer association, which already treats Industry 4.0 as one of its priorities and presents the 5-point action plan to implement it (MEDEF, 2017a, p. 5):

> (1) Technology sector: make France the 'Silicon Valley' of Europe around the technologies and platforms of the Internet of Things sector; (2) Industrial ecosystem: create an attractive and competitive ecosystem in France around prototyping, pre-industrialization and manufacturing of Internet of Things solutions; (3) Businesses: support 100,000 French small and medium-size enterprises in their transformation towards the 'Smart economy': the METAMORPHOSE Program (awareness, training, support and financing); (4) Attractiveness: make France "business friendly" to attract investors and promote the growth of start-ups, small and medium-size enterprises and large companies; (5) Communication: implement an international communication strategy around their vision and their 'smart economy' strategy.

The actions listed by MEDEF can be seen as challenging and extensive investments that are necessary for retaining the competitiveness of the French economy, however, they are not presented in such a way by the

Table 7.3 The number of documents that support, contradict, or are unrelated to H2, H3 and H4

Results for H2	The number of documents that:			The percentage of documents that:		
	Support	Contradict	Are unrelated	Support (%)	Contradict (%)	Are unrelated (%)
France—employers	18	0	64	21.95	0.00	78.05
Germany—employers	76	0	105	41.99	0.00	58.01
Poland—employers	41	2	64	38.32	1.87	59.81
UK—employers	9	0	11	45.00	0.00	55.00
Results for H3	The number of documents that:			The percentage of documents that:		
	Support	Contradict	Are unrelated	Support (%)	Contradict (%)	Are unrelated (%)
France—employers	33	0	49	40.24	0.00	59.76
Germany—employers	71	0	110	39.23	0.00	60.77
Poland—employers	38	0	69	35.51	0.00	64.49
UK—employers	8	0	12	40.00	0.00	60.00
Results for H2	The number of documents that:			The percentage of documents that:		
	Support	Contradict	Are unrelated	Support (%)	Contradict (%)	Are unrelated (%)
France—employers	5	0	77	6.10	0.00	93.90
Germany—employers	0	0	181	0.00	0.00	100.00
Poland—employers	15	0	92	14.02	0.00	85.98
UK—employers	0	0	20	0.00	0.00	100.00

association. Thus, such messages were neither considered as supporting the hypothesis, nor contracting it.

There are also two messages that contradict H2, which were published by the Polish Craft Association (*Związek Rzemiosła Polskiego*), which represents small business. One of these messages is an interview with the president of this association, where he states that (Związek Rzemiosła Polskiego, 2016):

> (…) in 30 years' time, most jobs will be done by robots, however the craft vocations will be exceptions, because in their case the individualised approach to consumers' needs matters.

In the second message (Związek Rzemiosła Polskiego, 2019) an expert of this association presents a similar statement concerning craft vocations, arguing that many consumers will prefer to be served by humans, not machines. However, this association also published five messages that are unequivocally consistent with H2, which indicates that the association's opinion concerning Industry 4.0 was still not unified in the analysed period.

Our third hypothesis predicted that one of the employer expectations is that the state will support them in improving employee skills. In the case of every analysed country, more than 35% of employer associations' messages explicitly support H3 (see Table 7.3). Such high support is not surprising if we bear in mind that the governments' strategies for industry digitalisation rather assumed that companies will retrain workers on their own and according to their needs, and for this reason, these strategies were predominantly focused on infrastructure and technology (European Commission, 2018, p. 12). Thus, in the case of employees' skills we have a situation where both parties (employers and governments) agree that improving these skills is crucial in implementing Industry 4.0, and both agree that the other party should pay more for it.

A quite surprising result was obtained for the fourth hypothesis, where we predicted that one of the employer expectations is to decrease the costs of hiring employees in order to be able to postpone the substitution of labour by capital. The obtained results indicate that, to a large extent, we were wrong. In the case of Germany and the UK none of the collected messages supported H4; in France, only a few; while in Poland it was around 14%, which, in comparison with the previous hypotheses, is a relatively low value. Such results may suggest that employer associations do not expect that the necessity to implement technological changes may be postponed long enough to make investment in a campaign for lowering the labour costs profitable. Bearing in mind that Poland lags behind other analysed countries in implementing Industry 4.0, and that its comparative advantage still largely relies on a cheap labour force (Ministry of Development Funds & Regional Policy, 2017, p. 2), the proposed explanation also helps to understand why it was Poland where we found the highest percentage of messages supporting H4.

As far as the trade unions are concerned, we found relatively strong support for our fifth hypothesis, predicting that unions tend to present Industry 4.0 as a challenge that can be mitigated by improving the employee skills (see Table 7.4). The percentage of messages supporting H5 was slightly lower than 30% only in France, while in other countries it was higher than one-third of the collected messages.

Surprisingly, two messages in Poland contradict H5. They were published by the Solidarity Trade Union (*Solidarność*) relatively early, in 2013 and 2014, respectively. We assessed them as contradicting H5 not because they undermine the necessity of retraining workers, but because they present technological changes in an unequivocally positive way: as a chance to create more high-quality jobs and improve working conditions. One of these messages states (Solidarność, 2013):

> (...) the government made a mistake when it decided to base the Polish comparative advantage on low labour costs and not on innovative industrial policy, new technologies, high-quality services or a highly-educated society. For this reason, Polish workers feel like "proles" that are nothing more than unwanted labour costs.

However, the messages published in later years by this trade union are much more cautious towards technological changes and indicate that, apart from many positive aspects, it may also bring serious social costs if it is not followed up by investments in employee skills. Such statements are consistent with H5.

Table 7.4 The number of documents that support, contradict, or are unrelated to H5, H6 and H7

Results for H5	The number of documents that:			The percentage of documents that:		
	Support	Contradict	Are unrelated	Support (%)	Contradict (%)	Are unrelated (%)
France—unions	129	0	308	29.52	0.00	70.48
Germany—unions	144	0	251	36.46	0.00	63.54
Poland—unions	20	2	31	37.74	3.77	58.49
UK—unions	24	0	14	63.16	0.00	36.84
Results for H6	**The number of documents that:**			**The percentage of documents that:**		
	Support	Contradict	Are unrelated	Support (%)	Contradict (%)	Are unrelated (%)
France—unions	49	0	388	11.21	0.00	88.79
Germany—unions	2	0	393	0.51	0.00	99.49
Poland—unions	5	0	48	9.43	0.00	90.57
UK—unions	6	0	32	15.79	0.00	84.21
Results for H7	**The number of documents that:**			**The percentage of documents that:**		
	Support	Contradict	Are unrelated	Support (%)	Contradict (%)	Are unrelated (%)
France—unions	95	0	342	21.74	0.00	78.26
Germany—unions	67	0	328	16.96	0.00	83.04
Poland—unions	7	0	46	13.21	0.00	86.79
UK—unions	15	0	23	39.47	0.00	60.53

In the case of the next hypothesis, the results are once more visibly diversified between countries. Here we predicted that trade unions would expect that expenditure on the labour market policy would be kept at a high level to limit the potential social costs caused by Industry 4.0. In the case of France, Poland, and the UK (see Table 7.4) the support for this hypothesis was relatively small, ranging from 9.43% messages in Poland to 15.79% in the UK. However, in the case of Germany, such support is practically non-existent: only two messages (among 395) were consistent with H6. Moreover, these two messages present only general expectations to somehow adapt the social security systems to the challenges of Industry 4.0. This is best evidenced by the following example (DGB, 2014, p. 2):

> The DGB welcomes the plans to expand the technical infrastructure. But beyond that, the unions lack clear statements about the requirements of a digital society. Such a future plan must 'set the course for a working world of the future', expects DGB chairman Reiner Hoffmann. (...) This includes adapting social security systems, occupational health and safety regulations and participation rights to mobile and digital work.

These results do not mean that trade unions consider the pessimistic forecasts about the percentage of jobs that will disappear due to Industry 4.0 as unrealistic (like Brynjolfsson and McAfee [2014], Ford [2015] or Frey and Osborne [2017]), because such forecasts are cited in the trade unions messages. It may simply reflect the fact that increasing the generosity of the labour market policy is considered to be the second-best solution for trade unions, while the expectation to increase the public or employer spending on improving the employee skills is the best solution. In consequence, publishing demands, on the one hand, to increase both the spending on helping the unemployed and, on the other hand, to retrain the employees, is not an optimal strategy for achieving the primary solution.

Finally, our last hypothesis (H7) predicted that another trade unions' expectation connected with Industry 4.0 was that any increases in the working time would be prohibited. The confirmation of H7 is particularly strong in the UK, where almost 40% of messages support it, but it is smaller in other countries where it ranges from 13.21% in Poland to 21.74% in France (see Table 7.4). The low support for this hypothesis does not mean that it should be rejected, because it is easy to find among the unions' messages such examples as the following, which was published by one of the German trade unions (DBB, 2019):

> When it comes to unlimited working, permanent availability and home office, people expect regulations and protection from us. It is also important to ensure that artificial intelligence will not be used for monitoring and selection.

Thus, as in the case of the previous hypothesis, it may be tentatively concluded that trade unions did not want working time to be increased, however, at the same time, they did not consider it as significant an issue as the necessity to improve employee skills (H5), or to be consulted by the government (H1), and thus opted not to focus their communication strategy on that topic.

It should be noted that many messages assessed as supporting H7 not only indicate that the working time should not be increased, but also demand that employees should work less thanks to robotisation. A representative example of such a demand can be found in the report published by the Trades Union Congress from the UK (TUC, 2018a, p. 21):

> And if new technology makes us richer, we can be ambitious about how we use that wealth to give us more time to spend with family and friends. We think it is time to put time back on the agenda – and it is clear that the public agree. When asked for their ideal working week, most people pick four days. Shorter working hours – without a reduction in living standards – should be on our agenda for the twenty-first century.

A similar statement can be found in the interview with the president of one of the Polish trade unions (OPZZ, 2018) where he indicates that, in the era of digitalisation, labour market regulations should explicitly give employees the right to turn off their phones and computers after working hours, which should be reduced to no more than 35-hour per week, without any salary reductions.

Discussion

It may be noticed that a large percentage of the messages has been classified as unrelated to the proposed hypotheses. To be more precise: 39% of all collected messages neither support nor contradict any of the proposed hypotheses. This is a consequence of the method employed to collect the messages, which required that whenever a message included at least one keyword it was included in the analysis. Thus, many of the analysed messages covered topics connected with Industry 4.0 only in a single or few sentences or used one of the keywords but in a context unrelated to any technical advancements. There are also many short messages that simply inform the readers what Industry 4.0 is without formulating any expectations. Moreover, some of the collected employer messages also expressed the expectation to make personal data protection law more flexible, however, we did not decide to present it as a separate hypothesis, because it was reflected only in a limited number of messages and is not related to the labour market as other hypotheses are.

Thus, neither can it be said that all the collected messages concern Industry 4.0, nor that we collected all the messages concerning Industry 4.0 published by the analysed organisations. However, the content of the messages published by particular organisations was very homogenous over time. This comes as no surprise, since a consistent communication strategy is something that may be expected from interest groups that attracted so many members that became the largest employer or employee organisations in their countries. Only in the case of two Polish organisations did we observe some evolution of the published statements over time, which led to the rejection of the two proposed hypotheses (H2, H5) in the case of just four messages. Thus, we are convinced that the employed method of gathering messages allowed us to comprehensively reproduce the statements of the analysed organisations on Industry 4.0.

Moreover, neither did we observe notable differences in the stances on Industry 4.0 between employer and employee organisations that operate in the same country. Thus, at least for France, Germany, and Poland, it can be claimed that the obtained results remain robust to potential reductions in the number of analysed organisations. At the same time, we observed meaningful differences in the published messages between the analysed countries. Thus, any potential extrapolations of our results to other countries should be avoided.

Conclusions

The accelerating pace of automating production processes in the manufacturing sector has inclined some authors to declare the beginning of the fourth industrial revolution. Even though this claim is controversial, the changes in production processes have already started to have a visible impact on the structure of labour demand in highly developed countries. The falling demand for workers who perform routine tasks (which are susceptible to automation) and unabated demand on highly skilled employees able to conduct non-routine tasks (which in some cases did not even exist a few years ago) puts pressure on employer- and employee-representing interest groups to react. Publishing messages is an example of such a reaction, the main advantage of which is its low cost. This encourages employee associations and trade unions to publish a lot of them, which makes them a reliable tool to reconstruct the organisations' stances on Industry 4.0 and its potential changes over time.

Thus, the conducted study analysed public messages formulated by employer associations and trade unions concerning the challenges posed by the recent advances in the manufacturing sector in France, Germany, Poland, and the UK in the years 2011–2019. The study has been based on a newly collected set of 1325 messages that were derived from the webpages of the 25 largest employee associations and trade unions in the analysed countries.

The conducted analysis indicates that the discussion concerning Industry 4.0 did not increase steadily over time, but rather one-year peaks in the interest on this topic can be observed, which happened as early as 2015 (in the case of French trade unions and German employers). The analysis also suggests that the content of the published messages varies predominantly between countries, not within them. This result applies both to employer associations and trade unions. This suggests that the reactions of such interest groups to technological changes is largely dependent on the labour market situation in particular countries.

In consequence, among the collected set of documents, we can find a varied set of expectations with respect to the state's policy on Industry 4.0. However, some expectations are characteristic for all analysed countries and dominate the whole collection of messages. Specifically, employer associations frequently present Industry 4.0 as an inevitable and challenging step that needs to be undertaken to sustain the competitiveness of their companies and the whole economy. At the same time, trade unions often underline that any policy reform related to Industry 4.0 must be consulted with and accepted by employee representatives. There is also one message that employer associations and trade unions agree upon and publish it as frequently as the two aforementioned ones. It states that in order to help the manufacturing sector benefit from Industry 4.0, the government should invest much more in workers' skills.

This expectation concerning workers' skills may inspire further research. Currently, the governments' policies for industry digitalisation focused more on infrastructure and technology than on the development of skills. In consequence, it will be worth checking whether and to what extent the pressure put on governments by employer associations and trade unions will lead to introducing educational reforms that respond to the technical advancements in the manufacturing sector.

Acknowledgements The authors would like to express their gratitude to Włodzimierz Lewoniewski for his indispensable help in collecting the messages for the analysis. Earlier versions of this study have been presented at the joint workshop organised by the Forum for Institutional Thought and WINIR on Institutions and survival: Social order for twenty-first century (Kraków, 20–21 Feb 2020), during the 32nd Annual EAEPE Conference 2020 (2–4 Sep 2020), at the Social Boundaries of Work conference (28–29 Oct 2020), and during the ICOFEP conference (19–20 Nov 2020).

The study has been financed within the Regional Initiative for Excellence programme of the Minister of Science and Higher Education of Poland, years 2019–2022, grant no. 004/RID/2018/19, financing 3,000,000 PLN.

References

Acemoglu, D., & Restrepo, P. (2018). The race between man and machine: Implications of technology for growth, factor shares, and employment.

American Economic Review, 108(6), 1488–1542. https://doi.org/10.1257/aer.20160696.

Acemoglu, D., & Restrepo, P. (2020). Robots and jobs: Evidence from US labor markets. *Journal of Political Economy, 128*(6), 2188–2244. https://doi.org/10.1086/705716.

Autor, D., Dorn, D., Katz, L. F., Patterson, C., & Van Reenen, J. (2017). Concentrating on the fall of the labor share. *American Economic Review, 107*(5), 180–185. https://doi.org/10.1257/aer.p20171102.

Barkai, S. (2020). Declining labor and capital shares. *The Journal of Finance, 75*, 2421–2463. https://doi.org/10.1111/jofi.12909.

BDA. (2017). Eine vernetzte Welt gestalten. Stabilität sichern—Zukunftsfähigkeit verbessern—Verantwortung übernehmen. *B20 EMPFEHLUNGEN FÜR DIE G20*. Berlin: B20 Germany. https://www.b20germany.org/fileadmin/user_upload/documents/B20/b20-summary-doc-de.pdf.

Belli, L., Davoli, L., Medioli, A., Marchini, P. L., & Ferrari, G. (2019). Toward industry 4.0 with IoT: Optimizing business processes in an evolving manufacturing factory. *Frontiers in ICT*, *6*(17), 1–14. https://doi.org/10.3389/fict.2019.00017.

Bongomin, O., Nganyi, E. O., Abswaidi, M. R., Hitiyise, E., & Tumusiime, G. (2020). Sustainable and dynamic competitiveness towards technological leadership of industry 4.0: Implications for East African community. *Journal of Engineering, 6*, 1–22. https://doi.org/10.1155/2020/8545281.

Brynjolfsson, E., & McAfee, A. (2014). *The second machine age: Work, progress, and prosperity in a time of brilliant technologies*. W.W. Norton & Company.

Butt, J. (2020). A strategic roadmap for the manufacturing industry to implement industry 4.0. *Designs*, *4*(11), 1–30. https://doi.org/10.3390/designs4020011.

Carbonero, F., Ernst, E., & Weber, E. (2018). *Robots worldwide the impact of automation on employment and trade* (ILO Working Papers No. 36). Genève: International Labour Organization.

CBOS. (2017). *Działalność związków zawodowych w Polsce* (Research Report No. 87). Warsaw: CBOS.

Czarzasty, J., Gajewska, K., & Mrozowicki, A. (2014). Institutions and strategies: Trends and obstacles to recruiting workers into trade unions in Poland. *British Journal of Industrial Relations, 52*(1), 112–135. https://doi.org/10.1111/j.1467-8543.2012.00919.x.

de Freitas Júnior, A. R., & da Silva, V. R. (2017). *The uberization of work and the legal regulation: The challenge of labor protection in semi-peripheral economies* (Working Paper from September 26, 2017). Labour Law Research Network.

de Spiegelaere, S., & Piasna, A. (2017). *The why and how of working time reduction*. ETUI.

Degryse, C. (2016). *Digitalisation of the economy and its impact on labour markets* (Working Paper No. 2016.02). Brussels: ETUI.

DBB. (2019, November 7). *Silberbach im Interview*. Digitalisierung: Schutz, Fortbildung und Freiräume für Beschäftigte. https://www.dbb.de/teaserdetail/artikel/digitalisierung-schutz-fortbildung-und-freiraeume-fuer-beschaeftigte.html.

DGB. (2014, July 28). *Einblick, 15/14*. https://www.dgb.de/einblick/ausgaben-archiv/2014.

Dribbusch, H., & Birke, P. (2019). *Gewerkschaften in Deutschland*. Friedrich-Ebert-Stiftung.

Emmenegger, P. (2014). *The power to dismiss: Trade unions and the regulation of job security in Western Europe*. Oxford University Press.

European Commission. (2018). *Digital transformation scoreboard 2018. EU businesses go digital: Opportunities, outcomes and uptake*. Luxembourg: Publications Office of the European Union.

European Commission. (2020). *Digital economy and society index (DESI) 2020*. Thematic chapters. https://ec.europa.eu/digital-single-market/en/desi.

Federal Ministry of Education and Research. (2020). *Industrie 4.0*. https://www.bmbf.de/de/zukunftsprojekt-industrie-4-0-848.html.

Fish, S. (1980). *Is there a text in this class? The authority of interpretative communities*. Harvard University Press.

Ford, M. (2015). *Rise of the robots: Technology and the threat of a jobless future*. Basic Books.

Frey, C. D., & Osborne, M. A. (2017). The future of employment: How susceptible are jobs to computerisation? *Technological Forecasting and Social Change, 114*, 254–280. https://doi.org/10.1016/j.techfore.2016.08.019.

Gordon, J. C. (2015). Protecting the unemployed: Varieties of unionism and the evolution of unemployment benefits and active labor market policy in the rich democracies. *Socio-Economic Review, 13*(1), 79–99. https://doi.org/10.1093/ser/mwu029.

Haipeter, T. (2020). Digitalisation, unions and participation: The German case of 'industry 4.0'. *Industrial Relations Journal*, *51*(3), 242–260. https://doi.org/10.1111/irj.12291.

Howell, C. (2005). *Trade unions and the state. The construction of industrial relations institutions in Britain, 1890–2000*. Princeton: Princeton University Press.

Huberty, M. (2015). Awaiting the second big data revolution: From digital noise to value creation. *The Journal of Industry, Competition and Trade, 15*, 35–47. https://doi.org/10.1007/s10842-014-0190-4.

IMF. (2017). *World Economic Outlook, April 2017: Gaining momentum?* International Monetary Fund.

Kagermann, H., Anderl, R., Gausemeier, J., Schuh, G., & Wahlster, W. (eds.). (2016). *Industrie 4.0 in a global context: Strategies for cooperating with international partners*. Monachium: National Academy of Science and Engineering (acatech).

Kramer, I. (2017, November 29). *Es gilt das gesprochene Wort—Sendesperrfrist: Redebeginn! Offenheit—Fairness—Veränderung. Rede von Arbeitgeberpräsident Ingo Kramer*. Berlin: BDA. https://www.arbeitgeber.de/www/arbeitgeber.nsf/res/9A1500A5FD202806C12581E7002DF57F/$file/2017-Pressefassung-Rede-IK.pdf.

Lohmann, S. (1995). Information, access, and contributions: A signaling model of lobbying. *Public Choice, 85*(3), 267–284. https://doi.org/10.1007/BF01048199.

MEDEF. (2017a). *Accélérer la transformation numérique de l'économie française. Synthèse des propositions du MEDEF*. Mouvement des entreprises de France.

MEDEF. (2017b). *Plan d'action pour la croissance et la transformation des entreprises*. Mouvement des entreprises de France.

Ministry of Development Funds and Regional Policy. (2017). *Strategy for responsible development for the period up to 2020 (including the perspective up to 2030)*. https://www.gov.pl/documents/33377/436740/SOR_2017_streszczenie_en.pdf.

Ministry of Labour, Employment and Economic Inclusion. (2018, September 6). *Mesure d'audience de la représentativité syndicale 2017*. https://travail-emploi.gouv.fr/dialogue-social/la-representativite-syndicale-et-patronale/article/mesure-d-audience-de-la-representativite-syndicale-2017.

Mueller, D. C. (2003). *Public choice III* (3rd ed.). Cambridge University Press.

Nerinckx, S. (2016). The 'uberization' of the labour market: Some thoughts from an employment law perspective on the collaborative economy. *ERA Forum, 17*, 245–265. https://doi.org/10.1007/s12027-016-0439-y.

OECD. (2019). *OECD Employment Outlook 2019: The future of work*. OECD Publishing.

OPZZ. (2018, July 31). *Krótszy tydzień pracy?—badania pokazują, że to się opłaca!* https://www.opzz.org.pl/aktualnosci/kraj/krotszy-tydzien-pracy-badania-pokazuja-ze-to-sie-oplaca.

Parviainen, P., Tihinen, M., Kääriäinen, J., & Teppola, S. (2017). Tackling the digitalisation challenge: How to benefit from digitalisation in practice. *International Journal of Information Systems and Project Management, 5*, 63–77. https://doi.org/10.12821/ijispm050104.

Pracodawcy, R. P. (2017, December 4). *Marzenie o Polsce high-tech.* https://pracodawcyrp.pl/media-o-nas/marzenie-o-polsce-high-tech.

PwC. (2017). *The economic impact of artificial intelligence on the UK economy.* PwC.

Santos, C., Mehrsai, A., Barros, A. C., Araújo, M., & Ares, E. (2017). Towards Industry 4.0: An overview of European strategic roadmaps. *Procedia Manufacturing, 13*, 972–979. https://doi.org/10.1016/j.promfg.2017.09.093.

Schnakenberg, K. E. (2017). The downsides of information transmission and voting. *Public Choice, 173*(1), 43–59. https://doi.org/10.1007/s11127-017-0462-8.

Schoreder, W., Greef, S., & Schreiter, B. (2017). *Shaping digitalisation. Industry 4.0-Work 4.0-regulation of the platform economy*. Berlin and Bonn: Friedrich Ebert Stiftung.

Schwab, K. (2015, December 12). *The fourth industrial revolution.* Foreign Affairs. https://www.foreignaffairs.com/articles/2015-12-12/fourth-industrial-revolution.

Scruton, R. (2007). *The Palgrave Macmillan dictionary of political thought* (3rd ed.). Palgrave Macmillan.

Solidarność. (2013, September 19). *Dialog społeczny trzeba zdefiniować na nowo.* http://www.solidarnosc.org.pl/aktualnosci/wiadomosci/kraj/item/5804-dialog-spoleczny-trzeba-zdefiniowac-na-nowo.

Ślusarczyk, B. (2018). Industry 4.0—Are we ready? *Polish Journal of Management Studies, 17*(1), 232–248.https://doi.org/10.17512/pjms.2018.17.1.19.

TUC. (2016, December 15). Living on the Edge: The rise of job insecurity in modern Britain. *Economic Report Series*. https://www.tuc.org.uk/research-analysis/reports/living-edge.

TUC. (2017, September 4). Shaping our digital future. *A TUC Discussion Paper*. https://www.tuc.org.uk/research-analysis/reports/shaping-our-digital-future.

TUC. (2018a). *A future that works for working people*. Trades Union Congress.

TUC. (2018b). *I'll be watching you. A report on workplace monitoring*. London: Trades Union Congress.

Tyson, L. (2006). *Critical theory today: A user-friendly guide* (2nd ed.). Routledge.

World Economic Forum. (2016). *Global Agenda. World Economic Forum Annual meeting 2016. mastering the fourth industrial revolution. Davos-Klosters, Switzerland 20–23 January*. Cologny, Geneva: World Economic Forum.

Zimmermann, A., Schmidt, R., Jugel, D., & Möhring, M. (2016). Adaptive enterprise architecture for digital transformation. In A. Celesti & P. Leitner (Eds.), *Advances in service-oriented and cloud computing* (pp. 308–319). Springer International Publishing.

Związek Rzemiosła Polskiego. (2016, October 28). *Rzeczpospolita: Jerzy Bartnik: Chcemy być partnerem w debacie gospodarczej*. https://zrp.pl/rzeczpospolita-jerzy-bartnik-chcemy-byc-partnerem-w-debacie-gospodarczej/.

Związek Rzemiosła Polskiego. (2019, October 24). *Konferencja pod patronatem RDS "Świat (bez) pracy"*. https://zrp.pl/konferencja-pod-patronatem-rds-swiat-bez-pracy/.

8

The Impact of Digitalization on Human Capital Skills and Talent Flows in the Financial Industry: A Graph Theory Approach

Héctor Díaz-Rodríguez, Miriam Sosa, and Alejandra Cabello

Introduction

The financial sector has key relevance for economic activity. It is essential for satisfying funding and investment needs, thus enhancing economic growth. During the last decades, the global financial sector has not only increased in size and importance, but also in terms of complexity. It is considered as one of the most dynamic areas in terms of technological innovation.

According to Statista (2021), the total value of investments in fintech (Financial Technology) companies worldwide was 67.1 billion US dollars

H. Díaz-Rodríguez · A. Cabello
National Autonomous University of Mexico, Mexico City, Mexico
e-mail: hectoreduardo12@comunidad.unam.mx

A. Cabello
e-mail: acr2001mx@yahoo.com.mx

M. Sosa (✉)
Metropolitan Autonomous University, Mexico City, Mexico

M. Ratajczak-Mrozek and P. Marszałek (eds.), *Digitalization and Firm Performance*,
https://doi.org/10.1007/978-3-030-83360-2_8

in 2015, and for 2019 it amounted to 135.7 billion. Globally, from 2015 to 2019, a total of 759,752 patents potentially linked with fintech were filed (WIPO, 2021).

As a result, the financial sector has presented growing and different requirements in terms of specialized labour force, and triggered changes in patterns, skills, positions and talent migration flows around the world. However, trend variations are diverse in each financial subsector. Thus, subsectors more susceptible to digital transformation have evolved, being identified as ejectors of traditional labour workers, and attractors of highly specialized skills.

This chapter analyzes labour market dynamics in the financial industry from an evolutionary skills theoretical perspective. Furthermore, it also examines migration talent flows and new skill patterns in the financial sector, employing a graph approach. The hypothesis put forward is that the financial sector is a pole of attraction for talent and that labour skills have increased and specialized in this sector. To test this hypothesis, the Digital Data for Development Database, provided by the World Bank and LinkedIn, is drawn on for the period (2015–2019).

The results are of the utmost importance for increasing understanding of the employment trends in the financial sector, in particular with regard to the labour force inflows and outflows from and to other economic sectors, talent migration among the financial subsectors, and variations in the skills and the abilities necessary to work in the financial sector. This evidence sheds some light on designing public policies related to the labour market, educational patterns and international labour affairs.

The chapter is structured as follows: section two presents the theoretical framework and a literature review, the third part develops the data and methodology, section four analyzes the results, and the last section concludes the chapter.

Literature Review

The relationship between economic growth and the development of skills and investment in human capital has been widely studied by economic theory. This research includes the classic theories of endogenous growth

(Becker, 1994; Barro y Lee, 1993, Romer, 1994), and the evolutionary theories in economics (Nelson y Winter, 1982; Dosi y Cimoli, 1994; Nelson et al., 2018).

Although macroeconomic models of endogenous growth that incorporate the role of education and knowledge in economic growth have served as an initial basis for country-level estimation (Sala-i-Martin, 1994), many of them have both conceptual and estimation problems (Zhao, 2019). Thus, the evolutionary theory of knowledge seems to better explain the processes of learning and knowledge generation, and how they impact economic growth.

This research is based on the evolutionary skills approach. This theory not only considers the knowledge skills of the individuals, but also the importance of the firm as a concentration and generation factor of knowledge, as well as the interaction of those factors on the macroeconomic and mesoeconomic levels (Harper, 2018; Nelson et al., 2018).

The evolutionary theory states that technological innovation is the result of cumulative knowledge in firms which are immersed in a competitive environment. As a result, new technical solutions appear (new products, services, processes, etc.), generating long-term extraordinary earnings (Dopfer & Potts, 2008).

Knowledge is a key factor in the innovation process. Thus, human capital formation is the basis of innovation and for the formation of technological skills. In this sense, social knowledge is materialized in technology through new process and products (Antonelli, 2008; Nelson, Dosi & Helfat, 2018; Pyka & Saviotti, 2018; Rosenberg, 1982).

According to an evolutionary theory of firms (Harper, 2018; Pyka & Saviotti, 2018; Rosenberg, 1982; Vromen, 2006), technology is just knowledge related to practical activities within an organization. As a result, technology is knowledge about certain techniques, methods and designs which triggered the productive conditions for the transformation process. On the other hand, for Antonelli (2008) technological change is the result of a cumulative process of knowledge. This process is necessary to offer new solutions to technical problems in a specific context.

Pavitt (2003) defines the process of technological innovation from three convergent and overlapping stages. In the first stage, agents form new knowledge or assimilate pre-existent knowledge. Secondly, knowledge is transformed into new ideas and materialized in items, services, process, etc. Finally, the market validates and accepts these ideas, recognizing the social utility of knowledge that incorporates these new products, services, procedures, etc.

According to Mokyr (2002), social knowledge can be divided into two essential parts: propositional knowledge, or the explanation of things, associated with scientific reasons, and prescriptive knowledge, or "know how" (technological knowledge). This latter category is directly related to the set of techniques that society develops to modify the environment. Hence, the crucial point is to convert propositional knowledge into prescriptive knowledge; the move from knowledge to solve-proposal.

It is important to state that there is no direct relation between the two kinds of knowledge; not all scientific knowledge evolves into technological knowledge. However, the greater scientific knowledge is, the better the possibilities of developing technological knowledge will be (Marengo & Pasquali, 2008).

Finally, the third phase implies a continuous process where, due to inadequacy, solutions must be adapted to the changing market. As these three stages are overlapping, dynamic organizations develop them in parallel with diverse products and processes. The skills generated as a consequence of this process tend to constantly improve, as new cognitive abilities are developed in both individuals and firms (Nelson et al., 2018).

According to Canibano and Potts (2019), changes not only occur in technology, firms and markets, but also in human capital and job positions. These last two factors co-evolve in a specific organizational environment.

Canibano and Potts (2019) and Dopfer and Potts (2008) adapt the axioms of evolutionary economic theory to analyze human capital, focusing on job positions as follows: (a) individual agents are knowledge carriers; (b) job positions are "slots", institutionally defined, where individuals fit; (c) like individual agents, job placements are knowledge structures, which in association with rules, determine unique firm capacities and; (d) individual agents and job assignment are knowledge processes that become more or less complex over time.

Evolutionary theory, based on these axioms, is a suitable theoretical framework for this research. Human capital is analyzed as a network knowledge where each job position is a node with a dynamic nature. Job placements evolve both qualitatively (how a particular activity is performed) and quantitatively (how many individuals are required for the activity).

From a micro-analytics perspective, for each individual agent, job assignments are interrelated stages in a trajectory known as a career. At each stage, individuals cumulate knowledge and experience. Careers are dependent on the path (path dependence). Thus, each individual embarks on an individual learning trail within a continuously transformed connections network (Dopfer et al., 2004).

At the mesoeconomic level, there is an evolutionary process where new job positions are discovered by the agents who explore knowledge networks. Individuals do not just have the ability to adapt to change, but also explore possible recombinations of knowledge, and this tends to change existing networks. In some cases, this process redefines and generates new job positions.

In the long run, new job assignments are gradually adopted in different contexts, and at the same time obsolete job positions tend to disappear. Finally, two phenomena occur: the retention of new job positions and redefinition in job markets. Redefinition implies the standardization of new activities; to guarantee the new permanence of new activities, new study programmes must be introduced in universities and technological centres (Berger & Frey, 2016; Cañibano & Potts, 2019; Foss, 2006; Otto, 1993).

The redefinition of jobs in the countries of the European Union has meant a greater demand for digital skills, so it is to be expected that a similar process will occur in other countries (Berger & Frey, 2016; Vasilescu et al., 2020).

In the macroeconomic scenario, the combination of new job trajectories reconfigures job dynamics, determining employment levels in an economy. At the same time, the employment level is determined by labour flows, which oscillate from the obsolete to new job assignments.

Islam, Jedwab, Romer and Pereira (2018) argue that factors of production could be misplaced across sectors, types of firms, and locations.

Services, cognitive occupations, the formal sector, and urban areas exhibit comparatively higher returns than non-services, manual occupations, the informal sector and rural areas.

According to Deloitte (2015), as digital technology diffuses across industries and occupations, the demand for ICT skills is expected to also increase outside the technology sector, especially in the financial sector, mainly for the following reasons:

1. To remain competitive, financial services have to keep up with digital transformation, adopting innovations and embracing digital changes, to improve efficiency and security, and to offer trustworthy platforms to carry out transactions (Mohamed & Ali, 2019).
2. Digital systems are becoming more widely used, representing a much faster, cheaper, and safer way when it comes to financial transactions.
3. Digital transformation and new technology adoption have changed the way of doing business and channels that offer banking and financial products and services are more intuitive and trustworthy (Wiliamson, 2016).

One way to achieve more efficient allocations of the factors of production is when human capital tends to be located in activities with the highest growth and wages. In the light of financialization and de-regulation processes (Sawyer, 2013), during the last 5 years the international financial system has experienced job growth rates twice as high as those in the rest of the world economy (Zhu et al., 2018).

Because of the growth rate, profitability, size and importance, the financial sector is immersed in a constant adaptive and changing process. Financial institutions are keen on promoting technological innovations to create new processes, products and marketing, and to develop distribution, management, and hedging risk strategies. To achieve that purpose, financial firms need all kinds of human capital specialized in different areas: artificial intelligence, management, telecommunications, psychology, marketing, law, etc. (Salvi et al., 2021; Tanda & Schena, 2019).

Despite the fact that financial institutions are demanding specialized human capital, each area of the financial sector has specific characteristics and peculiarities that must be described in order to understand the dynamics of the entire sector. Here we divide the financial sector based on the ISIC classification used by the World Bank and LinkedIn (see the section on data and methodology).

For example venture capital & private equity require knowledge about a firm's valuation, mergers and acquisitions process, acquisition funding alternatives, strategies and techniques to enhance the value of private market assets, and skills to anticipate the future of the investments to predict the private market landscape.

Capital markets are very dynamic; they give high-frequency information (prices every second). So, they need human resources to be able to do the following: programme and design artificial intelligence systems to execute buy and sell orders automatically, maintain databases, analyze fundamentals to reinforce asset allocation decisions, manage portfolios, interpret financial information, develop financial terms and conditions, review investment value and run different mathematical models to forecast the bourse's future behaviour (Great sample resume webpage, 2021).

Singh (2012, p. 4) defines investment management as the "*study of individual securities and their properties and the risk and return faced by them*". This is closely related to capital markets, but it is an activity which goes beyond buying and selling. It includes planning a short- or long-term strategy for acquiring and positioning portfolio holdings. It can also include banking, budgeting and tax services and duties. An investment manager should handle all business related to portfolio monitoring, performance measurement, and regulatory and client reporting (Nerdwallet website, 2021).

The insurance industry addresses an increasingly competitive environment. So, this industry requires to be aligned with customers' needs. This industry faces another big challenge, new risks are emerging all the time, and some of them cannot be foreseen. Thus, adaptive and precise models are required to diminish costs, increase profits and secure market share and permanence.

According to the website Collegrad (2021), 42% of insurance workers are in office and administrative support jobs, and these positions require skills and knowledge unique to the industry, such as those provided by international certifications. About 29% are in management or business and financial operations: claims adjusters, appraisers, examiners, and investigators are some of these positions, and they require very specialized knowledge of topics such as legal dispositions, terms and conditions, and internal procedures. 17% of the workers are engaged in sales activities and 11% are in professions and occupations related to computer and mathematical science.

According to Hakim (1985, p. 2) "*investment banking is primarily concerned with designing and underwriting new securities, and selling them to ultimate investors*". Morrison (2007, p. 3) argues that "*the investment bank's key role is in arranging the issuance of new securities by corporations and entrepreneurs in need of new capital*".

Investment banking is an industry which requires knowledge of popular investment vehicles and an interest in current relevant news, critical issues and international events. In terms of the abilities required, it is important that the individuals should be able to develop different types of financial models to value debt and equity for mergers, acquisitions and capital raising transactions; to analyze financial data; to perform valuations; and to know all the affairs related to the initial public offer (IPO) process (webpage Corporate Finance Institute [CFI], 2021).

In financial services, workers deal with a great amount of information on a daily basis. Thus, it is important to have certain skills to utilize the information for advice or for making decisions. Some of the skills needed in this kind of job are as follows: analytics, technical and software knowledge, leadership and influencing, team working, communication skills and problem solving (The London Institute of Banking and Finance website, 2019).

Banking is an industry which incorporates different services and products, such as: checking accounts, saving accounts, fixed-term deposits, commercial loans, mortgage credits, personal loans and credit cards (Ibarra, 2020). The skills required are very varied. They include knowledge about the promotion, opening, managing and optimizing of different types of bank accounts, as well as having experience in sales, communication skills, and marketing and industry awareness. Specialized workers, in addition to the above-mentioned skills, need to know how to design, optimize and programme an app or website, they also need to develop models to analyze the customer's behaviour and propose new products according to their different needs (website Give a grad a go, 2019).

Due to the above, the financial sector has become a pole of attraction pole, for a highly specialized labour force, but also a sector that eliminates obsolete human capital, which has been partially or completely substituted by apps and machines. Following this line of research, the chapter aims to analyze the dynamics, changes, inflows and outflows in the labour market associated with financial sector.

At this point, it is important to note that the financial sector has been radically transformed in recent years, as a result of the globalization and financialization processes, which have transformed the skills required to work in this sector.

As a result of the more intensive use of technology in the financial sector, the labour market requires new skills.

According to Mosteanu (2020), the main challenges in digitizing the financial sector resulted from the reconstruction of the design of organizations which have started to use financial technologies, and this entails new educational specializations and developing new skills and competences to meet the challenges of different and new job requirements.

Data and Methodology

The data source is the Digital Data for Development database, which has been developed by the World Bank and LinkedIn. The data survey is collected from more than 100 countries with at least 100,000 LinkedIn members each, distributed across 148 industries and equipped with 50,000 categories and skills. The database was selected for this research due to its advantages above other traditional and government statistics. It captures new trends and opportunities (Zhu et al., 2018).

We employ two variables: the migration talent between industries and the skills required by industries from 2015 to 2019.

Database Digital Data for Development use ISIC Classification; According to ISIC Classification, financial sector includes the following activities (1) Venture Capital & Private Equity, (2) Capital Markets, (3) Investment Management, (4) Insurance, (5) Investment Banking, (6) Financial Services, (7) Banking.

Graph Theory

In mathematics and computer science, graph theory analyzes the mathematical structures used to model pair-wise relations between objects from a collection. A graph is defined as an abstract illustration of a network. It is formed by a set of N nodes, (industries and skills), and of L edges or links (inflows and outflows from and to each sector, and skills needs (Bollobás, 2004; Biggs, 1993).

The information about the graph's relative connectivity structure is stored in the adjacency matrix A. When a weighted and directed edge exists from node i to j, the corresponding entry of the adjacency matrix is Aij $\neq$ 0; otherwise Aij = 0 (Newman, 2018).

Graph theory has been applied in multiple fields due to its benefits, above all, due to the easy way to observe the structure, hierarchies, links and the direction of the relationship among diverse objects or phenomena. It is important to emphasize that this approach also allows the nodes' behaviour to be predicted (Sanchez-Ante, 2013; Mitchell, 2009; Newman, 2018).

Node Strength

The simplest attribute of a node is its weighted degree, or strength, which means the sum of the weights of the total number of links established with other edges. This amount is subdivided into the in-strength, din, and out-strength, dout, when directed relationships are being measured. The formulation of the in-strength index can be described as follows:

$$d_{in}(i) = \sum j \in V^{A_{ji}} \tag{8.1}$$

Equation (8.1) is the total strength of the links coming into the vertex i. V is the set of available nodes (flows or skills) and Aij denotes the directed edge from node j to node i, with a weight given by the relative node's pair-wise. Interactions that do not reach statistical significance are set to zero. The value of a given in-strength will depend on the intensity of the linear pairwise between two nodes (Bollobás, 2004; Biggs, 1993; Newman, 2018). For the out-strength:

$$d_{out}(i) = \sum j \in V^{A_{ji}} \tag{8.2}$$

Equation (8.2) denotes the total strength of the links going out from vertex i. It should be noted that Aj,i ≠ Ai,j because of the asymmetry of the out and in flows. Figure 8.1 shows an example of in- and- out strengths. In the example, a 5 node (N) network with 6 edges (E) is described for simplicity. An alternative form for presenting a node is the relative adjacency matrix, shown on the right, with G = (N,E) and, where N = 5 and E = 6, represented as follows (Sandoval Cabrera et al., 2019; Mitchell, 2009):

$$N = \{A, B, C, D, E\} \tag{8.3}$$

$$E = \{(A, C), (B, C), (C, D), (C, E), (D, B), (E, A)\} \tag{8.4}$$

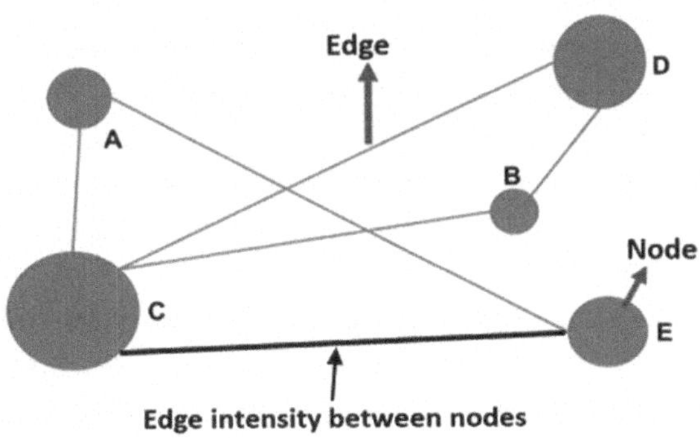

Fig. 8.1 Graph representation

Where,

$$W_{ij} = \begin{Bmatrix} 1.ifi, jarelinked \\ 0, ifi, jarenotlinked \end{Bmatrix} \tag{8.5}$$

$$i, j = 1, \ldots, n$$

$$W_{ij} = W_{ji} \tag{8.6}$$

A graph theory extension can be established through weighted networks. This kind of approach allows valued edges to be shown (Newman, 2018). Thus, each edge represents the intensity, as the higher the intensity of the relationship, the wider the edge between the nodes (see Fig. 8.1). Additionally, the nodes' size in Fig. 8.1, is associated to different values in each node.

Results Analysis

The Data Base Digital Data for Development joins the skills reported by LinkedIn users in 5 big sets: (1) Business Skills, (2) Disruptive Tech Skills, (3). Soft Skills, (4). Specialized Industry Skills, and (5). Tech Skills. As a first approximation of talent migration at the regional level, analyzing the human capital expulsion and attraction by type of skill in each region, the results show that migration talent occurs from developing and non-developed countries to developed ones. Thus, Europe and Central Asia are big talent importers for all the skill sets, followed by East Asia and Pacific and North America. In contrast, Latin America is an ejector of talent in all the ability groups, followed by the Middle East and North Africa.

This interesting fact has important implications for human capital formation policies. It implies that the expenditure in human resource generation is incurred by developing countries, but it is exploited by developed nations. In this sense, scarce public resources are focused on developing a highly qualified labour force, but developing and non-developed countries lack labour markets and professional opportunities for them.

Table 8.1 Panel A shows the global employment trends from 2015 to 2019. It presents a comparative analysis of employment growth based on the International Standard Industrial Classification (ISIC). It can be observed that there was a generalized slowdown, as a result of the anticipated economic crisis, even before the COVID19 pandemic.

Despite the slowdown, differentiated behaviour is observed in each economic activity, some with more growth than others. This is the case with FIRE (Finance, Insurance and Real Estate) and the Entertainment and Amusement sectors. On the other hand, the manufacturing and scientific and technical sectors have lost dynamism.

Among the general trends, those that stand out are the reduction of economies' capability to create labour positions, and the job rate growth

Table 8.1 Employment growth by ISIC sector, 2015 and 2019

Panel A. Employment growth by ISIC activity, 2015 and 2019

ISIC SECTOR	**Growth_rate_2015**	**Growth_rate_2019**
Financial and insurance activities	1.4%	0.7%
Manufacturing	1.2%	0.2%
Arts, entertainment and recreation	0.8%	0.4%
Information and communication	0.7%	0.2%
Professional scientific and technical activities	0.2%	-0.1%
Mining and quarrying	0.0%	0.3%
Total	**0.7%**	**0.2%**
Panel B. Employment Growth Rate in Financial and Insurance Sector by Economic Activity		
Economic Activity	**Growth_rate_2015**	**Growth_rate_2019**
Venture Capital & Private Equity	6.2%	5.0%
Capital Markets	4.7%	3.1%
Investment Management	3.1%	1.7%
Insurance	1.2%	0.4%
Investment Banking	2.1%	0.4%
Financial Services	0.8%	0.3%
Banking	0.0%	-0.1%
Total	**1.4%**	**0.7%**

Source Authors with data from Digital Data for Development, World Bank and LinkedIn

has slowed from 0.7% in 2015 to 0.2% in 2019. Nevertheless, despite the slowdown, financial activities and insurance industries sustained their activity levels.

To analyze changes in growth patterns, Table 8.1 Panel A desegregates the growth rates in financial sector areas. As is evident, Venture Capital & Private Equity is by far the area with the largest employment growth, followed by Capital Markets. In contrast, Banking and Financial services did not present significant variations over the last 5 years.

In order to understand the inter and intra sectorial trending generated by technological change, it is necessary to incorporate a migration talent variable, employing graph theory with Cytoscape Software. This allows us to examine the flow of talents direction and how human capital skills influence that phenomenon.

Figure 8.2 shows the international migration talent flows of the financial and insurance sector. It allows three dimensions to be analyzed: the first is constituted by the node size, which represents the increase in employment (the job growth rate in each sector for 2019).

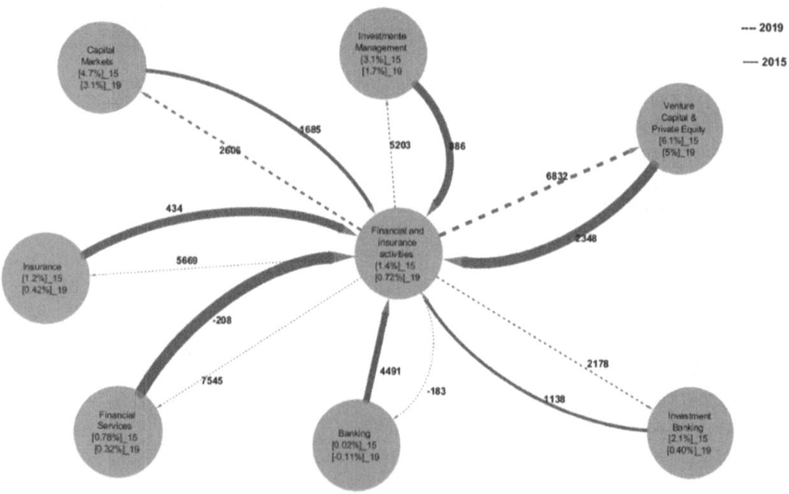

Fig. 8.2 Talent migration in Financial Services, 2015 and 2019

Secondly, the edge indicates if the flow is positive or negative. Finally, the third dimension is represented by the width of the edge, which also represents the magnitude of the talent migration flow between activities.

For example, in Venture Capital and Private Equity, the size of the node represents an increase in the job growth rate of about 5% in 2019, the green tonality of the edge means that the migration flow is positive in net terms, and the width indicates the migration of 6.8 million talented workers in 2015 and 2.3 million in 2019.

In Fig. 8.2, three subsectors stand out due to their dynamism in terms of employment growth rate: Venture Capital & Private Equity, Capital Markets and Investment Management. In contrast, the rest of the subsectors present almost zero growth. This fact shows which are the subsectors where technological change has allowed higher automation process.

This trend could be explained by the growing market share of institutional investors, which are organizations that pool together funds on behalf of others and invest in a variety of financial assets. Some institutional investors are: banks, credit unions, pension funds, insurance companies, hedge and mutual funds, REITS, etc. According to SEC (2018), institutional investors own about 80% of equity market capitalization.

According to Willis Towers Watson (2017), in 2016 the top 500 global asset managers together had US$81.2 trillion in assets under their management, which is slightly more than global GDP. Continuous growth and dynamism are also evidenced by the GDP share of the institutional investors in OECD countries, in 2008 institutional investors assets represented 239% of OECD countries' GDP, and in 2018 it was 337%.

In terms of talent attraction, it is possible to observe how all the subsectors present positive flows in 2015, while in 2019 the financial sector diminishes its attraction strength and inflows are reduced. In some cases, inflows are even in red numbers.

Despite the slowdown in employment increase, Financial Services presented the highest level of talent migration: 7.5 million workers got a position in that subsector in 2015. Gradually, the talent migration flow lost dynamism, and by 2019 Financial Services was losing talent.

In 2015, the second most important activity, in terms of talent attraction, was Venture Capital & Private Equity. The width of the edge shows a subsector which received 6.8 million professionals, and in 2019 2.3 million. Finally, the migration talent inflow for the insurance subsector was of the order of 5.6 million workers in 2015, and of 434 thousand in 2019.

Labour Force Skills in Financial Sector

Migration trends are shown in Figs. 8.3 and 8.4, they allow us to analyze where is the talent moving to, and whether it is in-between or out of the financial sector, globally. These mobility trends impose important challenges: firstly, when a worker migrates from one activity to another, he needs to develop different skills, in some cases, those abilities are dissimilar to those required in the original sector. If the labour force is aware of what those skills are, the incorporation process for the new sector will be easier and his knowledge has practical value, from the point of view of human capital.

In the second place, from a public policy perspective, if financial sector employers know the required skills in the financial sector, they can

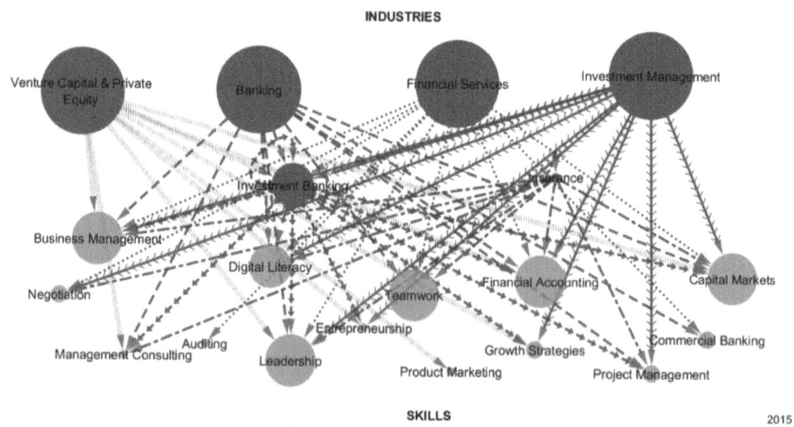

Fig. 8.3 Financial and Insurance Services Skills Needs, 2015

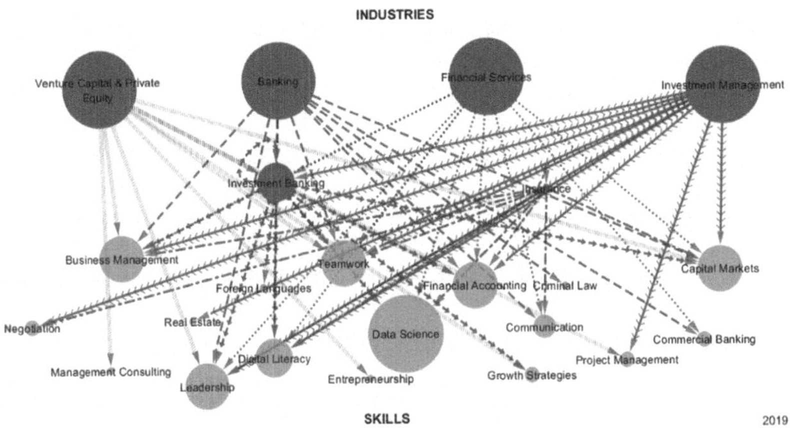

Fig. 8.4 Financial and Insurance Services Skills Needs, 2019

guide the government and private education institutions with regard to basic and specialized topics needed in capacitation programmes, syllabus, professional careers, etc. This has an enormous value for the design of educational policy.

This section analyzes the skills required by the financial sector. In general, the skills can be grouped according to their characteristics. The World Bank aggregates skills in 5 big sets, from the basics to specialized abilities and their relation to technology, business core, or their potential to generate disruption.

If World Bank classification is taken into account, key differences are observed in the skills required to work in the financial sector, in comparison with the necessary skills to perform in other sectors. As a consequence, an accelerated digital process is evident in the financial sector.

To estimate the skills, the 10 most required abilities are considered for each subsector.

The estimation of the required skills is as follows:

For each sector the (Wi,s) the weight represents how distinctive and representative each ability S is, in industry i:

$$w_{i,s} = m_{i,s} * \ln(\frac{N}{n_s}) \tag{8.7}$$

where m_(i,s) indicates the number of industry members i, with the ability s, N is the total amount of industries and n_s the total number of industries with the ability s.

For each ability a score is assigned, skills are ranked from 10 (the most required) to 1 (the least required). Scores are aggregated for the skill sets. Table 8.2 presents the comparative information for the financial sector and the rest of the big sectors in the ISIC classification.

The results in Table 8.2 allow us to examine two relevant aspects: (i) the skills to perform in the Financial Sector and Insurance activities (and to compare those competencies with the rest of the abilities required in other sectors of the International Standard Industrial Classification (ISIC)) and; (ii) the evolution of the skills and abilities required in each sector over time.

The most important abilities for the financial sector are business skills (71% of the total of the competencies), and among the most important are: Accounts Payable, Advertising, Auditing, Bookkeeping, Business Management, Capital Markets, Commercial Banking, Competitive Strategies, Corporate Communications, Customer Service Systems and Digital Marketing. In the second place are the soft abilities, related to general skills such as Communication, Leadership, Negotiation, Teamwork, Time Management, Writing, which constitute the 21% of the required skills to work in the financial sector.

Skills related to disruptive technologies, technological abilities, and those closely related/exclusive to the financial sector, only represent 8% of the total of the abilities required by this sector. However, it is important to highlight that there is a variation in the relative importance of the required abilities in the financial sector, as a result of the digitalization process.

Table 8.2 also shows that, despite Business Skills being the group of abilities with greater importance for the financial sector, they lost their

Table 8.2 Skills groups by ISIC Activity

ISIC ACTIVITY	Business Skills		Disruptive Tech Skills		Soft Skills		Specialized Industry Skills		Tech Skills	
	2015	2019	2015	2019	2015	2019	2015	2019	2015	2019
Arts, entertainment and recreation	29	10			45	73	361	337	115	130
Financial and insurance activities	**261**	**212**		**4**	**54**	**82**		**9**	**15**	**23**
Information and communication	139	66	57	77	71	91	249	273	364	373
Manufacturing	253	116	35	25	128	181	304	346	50	102
Mining and quarrying	31	20			20	30	51	45	8	15
Professional scientific and technical activities	347	248	32	54	132	218	521	486	178	204
TOTAL	**1060**	**672**	**124**	**160**	**450**	**675**	**1486**	**1496**	**730**	**847**

Source Authors with data from Digital Data for Development, World Bank and LinkedIn

relative importance from 2015 to 2019. On the other hand, Soft Skills and Tech Skills are becoming more required abilities in the financial sector. They are general activities with a transversal character to be used in practically all the subsectors. This change has occurred in the context of the technological migration of financial process.

Another clear trend related to professional skills of the financial sector is the higher demand for abilities related to disruptive technologies: Data Science, Development Tools and Human Computer Interaction. In the same line, Digitalization, Robotics and Data Science seem to be consolidated trends, not just in the financial Sector, but all other economic areas, as a fundamental part of the digitalization process.

The evolution of the required skills goes together with the adoption rate of certain financial services and the challenges that it poses for Financial Technologies (Fintech). As can be observed in Table 8.3, the financial services with higher adoption rate from 2015 to 2019 are: money transfer and payments, savings and investments, budgeting and financial planning, insurance and borrowing. It is significant that the insurance industry has broken the digital taboo, by enhancing new sales channels through Fintech. In contrast, borrowing is the activity with the lowest digital adoption. This fact could be explained by regulatory and cultural patterns.

Figures 8.3 and 8.4 present the necessary abilities to work in the financial sector in 2015 and 2019, respectively.

In Fig. 8.3, two patterns can be observed: (i) there is a set of structural fundamental abilities that take up a position of employment in the financial sector, all of them are related to Business Management, (skills such as

Table 8.3 Comparison of Fintech categories ranked by adoption rate from 2015 to 2019

FINANCIAL SERVICE	2015 (%)	2017 (%)	2019 (%)	RANK
Money transfer and payments	18	50	75	1
Savings and investments	17	24	48	2
Budgeting and financial planing	8	20	34	3
Insurance	8	10	29	4
Borrowing	6	10	27	5

Source Own elaboration with estimation results

Management, Strategic Planning, Strategy, Change Management, Business Planning, Business, Process Improvement, Vendor Management, Business Process, Outsourcing, Small Business), Capital Markets (Risk Management, Portfolio Management, Financial Modelling, Due Diligence, Financial Risk, Capital Markets, Valuation, Financial Markets, Equities, Trading), Financial Accounting (Financial Analysis, Financial Reporting, Financial Accounting, Corporate Finance, Financial Statements, U.S. Generally Accepted Accounting Principles (GAAP), Balance Sheet, Taxations, Target Costing, Consolidated Financial Statements), and Leadership (Leadership, Team Leadership, Team Building, Team Management, Cross-functional Team Leadership, Organizational Leadership, Strategic Thinking, Strategic Leadership, Self-confidence, Technical Leadership).

(ii) Emerging skills, which were marginal in 2015, but in 2019 became the key skills for the financial sector, such as teamwork, communication (communication in digital media), data science and project management.

Figure 8.4 shows the skills required to work in the financial sector in 2019. It can be observed that there was an increase in the importance of teamwork skills (which includes skills such as: Teamwork, Cross-functional Coordination, Build Strong Relationships, Cross-team Collaboration, Cross-Functional Team Building, Cooperative, Sociability, Group Presentations, Collaboration Solutions, Collaborative Work), and Foreign Languages (which includes a Second Language and Business English), both of which are necessary to work in a more integrated financial sector globally.

But perhaps the most important characteristic of Fig. 8.4 is the appearance of new skills, which were not required to work in the financial sector in 2015 but which in 2019 are of the greatest importance. Such abilities are associated with Data Science, which includes specific skills such as Data Analysis, SQL, Analytics, Statistics, R, IBM SPSS, PL/SQL, Tableau, Statistical Data Analysis, Big Data.

The increased demand for data science skills is an indicator of the current complexity of the financial sector, which seeks to make better use of the great amount of information available. According to Oracle (2020), modern technology has allowed the creation and storage of increasing amounts of information, and as a result, the volume of data exploded. It is estimated that 90% of the data in the world was created in the last two years.

For this reason, the financial sector increasingly demands skills that make it possible to take advantage of the great amount of information available, mainly data science.

The relative importance of the abilities in each subsector (Figs. 8.3 and 8.4) can be measured by Betweenness centrality, which quantifies the number of edges or connections that one node has with the rest of the nodes in the graph.

That measure is not an intrinsic attribute of the nodes, but is a structural value assigned from the location as a fundamental value to determine its value in the graph. Centrality is defined as follows:

$$D = D_j^{in} + D_i^{out} \tag{8.8}$$

where:

$$D_j^{in} = \sum_{j=1}^{n} x_{ij} \tag{8.9}$$

$$D_i^{out} = \sum_{i=1}^{n} x_{ji} \tag{8.10}$$

Table 8.4 measures the Betweenness centrality of the financial subsectors, the outflows (outdegree) and the inflows (indegree) of the required skills for each subsector. Outdegree data reveal growth in all the nodes available from 2015 to 2019, which means that in the financial sector there was an increase in human capital needs in quantitative and qualitative terms, consolidating as a dynamic, human labour attractor, a complex sector that is intensive in technology. In this sense, the human capital needs were diversified, incorporating skills related to the digitalization processes: Digital communication, Data Science and Project Management, the latter being a more general ability.

It is important to notice that the Teamwork skills had a better ranking in 2019, which could be because the increasing complexity in this

Table 8.4 The degree of centrality of Financial Activities, 2015 and 2019

Financial and Insurance Services Skills Needs							
The degree of centrality of Financial and insurance activities							
2015				**2019**			
Industries	***Outdegree***	***Skills***	***Indegree***	***Industries***	***Outdegree***	***Skills***	***Indegree***
Banking	10	Business Management	6	Banking	10	Business Management	6
Financial Services	10	Capital Markets	6	Financial Services	10	Capital Markets	6
Insurance	10	Financial Accounting	6	Insurance	10	Financial Accounting	6
Investment Banking	10	Leadership	6	Investment Banking	10	Leadership	6
Investment Management	10	Digital Literacy	5	Investment Management	10	Teamwork	6
Venture Capital & Private Equity	9	Investment Banking	5	Venture Capital & Private Equity	10	Digital Literacy	5
Nodes available	*16*	Management Consulting	4	*Nodes available*	*19*	Investment Banking	5
		Project Management	4			Communication	3
		Entrepreneurship	3			Data Science	3
		Growth Strategies	3			Commercial Banking	2
		Negotiation	3			Growth Strategies	2

(continued)

Table 8.4 (continued)

Financial and Insurance Services Skills Needs							
The degree of centrality of Financial and insurance activities							
2015				**2019**			
Industries	*Outdegree*	*Skills*	*Indegree*	*Industries*	*Outdegree*	*Skills*	*Indegree*
		Teamwork	3			Negotiation	2
		Commercial Banking	2			Project Management	2
		Auditing	1			Criminal Law	1
		Insurance	1			Entrepreneurship	1
		Product Marketing	1			Foreign Languages	1
		Nodes available	*6*			Insurance	1
						Management Consulting	1
						Real Estate	1
						Nodes available	*6*

Source The authors' own elaboration, based on Mitchell (2009)

sector requires highly coordinated activities between different specialists: accountants, managers, economists, actuaries, software developers, designers, marketers, etc.

In the context of the development of high-tech industries and the formation of the digital economy, human capital has emerged as the most competitive and unique resource. The digitalization processes have had an impact on the formation and development of human capital. As it is noticed in our analysis, human capital is characterized by the great importance of digital skills and abilities, ICT literacy, electronic skills, the ability to work in teams and leadership.

Digitalization influences the human capital of financial institutions in a twofold way: both qualitative and quantitative change. It involves individuals in a new digital environment, facilitating communication and creation processes, becoming more intuitive and familiar with digital technologies. This process of "digital literacy" favours the rapid adoption of new applications and tools, i.e. digitalization fosters the ability to adapt to fast-changing environments in which the propensity for continuous learning will be the employee's competitive advantage (Zaborovskaia et al., 2020).

The ability to learn quickly and continuously provides the worker with a constant flow of knowledge, which is potentially transferable to technical and technological improvements in financial institutions. The quantitative results are tangible in the increased information processing capacity, efficiency, and optimization of diverse processes that, without digital technologies, would be impossible or would take exponential time.

Conclusions

The results demonstrate that at the global level, there is a talent migration from non-developed countries to developed economies. Europe and Central Asia, East Asia and Pacific, and North America, are the importers of talent, while Latin America and the Caribbean, and the Middle East and North Africa, are ejectors of talent. This fact has very important implications in terms of educational policy and the human resources balance sheet. Emerging and developing countries are spending scarce resources in training and professionalizing human labour, but they do not take advantage of the final product, because they do not have the employment capacity to absorb all the human resources they are preparing.

During the period of study, 2015–2019, an economic slowdown occurred. This was reflected in the employment growth dynamism. In general terms, the employment level decreased. Nevertheless, the financial sector turned out to be one of the most dynamic sectors in terms of the higher employment rate.

As a result of digitalization in financial services, some subsectors became attractors and ejectors of talent. Three subsectors are highlighted due to their dynamism, in terms of the increase in employment: Venture Capital & Private Equity, Capital Markets and Investment Management.

With regard to skills, there is a variation in the relative importance of the required abilities in the financial sector, as a result of the digitalization process. Quantitative and qualitative changes are observed in the required skills, increased demand for abilities related to disruptive technologies: Data Science, Development Tools, Human Computer Interaction, Digitalization, Robotics and Data Science.

The Emerging skills which in 2019 became key factors for the financial sector were related to Data Science, including the use of tools such as Data Analysis, SQL, Analytics, Statistics, R, IBM SPSS, PL/SQL, Tableau, Statistical Data Analysis, Big Data. The use of these complex tools allows the Financial Sector to make better use of the great amount of information, in order to promote decision making and rapid responses.

One of the main challenges of the financial sector is organizational redesign for the purpose of using new financial technologies. To achieve this goal, universities should cooperate with the business sector to create new educational specializations and to develop new abilities and skills needed to meet the requirements of new job positions. Another important goal is financial inclusion, which has been hindered, above all in emerging countries, by structural problems related with economic disparity, such as lack of financial literacy and Information and Communication Technologies penetration.

An educational policy recommendation for emerging markets is to analyze the labour market and strategically decide which professional and technical careers will be developing, according to the development plans and long-run national projects. As a result, non-developed countries would spend resources on their needs, reassigning funds in other national priorities.

The future research agenda could extend the analysis to employing another approach, examining diverse economic sectors, or including different variables, such as profits, investment, the number of patents. Finally, it is also important to analyze the public policy about education and the formulation of strategic programmes, assigning resources according to each country's needs.

References

Antonelli, C. (2008). *Localized technological change. Towards the economics of complexity*. Routledge.

Barro, R., y Lee, J. (1993). International comparisons of educational attainment. *Journal of Monetary Economics, 32*(3), 363–394.

Becker, G. (1994). Human capital revisited. In *Human capital: A theoretical and empirical analysis with special reference to education* (3rd ed., pp. 15–28). The University of Chicago Press.

Berger, T., & Frey, B. (2016). *Digitalisation, jobs and convergence in Europe: Strategies for closing the skills gap* (Vol. 50). Oxford Martin School.

Biggs, N. L. (1993). *Algebraic graph theory*. Cambridge University Press.

Bollobás, B. (2004). *Extremal graph theory*. Courier Corporation.

Cañibano, C., & Potts, J. (2019). Toward an evolutionary theory of human capital. *Journal of Evolutionary Economics. No., 29*, 1017–1035.

CFI e "Investment Banking Job description". (2021). https://corporatefinanceinstitute.com/resources/careers/jobs/investment-banking-job-description/ (Accessed 25 May 2021).

Collegrad. (2021). *Insurance industry: Jobs, salary and education information.* https://collegegrad.com/industries/insurance#employment

Deloitte. (2015). *From brawn to brains: The impact of technology on jobs in the UK*. Deloitte.

Dopfer, K., & Potts, J. (2008). *The general theory of economic evolution.* Routledge.

Dosi, G., & Cimoli, M. (1994). De los paradigmas tecnológicos a los sistemas nacionales de producción e innovación. *Comercio Exterior, 44*(8), 669–682.

Foss, N. (2006). *The emerging knowledge governance approach: Challenges and characteristics* (Working Paper: Danish Research Unit for Industrial Dynamics, No. 06–10).

Give a grad a go. (2019). https://www.giveagradago.com/news/2019/06/banking-graduate-jobs-what-skills-do-i-need/402. (Accessed 25 May 2021).

Great sample resume. (2021). https://www.greatsampleresume.com/job-responsibilities/finance/capital-markets-analyst#:~:text=Provide%20support%20to%20capital%20markets,pitches%20and%20provide%20required%20materials.&text=Prepare%20presentations%20for%20all%20investors,analyze%20all%20market%20intelligence%20programs (Accessed 25 May 2021).

Hakim, J. (1985). *Latin America's financial crisis: Causes and cures. Latin America and the world recession* (pp. 17–37). Cambridge: Cambridge University Press.

Harper, D. A. (2018). Innovation and institutions from the bottom up: An introduction. *Journal of Institutional Economics, 14*(6), 975–1001.

Ibarra, D. (2020). México: Banca y temas relacionados. *Economía UNAM, 17*(49), 16–45.

Islam, A., Jedwab, R., Romer, P., & Pereira, D. (2018). *Returns to experience and the misallocation of labour* (Working Paper).

Kurt, D., Foster, J., y Jason, P. (2004). Micro-meso-macro. *Journal of Evolutionary Economics, 14*, 263–279.

Marengo, L., & Pasquali, C. (2008). El mercado, la empresa y la primacía del conocimiento.In R. Viale (Comp.), *Las nuevas economías. De la economía evolucionista a la economía cognitiva: más allá de las fallas de la teoría neoclásica* (pp. 65–78). México: FLACSO.

Mitchell, M. (2009). *Complexity: A guided tour.* Oxford University Press.

Mohamed, H., & Ali, H. (2019). *Blockchain.* CPI books GmbH, Leck.

Mokyr, J. (2002). *The gifts on athena. Historical origins of the knowledge economy.* Princeton University Press.

Morrison, E. R. (2007). Bankruptcy decision making: an empirical study of continuation bias in small-business bankruptcies. *The Journal of Law and Economics, 50*(2), 381–419.

Mosteanu, N. R. (2020). Finance digitalization and its impact on labour market. *Technium Social Sciences Journal, 8*, 598.

Nelson, R. R., Dosi, G., & Helfat, C. E. (2018). *Modern evolutionary economics: An overview*. Cambridge University Press

Nerdwallet. (2021). https://www.nerdwallet.com/article/investing/what-is-investment-management (Accessed 25 May 2021).

Newman, M. (2018). *Networks*. Oxford University Press.

Otto, K. (1993). The national system of technical innovation in germany. In N. Innovation (Ed.), *Richard Nelson* (pp. 115–157). Oxford University Press.

Pavitt, K. (2003). *The process of innovation,* en Electronic Working Paper Series SPRU, Inglaterra.

Pyka, A., & Saviotti P. (2018). *Evolutionary perspective on lung run economic development*. The Economics of Knowledge, Innovation and Systemic Technology Policy.

Romer, P. M. (1994). The origins of endogenous growth. *Journal of Economic Perspectives, 8*(1), 3–22.

Rosenberg, N. (1982). *Inside the Black Box*. Cambridge University Press.

Sanchez-Ante, G. (2013). *Sistemas inteligentes: Reportes finales Ago-Dic 2013.* Reporte Tecnico RT-0002-2013.

Sandoval Cabrera, S., Morales Sánchez, M. A., & Díaz Rodríguez, H. E. (2019). Estrategia de escalamiento en las cadenas globales de valor: el caso del sector aeroespacial en México. *Entreciencias: diálogos en la sociedad del conocimiento, 7*(20), 35–52.

Sala-Martin, X. (1994). Cross-sectional regressions and the empirics of economic growth. *European Economic Review, 38*(3–4), 739–747.

Salvi, A., Vitolla, F., Rubino, M., Giakoumelou, A., & Raimo, N. (2021). Online information on digitalisation processes and its impact on firm value. *Journal of Business Research, 124*, 437–444.

Sawyer, M. (2013). What is financialization? *International Journal of Political Economy, 42*(4), 5–18.

Statista. (2021). *Total value of investments into Fintech companies worldwide from 2010 to 2019 (in billion U.S. dollars).* https://www.statista.com/statistics/719385/investments-into-Fintech-companies-globally/. Accessed 7 March 2021.

SEC. (2018). *U.S. securities and exchange commission.* Accessed 7 June 2020.

Singh, S. (2012). Investor irrationality and self-defeating behavior: Insights from behavioral finance. *Journal of Global Business Management, 8*(1), 116.

Tanda, A., & Schena, C. M. (2019). *FinTech, BigTech and banks: Digitalisation and its impact on banking business models.* Springer.

The London Institute of Banking and Finance web site. (2019). *The top skills you need to work in financial services.* https://www.libf.ac.uk/news-and-ins

ights/news/detail/2019/11/21/the-top-skills-you-need-to-work-in-financial-services (Accessed 25 May 25 2021).

Vasilescu, M. D., Serban, A. C., Dimian, G. C., Aceleanu, M. I., & Picatoste, X. (2020). Digital divide, skills and perceptions on digitalisation in the European Union—Towards a smart labour market. *PloS one, 15*(4), e0232032.

Vromen, J. (2006). *Organizational routines and individual skills. Beyond analogy (pp. 1–18).* Erasmus Institute for Philosophy and Economics, Working Papers, (enero).

Williamson, B. (2016). Digital education governance: Data visualization, predictive analytics, and "real-time" policy instruments. *Journal of Education Policy, 31*(2), 123–141.

Willis Towers Watson. (2017). *The world's 500 largest asset manager—year end 2016*. https://tinyurl.com/ycketcgk (Accessed 23 January 2021).

WIPO. (2021). *Technology trends 2021.* https://www.wipo.int/publications/en/details.jsp?id=4541

Zaborovskaia, O., Nadezhina, O., & Avduevskaya, E. (2020). The impact of digitalization on the formation of human capital at the regional level. *Journal of Open Innovation: Technology, Market, and Complexity, 6*(4), 184.

Zhao, R. (2019). Technology and economic growth: From Robert Solow to Paul Romer. *Human Behaviour and Emerging Technologies, 1*(1), 62–65.

Zhu, T., Orlowski, J., & Fritzler. (2018). *Data insights: Jobs, skills and migration trends methodology and validation results.* World Bank Group. http://documents1.worldbank.org/curated/en/827991542143093021/pdf/World-Bank-Group-LinkedIn-Data-Insights-Jobs-Skills-and-Migration-Trends-Methodology-and-Validation-Results.pdf

9

East Asia and East Africa: Different Ways to Digitalize Payments

Qing XU

Introduction

Digitalization encourages traditional financial services providers to innovate in order to achieve more reliable, convenient, and secure real-time payment. An adequate payment system is an essential component of a country's monetary and financial system, and is crucial for national economic development. To improve the security and efficiency of payment systems requires the development of an appropriate regulatory regime, more extensive access and low-cost settlement for financial institutions, improved liquidity-saving mechanisms, and more stable and better-organized markets for delivering and pricing various payment services to users (Pacifici & Pozzi, 2004; Summers, 1994).

Including software, hardware, networks, collection, storage, transmission, processing, and presentation of information, the term Information

Q. XU (✉)
Université Côte d'Azur-GREDEG-CNRS, Valbonne, France
e-mail: qing.xu@univ-cotedazur.fr

M. Ratajczak-Mrozek and P. Marszałek (eds.), *Digitalization and Firm Performance*,
https://doi.org/10.1007/978-3-030-83360-2_9

and Communication Technologies (ICTs) refers to a comprehensive range of IT technologies that address and manage electronic data. The financial innovation of ICTs encourages dramatic changes in the current financial industry: digitalization could diminish the marginal costs of financial institutions, lead to buoyant economies of scale, and improve efficiency in financial services (Ramanzan, 2021). The research of Alshubiri et al. (2019) demonstrates that ICTs could facilitate the interactions and operations of financial institutions through their digital networks, resolve time constraints and reduce distance to increase the efficiency of financial and economic activities. The rapid growth of ICTs has changed the payment systems in many emerging and developing countries, and increased people's familiarity with technology and its use for everyday activities (Pradhan et al., 2018; Waverman et al., 2005).

The research of EMR (2020) and Mordor Intelligence (2020) show that the mobile payments market was valued at USD 1449.56 billion in 2020, and is expected to reach USD 5399.6 billion by 2026. AliPay, WeChat Pay, PayPal, Samsung Pay, Apple Pay, Amazon Pay, and Google Pay, are among the best-known global mobile payment applications. Use of m-payment solutions can allow developing countries to leapfrog traditional card-based payment systems. There are three features of a successful cashless payment implementation: (1) the digitalization of the local implementation environment; (2) the relative novelty of a given payment technology solution in a country at a specific point in time; and (3) the development status of the national infrastructure (Dennis et al., 2021).

Despite financial digitalization, in Europe, most of the new digital payment solutions are still primarily based on traditional cards or bank transfers, which are offered by banks, card companies, and financial technology firms (European Commission, 2020). The digital revolution has prompted few changes apart from opportunities to use credit cards and specific applications, such as PayPal, to make online payments. However, in East Asia and in East Africa, the widespread diffusion of mobile devices and innovative businesses has made radical changes to both distant and proximate payments.

The Digital 2020 Report (Hootsuite/We Are Social, 2020b) shows: (i) that Internet penetration rates reached 63% in East Asia and 23%

in Africa; and (ii) that the mobile connectivity ratios (this value might exceed 100%, due to individual use of multiple connections), by region, were 114% in East Asia and 60% in East Africa. Although the levels and forms of adoption are different in these regions, in both cases the advances of digitalization have changed habits and reorganized the payment 'industry', whereas in Western developed countries neither of these aspects has changed.

This chapter discusses how the successful adoption of m-payment technologies differed in both regions, for example, why it did not involve the same kind of operators and the same technical solutions. Second section presents a classification of mobile payment operational models. Third section presents the general background of m-payment in East Asia and East Africa. Fourth and fifth sections highlight different development paths and adoption models of m-payment in East Asia and East Africa. We consider the consequences of these differences for each region's current and future financial intermediation and financial systems. Finally, we make concluding remarks and offer some reflections on other world regions.

The Classification of Mobile Payment Operational Models

Mobile payment models can be classified according to different types of service providers. Miao and Jayakar (2016), Téllez and Zeadally (2017) show that the mobile payment value chain can include financial services providers (such as banks, financial institutions, etc.), third-party payment services providers (e.g., Alipay, WeChat Pay, Google Wallet, Paypal), mobile operators, service providers (such as transport companies, public utility companies, etc.), equipment providers (such as manufacturers of mobile phones and chips and terminal equipment providers), system integrators, merchants, and mobile phone consumers.

Table 9.1 shows that bank-led, mobile network operator-led, third-party platform-led, and hybrid models, are the four main types of mobile payment operational models (Chaix & Torre, 2011; Koch et al., 2020;

Table 9.1 Classification of mobile payment operational models)

Types of mobile payment operational models	Description
1. Bank-led model	Banks offer mobile payment services independently, are responsible for transactions and retain all the profit. Mobile operators are responsible only for providing the information access channel; they do not participate in the operation and management of the payment system
2. Mobile operator-led model	The mobile account is considered the payment account and is linked to the user's telephone number. Mobile transaction charges are collected directly by mobile operators. Payments are deducted directly from the mobile account
3. Third-party payment platform-led model	Third party online payment platforms are independent of banks and other financial institutions; they play an intermediary role and are responsible for transactions. They connect consumers, banks and merchants, provide lower cost banking services and increase the trading parties' trust
4. Hybrid models	Mobile operators and banks work together to provide the mobile payment service. This model exploits the mobile operator's network and customer relationships and the banks' electronic payment technology, security and credit management expertise, and overcomes the limitations of both these parties

Ondrus & Pigneur, 2006; Miao & Jayakar, 2016; Mishra & Bisht, 2013; Zhao & Sun, 2012).

The bank-led mobile payment model has a high level of bank involvement and a low level of mobile operator involvement. The mobile network operator-led model has a high level of mobile operator involvement and a low level of bank involvement. The third-party platform-led model means third-party online payment platforms work as independent intermediaries with a low bank or mobile operator involvement. The hybrid model involves financial institutions and mobile operators collaborating in the management of tasks.

The General Background of M-payment in East Asia and East Africa

The universalization of the Internet has enabled rapid expansion and the adoption of smartphones, allowing m-payment by electronic devices, as well as payments and receipt of money without the need for traditional cash or cheques (Chawla & Joshi, 2019). Téllez and Zeadally (2017) summarize by suggesting that m-payment can be widely accepted by satisfying the following conditions: (1) simplicity and usability, (2) universality, (3) interoperability, (4) security, privacy and trust, (5) low transaction cost and convenience, and (6) accessible globally. Tiago et al. (2016) demonstrate that compatibility, perceived technology security, performance expectations, innovativeness, and social influence could, directly and indirectly, affect the adoption and recommendation of m-payment.

The advantages that m-payment provides are lowering transaction costs significantly and increasing financial transparency, improving business record-keeping, and reducing cash-related fraud (Ligon et al., 2019; Setor et al., 2021; Staykova & Damsgaard, 2015). Singh et al. (2019) suggest there are ten success factors related to the adoption of digital payment: the perceived ease of use, perceived functional benefits, awareness, availability of resources, governmental policy, performance expectancy, social impact, price value, experience and habit, and risk-taking capability. Debit/credit cards, mobile payments, and online payment systems are standard digital payment solutions (Iman, 2018) and m-payment is the main digital payment method in several developing countries, such as China, South Korea, Kenya, Indonesia, and Brazil (Maurer, 2012; Setor et al., 2021).

China and South Korea are cashless payment solution leaders in East Asia. Chinese e-commerce will account for 11.6% of Chinese GDP in 2022 and, based on a robust national infrastructure, South Korea will be the top cashless country in 2022 (Global Data, 2020). By 2025, the Japanese government intends to increase cashless payments from the current 20% to 40% of all transactions by 2025 (*South China Morning Post*, 2021). According to the 2018 Asian Digital Transformation Index (Economist Intelligence Unit, 2019), Japan is ranked 3rd for digital infrastructure (58.9), with South Korea (54.3) and China (35.7) in 4th and 8th places, respectively. The Digital 2020 April Global Statshot Report ranks South Korea 2nd and China 4th for mobile Internet connection speed (Hootsuite/We Are Social, 2020a).

China had experienced a payments revolution: mobile payments have diffused rapidly in the space of less than a decade. In 2019, the value of mobile payment transactions in China increased by 25% compared to 2018, to reach RMB347.11 trillion (People's Bank of China, 2020). Tencent's WeChat Pay and Alibaba's Alipay system dominate China's mobile payment market.

South Korea also has a well-established mobile or m-payment infrastructure and has recently become the first walletless nation. The transaction value of mobile wallet payments was KRW143.4 trillion (USD124.2 billion) in 2019, increased by 79% compared to 2018 (Global Data, 2021). South Koreans prefer to use smartphones to make both online and offline payment, by using Kakao Pay, Naver Pay, Samsung Pay, and tec.

The use of m-payment has developed more rapidly in Japan than in Western developed countries. The Yano Research Institute (2018) estimates that the Japanese domestic mobile payment transaction will increase from JPY1.303 trillion in 2018 to JPY1.66 trillion in 2019. PayPay, LINE Pay, Origami Pay, D-barai, merPay, Pixiv, Apple Pay, and Google Pay are popular Japanese mobile payment services.

The story of the adoption and use in East Africa took a different form than in Asia: in this case, the M-Pesa/Safaricom model played a leading role: Kenya was associated with this initiative mostly because Safaricom was a Kenyan company. The Safaricom/Kenyan experience was then repeated in neighboring countries: the more Safaricom was present there, the faster the adoption was, until different regional operators proposed the same range of services as M-Pesa. Between China, South Korea and Japan, service providers, uses and even technologies differ. In contrast, in East Africa, there is a dominant operator, the same use and technology among countries.

In East Africa, mobile payments have been an essential part of life for more than ten years. For example, in Kenya, Tanzania, and Uganda, the number of m-payment accounts has overtaken the number of bank accounts and the volume of m-payments continues to show strong growth. The Central Bank of Kenya announced that in 2019 mobile money transactions in Kenya were valued at USD38.5 billion, almost half of Kenya's GDP. East Asian countries have followed various paths of digital payment development with different operators. In contrast, East African countries demonstrated similar development models. M-Pesa and its mother company Safaricom have initiated a model where distant transfers are more common than proximity payments, where telephonic operators, with or without local banks as partners, never left the lead to Internet service providers, where national frontiers played few roles in the extension of technical services.

M-payment in East Asia

M-payment in China

The General Background on M-payment in China

Historically, China was a cash economy and the exchange model was cash dominated (Klein, 2019; Torre & Xu, 2019). However, the largest Chinese currency note is RMB100 (around USD15), whereas the US has USD100 bills and European countries have Euro500 notes. As a result, cash payment has become inconvenient for high-value transactions in China.

In addition, the adoption of card-based terminals in China was not in line with the issuing of bank cards. China has a large card network with 8.95 billion cards, of which 8.17 billion are debit cards and only 778 million are credit cards (People's Bank of China, 2021). However, the adoption of card-based point-of-sale or POS terminals by Chinese merchants has been slow. At end of 2020, there were only 30.89 million POS terminals in China (People's Bank of China, 2021). The reluctance of merchants to acquire POS terminals and the problems related to cash payments triggered the development of an alternative payment method.

Compared to South Korea and Japan, China is a latecomer in the ICT sector. However, following years of technological innovation and development, China's digital payment market made dramatic progress and in 2020 China became the leader of digital payments. One of the peculiarities of the Chinese economy has been its rapid adoption and widespread diffusion of mobile payments. According to the 47th China Statistical Report on Internet Development, released by the China Internet Network Information Center (2021, p. 49), by the end of 2020, the number of Chinese mobile payment users had reached 853 million, an increase of 87.44 million since March 2020, and accounted for 86.5% of Chinese mobile netizens. Mobile payments enabled by smartphones and Quick Response (QR) codes have caused disintermediation in China's banking system (Klein, 2019).

The 2020 Communications Industry Statistics Bulletin, published by the Ministry of Industry and Information Technology of the People's Republic of China (2021), states that, at the end of 2020, there were around 1.59 billion mobile phone users in China, and mobile phone coverage in China had reached 113.9 sets per 100 people. According to the People's Bank of China (2021) statistics, at the end of 2020, digital payments were continuing to grow. During those three months: (i) Chinese banks processed 235.225 billion electronic payments, representing a total of RMB2711.81 trillion (around USD393 trillion, using average closing price of 2020 China/US Foreign Exchange Rate was 6.9), including 123.22 billion mobile transactions with a total value of RMB432.16 trillion (around USD62.6 trillion), respective year-on-year increases of 21.48% and 24.5%; (ii) non-bank entities processed 827.29 billion electronic payments amounting to RMB294.56 trillion yuan (around USD42.7 trillion) and respective year-on-year increases of 14.9% and 17.88%.

Two leading Chinese digital economy players, Alipay—created by Alibaba (China's version of Amazon), and WeChat Pay—launched by Tencent (China's version of Facebook), have experienced very successful mobile payment innovation and adoption (Klein, 2019; Torre & Xu, 2019, 2020; Yiping et al., 2020). In 2019, Alipay and WeChat Pay were first-tier corporations and accounted for almost 93.8% of the third-party payment market (iResearch Consulting Group, 2020). WeChat is ranked 5th in the global ranking of mobile apps based on average monthly active users, and Alipay is ranked 7th (Hootsuite/We Are Social, 2020a). WeChat Pay and Alipay dominate the Chinese mobile payment market as the primary payment method for most Chinese people, with cash second and debit/credit cards third (Steven, 2017).

Alipay

Alipay, one of China's largest digital payment platforms, provides complete digital payment, digital finance and digital daily life services. It was created in 2004, initially as the financial department of the Alibaba Group's online platform, Taobao.com, to try to resolve the trust issues between buyers and sellers in online transactions, and to act as an e-wallet and a one-stop payment portal. Alipay increased trust between e-commerce sellers and buyers, facilitated online business, and underpinned the expansion of e-commerce in China.

Alipay launched its Alipay mobile payment App in 2009 and its QR code payment system in 2011 (Ant Group Co. Ltd, 2020, p. 135). In 2013, it launched Yu'ebao to offer Alipay users the opportunity to invest in Alipay's money market fund at the very low purchase threshold of RMB1, around Euro0.13 (Ant Financial Services Group, 2019). Huabei and Jiebei were created in 2014 and 2015 respectively: the former works like a bank credit card and focuses on quick consumer loans for purchases using e-commerce platforms, such as Taobao.com and Tmall.com (China's version of Amazon); the latter is similar to a bank loan and is used to finance almost anything, from travel to education. At the beginning of 2015, Alipay implemented Zhima Credit, a credit-scoring service: high-scoring users have easier access to loans and a more trustworthy profile on e-commerce sites in the Alibaba Group. The AntChain Blockchain-as-a-Service (BaaS) open platform was launched in 2018, to provide an open collaboration platform and convenient services for both enterprises and individuals worldwide, and more equal opportunities. Alipay has developed from a simple payment tool to a one-stop digital daily life platform that offers digital finance, government affairs services, local life services, and other services in various sectors. By end of June 2020, Alipay had operations in more than 200 countries and regions, over 1 billion annual active users (numbers of people using the Alipay App in the previous 12 months), and more than 80 million monthly active merchants (merchant accounts that completed at least one transaction during that month) and over 2,000 financial institution partners (Ant Group Co. Ltd, 2020).

Focusing on individual consumers and small businesses whose financial requirements are substantially underserved in China, Alipay cooperates with financial institution partners and implements digital financial solutions for its participants. For individual consumers, Alipay provides digital payments, consumer credit, asset management and insurance services, and daily life services provided by third parties, such as food delivery, transportation, entertainment, and access to municipal resources. For business clients, Alipay offers collection and payment services and digital finance, for example, SMB or Server Message Block credit and investment products. Financial institutions use the Alipay platform to distribute credit, investment, and insurance products.

WeChat Pay

WeChat started as a simple messaging App (China's version of WhatsApp) and was launched by Tencent in 2011 as Weixin (Mandarin for micro-message). It was developed to provide services similar to

Facebook, WhatsApp, Instagram, Uber, Apple pay, etc. WeChat now combines functions including instant messaging, voice and video calls, social space (WeChat Moment), short videos (WeChat Channel), e-commerce (WeChat Business), mini-programs, online games, digital payment (WeChat Pay), asset management, ebooks (WeChat Reading), a corporate communication, and office tool (Enterprise WeChat), etc.

The initial features offered by WeChat were the basic text messaging, voice clip creation, and photo sending services. In August 2011, it added video clips and a 'find nearby users' function. WeChat launched its voice and video calls function and went international in 2012 with updated versions in the English, Thai, Vietnamese, Indonesian, and Portuguese languages. Several revolutionary features were introduced in 2013, for example, WeChat Pay, WeChat Official Accounts, WeChat Emojis, and WeChat Games.

In China, there is a tradition of giving red envelopes containing money as new year, birthday and wedding gifts, especially from parents to children, and from other family members. During the 2014 Spring Festival, WeChat introduced its WeChat Red (virtual) Envelope, and more than 8 million Chinese people sent over 40 million WeChat Red Envelopes of good wishes to relatives and friends. The popularity of this digital exchange' seeded the WeChat Pay accounts of many customers with initial funds and further increased WeChat Pay's penetration (Torre & Xu, 2020). Since then, WeChat has become a very popular, multi-functional social media app and has been downloaded by almost every Chinese mobile phone user.

Tencent (2021) announced that, at the end of 2020, there were 1.225 billion active monthly WeChat users. In less than ten years, WeChat had evolved from a real-time communication application to a communication and social network platform that meets the digital needs of more than 1.2 billion users. Every day, more than 120 million users post content on WeChat Moment, 360 million users read WeChat articles, and around 400 million users employ mini programs (Tencent, 2021). In addition, Enterprise WeChat has become indispensable as a communication tool for remote office working and serves more than 5.5 million corporate customers (Tencent, 2021).

QR Code Adoption in China

QR codes are modern two-dimensional bar codes with large data storage capacity for information such as contact details and digital payments. They differ from the linear product barcodes in terms of their huge data storage capacity, scanability using a screen, readability (even if slightly damaged), and data encryption which provides security.

QR codes are an essential component of China's digital payment revolution. In the third quarter of 2020, transaction amounts related to QR code payment reached around RMB10 trillion, an increase of 19.4% compared to the previous three months (iResearch Consulting Group, 2021). Both Alipay and WeChat Pay make extensive use of the QR code: app users employ them for their personal accounts and merchants use them in their stores, on products, and for advertisements.

QR codes enable merchants to access payment systems without using an Internet connection; only the payer needs to be connected for the payment transaction. Merchants need to supply a printed QR code that the consumer can scan using a smartphone and go online to process the payment transaction. This lowers the merchant's costs and increases the payment benefits (e.g., speedier payment process), further facilitating m-payment adoption (Yan et al., 2021).

M-payment in South Korea

The General Background of M-payment in South Korea

South Korea has a well-developed digital payment market and high levels of smartphone adoption and Internet penetration. The Asia Pacific e-Commerce and Payments Guide 2020 states that in 2019 Internet penetration in South Korea was 91.8% and smartphone penetration was 88.5% (Rapyd, 2020).

Prior to 2014, South Korea's mobile payment industry was strictly controlled. This resulted in a much lower demand for e-payment services in Korea compared to some other countries and in the continuing use, by Korean consumers, of traditional financial methods, such as credit cards and Internet banking. In 2015, the regulation changed and South Korea became a more creative and innovative environment for the Fintech industry. Financial systems were restructured to fit the online and mobile environment, supported by funding for fintechs, and the barriers to electronic financing were lowered (MSIP and KISA, 2015). In April 2015, the Ministry of Science, ICT and Future Planning (MSIP) announced a strategy aimed at reducing the use of the ActiveX framework by private sector finance, education and entertainment organizations, and promoting more convenient digital payment methods.

Korean users register their credit cards on Naver Pay (introduced in 2015 by Korea's leading portal site operator, Naver) or Kakao Pay (launched in 2014 by the internet giant Kakao) to enable online shopping; this is similar to the US Paypal system. In 2015, the smartphone manufacturer, Samsung Electronics, launched Samsung Pay, which uses Near Field Communication (NFC) and magnetic secure transmission technologies. In 2018, Kakao Pay launched a QR payment option and the South Korean government implemented Zero Pay.

The potential offered by Fintech developments has resulted in many traditional Korean financial institutions, technology companies, and even government launching mobile payment services. The Korean government has a strong incentive to achieve a cashless transformation and the Bank of Korea's Coinless Society Project, launched in April 2017, has further promoted FinTech payments.

According to the survey of Rapyd (2020), around 36% of South Koreans have opted for mobile payments (or what Koreans call 'simple' payments, via Kakao Pay, Samsung Pay and Naver Pay, compared with 30% who prefer domestic card payments, 15% who prefer international card payments and 13% who favor bank transfers. The transaction value of mobile wallet payments grew from KRW12.0 trillion (USD10.4 billion) in 2016, to an estimated KRW209.7 trillion (USD181.6 billion) in 2020, and is expected to reach KRW581.3 trillion (USD503.5 billion) in 2024 (Global Data, 2021).

Kakao Pay and Naver Pay

Simple payments allow South Korean consumers to pay for goods and services easily, both online and offline. Kakao Pay is used by 41% of consumers, Naver Pay 34%, and Samsung Pay by 32% (Rapyd, 2020). According to a Rakuten Insight survey of e-payment usage, around 84% of respondents had made at least one transaction using an e-payment method, with the most popular among South Korean respondents, being Naver Pay (53% of respondents), followed by Kakao Pay and Samsung Pay (respectively around 50 and 40% of respondents) (Statista, 2021).

Kakao Pay, South Korea's top ranked mobile payment service provider, was launched in April 2014 as a fintech subsidiary of Kakao. By the end of 2019, Kakao Pay had more than 20 million active monthly users, over 30 million accumulated users, and a turnover in 2019 of around 40 billion dollars (KRW48 trillion) (Kakao, 2020). Kakao is one of the largest Internet companies in South Korea and provides a range of services such as instant messaging (Kakao Talk), image, video, and music sharing (Kakao Story), a music app (Kakao Music), a mobile fashion service (Kakao Style), a mobile e-wallet (Kakao Pay), a mobile bank (Kakao Bank), investment and venture capital (Kakao INV and Kakao Ventures), etc. Kakao Pay is incorporated with Kakao Talk and allows Kakao Talk users to pay for e-commerce products and services through the messaging app. It aims to lead the wallet-free society revolution, to allow economic activities to take place anytime, anywhere with the intermediation of a smartphone. It has extended its services with the addition of innovative life finance services such as online and offline payments, remittances, memberships, bills and authentication. In February 2017, Ant Financial Service Group (the parent company of Alipay) invested USD200 million in Kakao Pay and became its second-largest shareholder. This strategic partnership enabled the use of a QR code payment service, compatible with Alipay, and facilitated international e-commerce at Alipay-supported stores and businesses abroad.

Naver Pay was launched in 2015, by Naver, South Korea's main web portal. It integrates online shopping, convenient in-app payments, electronic financial transaction functions, etc. Naver has a large market share and receives 30 million visits daily on average. The number of monthly users of NAVER Pay reached 12 million at the end of 2019 (Naver, 2020) and in that same year, Naver decided to make Naver Pay a separate entity. Naver Financial is an innovative financial platform offering exceptional services.

M-payment in Japan

The General Background of M-payment in Japan

Unlike developments in China and South Korea, in Japan digital payment advances have been slow. In Japan, more than 80% of transactions still involve cash; fewer than 20% of transactions use cashless payment methods, such as credit cards, electronic money, and mobile payments. This historical 'preference for cash', which is observed, also, in Germany, has reduced the use of credit cards for small and medium-sized payments. In 2004, Japan launched a mobile wallet, a world mobile commerce innovation created by NTT DotCoMo (Japanese mobile operator); however, Japan's ageing population remains strongly linked to cash (PYMNTS, 2020).

The Japanese government has been making huge efforts to promote digital payment. In 2017, the Ministry of Economy, Trade and Industry issued a policy document entitled Cashless Vision, which set a target of 40% of digital payments in 2027 from the 2017 level of 18%. The Yano Research Institute (2018) estimates that the Japanese domestic mobile payment transaction will grow from JPY1 trillion in 2017 to JPY4.3 trillion in 2023.

In 2019, the Japanese government launched its Cashless project: until the end of June 2020 the government-funded rebate amounts to 2% of the total purchase amount at major retailers and 5% at small- and medium-sized merchants and is available, and consumers can take advantage of the discount by using any of a wide range of payment options, such as credit, debit, prepaid and transit cards, Apple Pay and Google Pay, plus QR mobile payments services such as Line Pay, PayPay and Rakuten Pay (Japan Cashless Promotion Council, 2019). These actions hugely boosted use of digital payment in Japan.

The Asia Pacific eCommerce and Payments Guide 2020 (Rapyd, 2020) shows that, in 2019, Japan was the second-largest e-commerce market in the Asia–Pacific region with a market value of USD150.1 billion and a mobile commerce market worth USD36.6 billion. In 2019 Internet penetration was 91% and smartphone penetration was 47% (Rapyd, 2020). By end of 2020, there were about 186 million mobile subscribers in Japan (Telecommunications Carriers Association, 2020).

PayPay and Rakuten Pay

Based on the July 2020 Smartphone Payment Usage Trend Survey of Mobile Marketing Data Laboratory (MMDLabo, 2020), the main payment methods were cash (90.2% usage rate), credit card (73.4% usage rate), smartphone payments (37.8% usage rate) including Near Field Communication (NFC) payments and QR code payments, public transport IC card (27.9% usage rate) and non-public transport IC card (21.6% usage rate). The survey results show, also, that 93.3% of respondents recognized QR code payments and 34.3% were QR code payment users and, among these, PayPay was the most used QR code payment (48.7%), followed by Rakuten Pay (15.7%), d Payment (13.4%) au Pay (10.3%), and LINE Pay (6.2%) (MMDLabo, 2020).

PayPay is a joint venture, established by SoftBank Group Corporation and Yahoo Japan Corporation, in autumn 2018. It offers smartphone payment services, using QR code technology, supported by India's largest digital payment company, Paytmm, a SoftBank investee (SoftBank, 2018). By the end of February 2021, PayPay had over 36 million users in Japan. On 1 March, 2021, the SoftBank Group Corporation completed a merger between its Japanese Internet business and the messaging service operator, Line Corporation. It intended to combine these entities' payment apps to give PayPay access to users of Line Corporation's messaging services (Alpeyev, 2021).

Rakuten is a Japanese e-commerce and online retailing company whose businesses include worldwide e-commerce, fintech, digital content, and communications. The Fintech Groupe offers a variety of services, such as digital payment (Rakuten Pay, Rakuten Point Card,

Rakuten Edy, etc.), Internet banking (Rakuten Bank), credit card issuing (Rakuten Card), online brokerage (Rakuten Securities) and insurance (Rakuten Insurance General Information Center, Rakuten Life Insurance, Rakuten General Insurance, etc.). In the last quarter of 2020, the Fintech Groupe's segmentation revenue accounted for 32.6% of the total revenue. In 2012, Rakuten introduced Rakuten Pay, primarily to support small and medium-sized businesses with no POS system and, in late 2016, launched the Rakuten Pay app (Rakuten Today, 2019).

Mobile Payment Operational Models in East Asia

In Section "The Classification of Mobile Payment Operational Models", we referred to the high level of bank involvement and low level of mobile operator involvement in the bank-led mobile payment model, and the high level of mobile operator involvement and low level of bank involvement in the mobile network operator-led model. The third-party platform-led model relies less on banks and mobile operators, and the hybrid model relies heavily on cooperation between banks and mobile operators.

WeChat Pay and Alipay belong to third-party payment platforms. Kakao Pay, Naver Pay and Samsung Pay also have little bank and mobile operator involvement. Therefore, China and South Korea are examples of third-party platform-led mobile payment models (see Fig. 9.1).

For the Japanese cases of PayPay and Rakuten Pay: PayPay, backed by SoftBank, Yahoo Japan, a 1996 joint venture between SoftBank and Yahoo, and Paytmm an investee of SoftBank. Rakuten launched Rakuten Bank, two years before implementing Rakuten Pay, and introduced Rakuten Card, which increased the penetration of PayPay. Both cases depend heavily on financial service providers—that is, banks. Thus, Japan is an example of a bank-based mobile payment model (see Fig. 9.1).

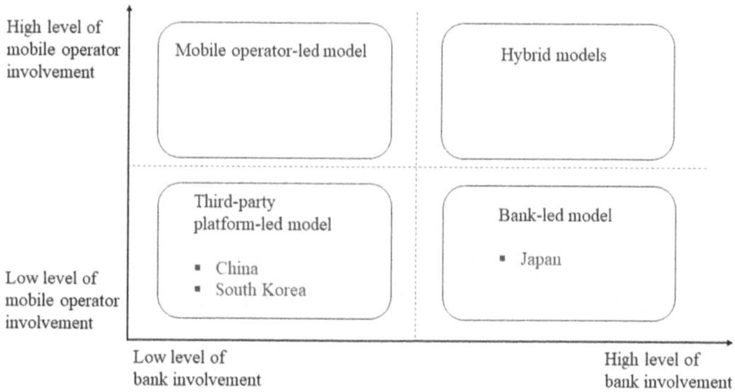

Fig. 9.1 A classification of mobile payment operational models in China, South Korea, and Japan

M-payment in East Africa

The Safaricom Kenyan Story

The Operator Centric Phase

The East Africa story of m-payment solutions began in Kenya as an initiative of Vodafone, still the leading m-payment operator in this part of Africa. In this country, which served as a testing ground for other experiences in East Africa, they initially proposed simple solutions able to work without any Internet connexion, and then they improved the service, in collaboration with local banks (Chaix & Torre, 2015; Jack et al., 2010; Mbiti & Weil, 2014).

In 2007, Safaricom, a Kenyan subsidiary of Vodafone, proposed an innovative service adapted to an environment where only first-generation mobile phones, with no Internet connection or advanced functionalities, were available. M-Pesa was implemented as a transfer service, enabling deposits and withdrawals of money from a network of agents, transfers of money to other users and non-users, bill payment, and purchase of phone minutes. Transmissions were based on unstructured supplementary service data technology, which had a low level of reliability, and 'certified agents' enabling both ends of the payments: one to transform notes into electronic signs and the other to transform codes into notes. Users were charged a small fee by the operator. The receiver of the transfer did not have to be registered with M-Pesa, although registration made the transfer order slightly cheaper. All the operations, from the transmission of the code to the contribution of the certified agents, were controlled by the mobile network operator and required no intervention from a financial agent. Therefore, this was an operator-centric model (or mobile operator-led model).

The success of this model (see Fig. 9.2), was huge and unexpected. Jack et al. (2013) state that the growth in these services in parts of the developing world has been remarkable, especially in Kenya: only five years after the launch of M-Pesa, at least 70% of households in Kenya have accessed M-Pesa, which became the country's largest mobile money product. One of the reasons for its success was that it enabled international transactions (Ntara, 2015) and allowed international transfers by immigrants (Metzger et al., 2019; Morawczynski, 2009). However, the main reason for its success was that it allowed local customers to make distant payments without having to use intermediaries. Network

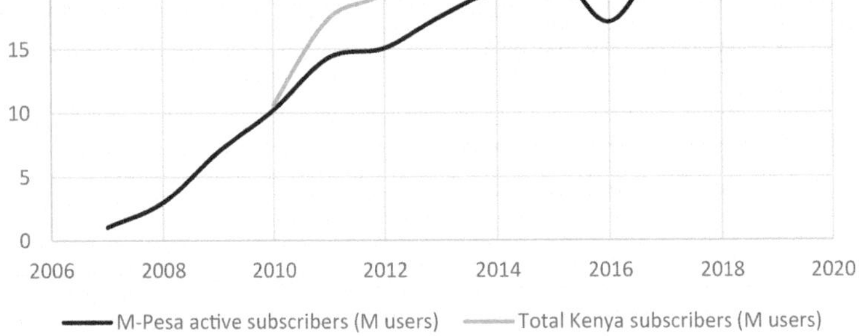

Fig. 9.2 The number of domestic Kenyan subscribers to M-payment (millions)

dynamics played an important role in its rapid adoption. Chaix and Torre (2015) point to the relevance of a mean field and microeconomic network settings for explaining the diffusion of the Safaricom innovation.

Hybrid Models: Bancarization and Financialization Led by Telephone Operators

Africa has the fastest growth in mobile payment, and mobile payment innovations contribute to economic development and financial inclusion in Africa (Ahmad et al., 2020; Aker & Isaac, 2010; Asongu et al., 2020; Demirguc-Kunt et al., 2018). Following the initial rather frugal solution, and based on its observation that one-third of M-Pesa accounts included otherwise unbanked individuals, Safaricom proposed partnerships with several banks to provide additional services. In 2012, it launched M-Shwari, a joint venture with the Commonwealth Bank of Australia. Users of m-payment services could access loans that were redeemable in 30 days, a rate of 7.5%, and could access saving accounts offering 5% interest. In 2013, Safaricom and Equity Bank launched M-Kesho, which was a more sophisticated version of M-Pesa. It offered access to several banking services without the need for account opening fees, minimum balances or monthly charges, as well as micro-saving, micro-credit, and micro-insurance services. M-Kesho accounts paid interest and withdrawals carried a very small cost. This new service provided Safaricom/Vodafone with an involuntary means to increase their client base through an asymmetric operator-bank partnership and offered an efficient way to bancarize Kenya.

The Diffusion of the Kenyan Model in Other East-African Countries

Following the success in Kenya, Vodaphone tried to apply the model in other countries. M-Pesa explains that its solution is now available in the Democratic Republic of Congo, Egypt, Ghana, Lesotho, and in the East-African countries Mozambique and Tanzania. The latter, a neighbour of

Kenya, was the first to access the M-Pesa service, in 2008, following an initiative by Vodacom, another subsidiary of Vodafone. In 2021, there are now 6 different operators offering m-payment solutions in Tanzania: the share of market of m-Pesa is around 40%, followed by Luxemburg's Tigo Pesa at around 30%, the Indian Airtel at 20%, and other minor operators with the last 10%. In this country, the M-Koba solution has recently been launched by Vodacom, in cooperation with TPB bank, to promote savings groups, to access loans, and share earnings.

M-payment has been the main driver of the increased financialization of Sub-Saharan Africa (Beck et al., 2018; Chaix & Torre, 2015; Dissaux, 2019; Llewellyn-Jones, 2016; Mazer & Rowan, 2016;). What is interesting is that Safaricom continued to offer the possibility to subscribe to its initial frugal service, despite the later versions being more secure and more sophisticated. The dual offer facilitated the adoption of full banking services by previously unbanked customers and was probably very relevant for the subsequent adoption of new banking services by new users.

In many countries, Vodafone was/is not dominant or the leader, but the same scenario as that applied than in Kenya was followed, only sometimes with a delay. MTN, the largest South African operator, launched the MMT (Mobile Money Transfer) in many African countries, including Uganda (see Fig. 9.3) and Rwanda in East Africa. In each case, the introduction of mobile payments under the MTN initiative has also impacted the financialization of economies. If Vodafone was the first mover, it was not the only telephonic operator able to supplement the banks in some of their areas of competence and to perpetuate an operator-centric model which seems so unsuitable in Asia.

For many years, East Africa was the leader in terms of implementation of mobile-money solutions; however, based on subscriber numbers, West Africa now dominates. In this region, which has the most French-speaking countries, the main operator is Orange, which uses a more advanced technology than Vodafone and has worked to create an international m-payment ecosystem among countries that use the same currency (CFA franc) linked to the euro via a fixed exchange rate system. Interoperability seems to be the key to Orange's success, in a world region

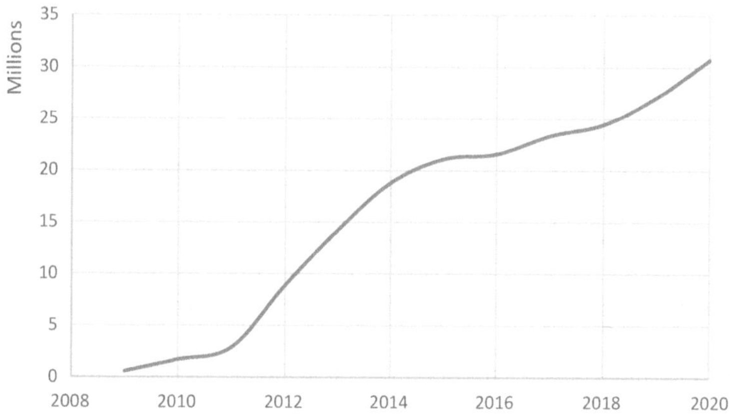

Fig. 9.3 The number of domestic Ugandan subscribers to M-payment (millions)

that includes countries that are too small to impose a national strategy (GSMA, 2019).

Mobile Payment Operational Models in East Africa

According to the classification of Ondrus and Pigneur (2006)–Chaix and Torre (2011, 2015), the East Africa mobile payment implementation model was clearly a successful operator centric framework (mobile operator-led model) (see Fig. 9.4), which, over time, evolved from an imaginative use of a frugal technology to the provision of more advanced financial services, but focused always on the specific needs of local populations.

However, in recent years, more and more banks in Africa are beginning to compete aggressively for mobile banking customers and partnering with mobile operators to facilitate mobile money transactions (Chironga et al., 2017). In 2020, Ecobank launched a digital payment service, Rapidtransfer International, for instant cross-border payments between Europe and the 33 African countries where Ecobank operates. In February 2021, Mastercard and MTN announced a strategic partnership, combining a Mastercard virtual payment solution linked to the MTN MoMo wallet, to enable millions of consumers in 16 countries

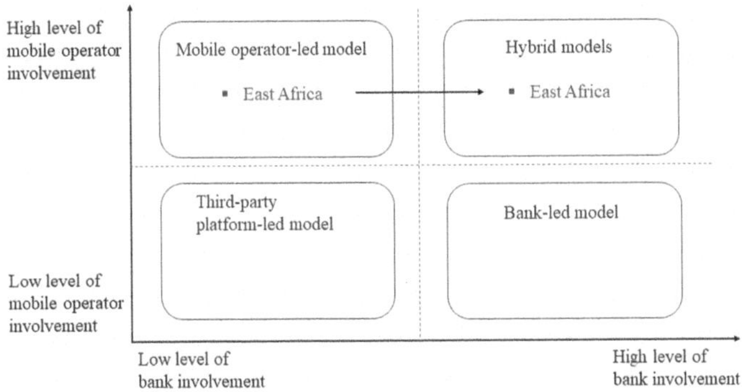

Fig. 9.4 A classification of mobile payment operational models in East Africa

across Africa to make global e-commerce payments safely and securely (MTN Group, 2021). Therefore, in my view the African traditional mobile operator-led model has moved toward a hybrid model with the involvement of more banks and mobile operators (see Fig. 9.4).

Conclusion

This chapter shows that, despite a common trend toward increased use of m-payment solutions, adoption patterns differ among continents, and the pace of adoption differs among countries—even on the same continent. In Asia, initially, distant payment was introduced to allow payments online using mobile phones in virtual marketplaces. However, it is proximity payment that has led to increased adoption of m-payment in this region. In Africa, only distant payments have remained attractive and led to new practices, despite not very secure technologies. These differences are likely due to the type of need and the level of development in these regions. In Asia, the business models were mostly introduced by the Internet service providers, which used m-payment to extend their activities into the finance, banking and insurance sectors. The emergence and economic success of fintechs in Asia owe much to this payment revolution. In Africa, which was an earlier adopter of m-payment before the diffusion of smartphones and 3G and 4G standards, it was the telephone operators who were best placed to provide the service and, despite the greater availability of mobile Internet, their supremacy has not been contested. This is due, in part, to their joint ventures with local banks in a bid to enlarge the range of services provided.

Based on the above, it is likely that the relative slowness related to the take-up of mobile payment in Western developed countries is due to a lack of encouragement from the market incumbents, that is, the major credit cards issuers. The improvements that have been made to their services have reduced the need for a transition to a technologically more advanced solution and limited the development for existing functionalities, such as generalizing the contactless payment in recent years. Since more and more travelers prefer using m-payment for travel-related services, especially Asian travelers, and since service providers could implement mobile payment options to attract and better serve travelers, it is a good opportunity for the tourism industry to be a pioneer in leading economic growth through mobile payment (Tangit & Law, 2021; World Travel & Tourism Council, 2019; Wu et al., 2021). Policymakers and regulators could encourage the implementation of m-payment to maximize the opportunities that mobile payment systems can bring to an economy. Additionally, mobile payment also impacts migrants' remittances (Darmon et al., 2016; Kosse & Vermeulen, 2014). Thanks to its low cost, convenience and security, m-payment facilitates the transfer of remittances from migrants to family members, distant family members, or even migrants themselves. Western developed countries could use m-payment to stimulate the safety, efficiency, and integrity of the international remittance market.

Acknowledgements The author wishes to thank Professor Milena Ratajczak-Mrozek, Professor Paweł Marszałek, and Professor Dominique Torre, for their remarks and suggestions which allowed the author to improve and clarify the content of this chapter.

References

Ahmad, A. H., Green, C., & Jiang, F. (2020). Mobile money, financial inclusion and development: A review with reference to African. *Journal of Economic Surveys, 34*(4), 753–792. https://doi.org/10.1111/joes.12372

Aker, J. C., & Isaac, M. M. (2010). Mobile phones and economic development in Africa. *Journal of Economic Perspectives, 24*(3), 207–232.

Alpeyev, P. (2021). *SoftBank to merge PayPay and Line Pay apps in Japan*. https://www.bloombergquint.com/business/softbank-is-said-to-merge-paypay-and-line-pay-apps-in-japan

Alshubiri, F., Syed Ahsan Jamil, S. A., & Elheddad, M. (2019). The impact of ICT on financial development: Empirical evidence from the Gulf Cooperation Council countries. *International Journal of Engineering Business Management, 11*, 1–14.

Ant Financial Services Group. (2019). *Ant Financial History*. https://www.antfin.com/history.htm

Ant Group Co. Ltd. (2020). *Ant Group IPO prospectus*. https://www1.hkexnews.hk/listedco/listconews/sehk/2020/1026/2020102600165.pdf

Asongu, S. A., Biekpe, N., & Cassimon, D. (2020). Understanding the greater diffusion of mobile money innovations in Africa. *Telecommunications Policy, 44*(8). https://doi.org/10.1016/j.telpol.2020.102000

Beck, T., Pamuk, H., Ramrattan, R., & Uras, B. R. (2018). Payment instruments, finance and development. *Journal of Development Economics, 133*, 162–186. https://doi.org/10.1016/j.jdeveco.2018.01.005

Chaix, L., & Torre, D. (2011). *Four models for mobile payments*. https://www.researchgate.net/publication/267917243_Four_models_for_mobile_payments

Chaix, L., & Torre, D. (2015). The dual role of mobile payment in developing countries. *Revue Economique, 66*(4), 703–727. https://doi.org/10.3917/reco.664.0703

Chawla, D., & Joshi, H. (2019). Consumer attitude and intention to adopt mobile wallet in India—An empirical study. *International Journal of Bank Market, 37*(7), 1590–1618. https://doi.org/10.1108/IJBM-09-2018-0256

China Internet Network Information Center. (2021). *The 47th China's Statistical Report on Internet Development*. http://www.cac.gov.cn/2021-02/03/c_1613923423079314.htm

Chironga, M., Grandis, H. D., & Zouaoui, Y. (2017). *Mobile financial services in Africa: Winning the battle for the customer* (McKinsey report). https://www.mckinsey.com/~/media/McKinsey/Industries/Financial%20Services/

Our%20Insights/Mobile%20financial%20services%20in%20Africa%20Winning%20the%20battle%20for%20the%20customer/Mobile-financial-services-in-Africa-Winning-the-battle-for-the-customer.pdf

Communication Authority of Kenya Annual. (2007–2019). *Communication Authority of Kenya annual reports.* https://ca.go.ke/downloads/publications/annual-reports/

Demirguc-Kunt, A., Klapper L., Singer D., Ansar S., & Hess J. (2018). *Base de données Global Findex 2017: Mesurer l'inclusion financière et la révolution technico-financière.* World Bank. https://openknowledge.worldbank.org/handle/10986/29510

Darmon, E., Chaix, L., & Torre, D. (2016). M-payment use and remittances in developing countries: A theoretical analysis. *Revue D'economie Industrielle, 156*, 159–183. https://doi.org/10.4000/rei.6469

Dennis, N., Robert, J. K., Paul, G., & Jonas H. (2021). Can we classify cashless payment solution implementations at the country level? *Electronic Commerce Research and Applications, 46.* https://doi.org/10.1016/j.elerap.2020.101018

Dissaux, T. (2019). Inclusion financière et liens sociaux: la monnaie entre marchandisation et mise en commun au Kenya. *Mondes en développement, 1,* 83–108. https://ideas.repec.org/a/cai/meddbu/med_185_0083.html

Economist Intelligence Unit. (2019). *The 2018 Asian Digital Transformation Index (ADTI).* http://connectedfuture.economist.com/wp-content/uploads/2018/12/ADTI-whitepaper.pdf

EMR. (2020). *Global Mobile Payment Market.* https://www.expertmarketresearch.com/reports/mobile-payment-market

European Commission. (2020). *Communication from the commission to the European Parliament, the council, the European economic and social committee and the committee of the regions on a Retail Payments Strategy for the EU.* https://eur-lex.europa.eu/legal-content/EN/TXT/PDF/?uri=CELEX:52020DC0592&rid=2

Global Data. (2020, January 13). *Top countries moving toward a cashless society by 2022.* Revealed by Global Data. London. https://bit.ly/3ntKrzQ.

Global Data. (2021). *Mobile wallet payments in South Korea to surpass US$500bn in 2024*. https://www.globaldata.com/mobile-wallet-payments-south-korea-surpass-us500bn-2024-reveals-globaldata/

GSMA. (2019). *2019 State of the Industry Report on Mobile Money.* https://www.gsma.com/sotir/wp-content/uploads/2020/03/

Hootsuite/We Are Social. (2020a). *Digital 2020 April Global Statshot Report*. https://wearesocial.com/blog/2020/04/digital-around-the-world-in-april-2020

Hootsuite/We Are Social. (2020b). *Digital 2020 China*. https://wearesocial-cn.s3.cn-north-1.amazonaws.com.cn/digital2020-china.pdf

Iman, N. (2018). Is mobile payment still relevant in the fintech era? *Electronic Commerce Research and Applications, 30*, 72–82. https://doi.org/10.1016/j.elerap.2018.05.009

International Monetary Fund (IMF). (2020). *IMF Annual Report 2020*. https://www.imf.org/external/pubs/ft/ar/2020/eng/downloads/imf-annual-report-2020.pdf

iResearch Consulting Group. (2020). *China's Third-Party Mobile Payment Industry Report 2020*. http://report.iresearch.cn/report/202004/3552.shtml

iResearch Consulting Group. (2021). *China's Third-Party Mobile Payment Industry Report 2020 Q3 & 2020 Q4e*. http://report.iresearch.cn/report/202101/3726.shtml

Jack, W., Suri, T., & Townsend, R. (2010). Monetary theory and electronic money: Reections on the Kenyan experience. *Economic Quarterly, 96*(1), 83–122.

Jack, W., Adam, R., & Tavnee, t. S. (2013). Transaction networks: Evidence from mobile money in Kenya. *American Economic Review, 103*(3), 356–361. https://doi.org/10.1257/aer.103.3.356

Japan Cashless Promotion Council. (2019). *Cashless point return business*. https://cashless.go.jp/

Kakao. (2020). *Kakao March 2020 investor relations*. https://t1.kakaocdn.net/kakaocorp/admin/ir/results-announcement/4586.pdf

Klein, A. (2019). *Is China's new payment system the future?* https://www.brookings.edu/research/is-chinas-new-payment-system-the-future/

Koch, J., Rövenich, K., &Dunkel K. (2020). *How Africa's growing mobile money market is evolving*. https://www.ey.com/en_gl/banking-capital-markets/how-africa-s-growing-mobile-money-market-is-evolving

Kosse, A., & Vermeulen, R. (2014). Migrants' choice of remittance channel: Do general payment habits play a role? *World Development, 62*, 213–227. https://doi.org/10.1016/j.worlddev.2014.05.002

Llewellyn-Jones, L. (2016). Mobile money: Part of the African financial inclusion solution? *Economic Affairs, 36*(2), 212–216. https://doi.org/10.1111/ecaf.12177

Ligon, E., Malick, B., Sheth, K., & Trachtman, C. (2019). What explains low adoption of digital payment technologies? Evidence from small-scale merchants in Jaipur, India. *PLoS ONE, 14*(7), 1–22. https://doi.org/10.1371/journal.pone.0219450

Maurer, B. (2012). Mobile money: Communication, consumption and change in the payments space. *Journal of Development Studies, 48*(5), 589–604. https://doi.org/10.1080/00220388.2011.621944

Mazer, R., & Rowan, P. (2016). Competition in mobile financial services: Lessons from Kenya and Tanzania1. *The African Journal of Information and Communication, 17,* 39–59. https://core.ac.uk/download/pdf/188771434.pdf

Mbiti, I., & Weil, D. N. (2014). *Mobile banking: the impact of M-Pesa in Kenya. National Bureau of Economic Research* (NBER Working Papers: 17129).

Metzger, M., Riedler, T., & Pédussel Wu, J. (2019). *Migrant remittances: Alternative money transfer channels* (IPE Working Papers 127/2019). Berlin School of Economics and Law, Institute for International Political Economy (IPE).

Miao, M., & Krishna, J. (2016). Mobile payments in Japan, South Korea and China: Cross-border convergence or divergence of business models? *Telecommunications Policy, 40*(2–3), 182–196. https://doi.org/10.1016/j.telpol.2015.11.011

Ministry of Industry and Information Technology of the People's Republic of China. (2021). *2020 Communications Industry Statistics Bulletin.* https://www.miit.gov.cn/zwgk/zcjd/art/2021/art_4920f2ae9aef45689cfc6da92d406f9b.html

Ministry of Science, ICT and Future Planning, Korea Internet & Security Agency (MSIP and KISA). (2015). *Korea Internet White Paper 2015.*

Mishra, V., & Bisht, S. S. (2013). Mobile banking in a developing economy: A customer-centric model for policy formulation. *Telecommunications Policy, 37*(6–7), 503–514. https://doi.org/10.1016/j.telpol.2012.10.004

Mobile Marketing Data Laboratory (MMDLabo). (2020). 最も利用しているQRコード決済サービス、トップは「PayPay」で48.7%、次いで「楽天ペイ」が15.7%、「d払い」が13.4%. https://mmdlabo.jp/investigation/detail_1873.html

Morawczynski, O. (2009). Exploring the usage and impact of "transformational" mobile financial services: The case of M-PESA in Kenya. *Journal of Eastern African Studies, 3*(3), 509–525. https://doi.org/10.1080/17531050903273768

Mordor Intelligence. (2020). *Mobile payments market—Growth, trends, and forecast (2020–2025).* https://www.mordorintelligence.com/industry-reports/mobile-payment-market

MTN Group. (2021). *Mastercard and MTN empower millions of consumers in Africa to make payments on global platforms.* https://www.mtn.com/mas

tercard-and-mtn-empower-millions-of-consumers-in-africa-to-make-payments-on-global-platforms/

Naver. (2020). *2019 NAVER Annual Report*. https://www.navercorp.com/navercorp_/ir/annualReport/2020/NAVER_2019AR_Design_TCG0604_ENG.pdf

Ntara, C. (2015). An analysis of M-Pesa use in international transactions. *European Journal of Business and Management, 7*(17), 73–79. https://doi.org/10.5120/ijca2016911020

Ondrus, J., & Pigneur, Y. (2006). Towards a holistic analysis of mobile payments: A multiple perspectives approach. *Electronic Commerce Research and Applications, 5*(3), 246–257. https://doi.org/10.1016/j.elerap.2005.09.003

Pacifici, G., & Pozzi, P. (2004). *Money-on-line.eu: Digital Payment Systems and Smart Cards*. FrancoAngeli. https://books.google.fr/books?id=P1EWAQAAMAAJ.

People's Bank of China. (2020). *The People's Bank of China overall operation of the payment system in 2019*. http://www.gov.cn/xinwen/2020-03/17/content_5492272.htm

People's Bank of China. (2021). *The 2020 overall operation of the national payment system*. http://www.pbc.gov.cn/goutongjiaoliu/113456/113469/4213347/2021032414491874847.pdf

Pradhan, R. P., Mallik, G., & Bagchi, T. P. (2018). Information communication technology (ICT) infrastructure and economic growth: A causality evinced by cross-country panel data. *IIMB Management Review, 30*(1), 91–103. https://doi.org/10.1016/j.iimb.2018.01.001

PYMNTS. (2020). *Bain Capital Technology's Bet On hey And Japan's Digital Payments Shift*. https://www.pymnts.com/digital-payments/2020/bain-capital-tech-japan-as-the-land-of-the-rising-digital-payment/

Rakuten Today. (2019). *Building Japan's cashless future: Koichi Nakamura*. https://rakuten.today/tech-innovation/japan-cashless-future.html

Ramanzan, E. (2021). The impact on digitalization on financial sector performance. In S. Bozkuş Kahyaoğlu (Ed.), *The impact of artificial intelligence on governance, economics and finance* (pp. 99–120). Springer Singapore. https://doi.org/10.1007/978-981-33-6811-8_6

Rapyd. (2020). *Asia Pacific eCommerce and Payments Guide 2020*. https://cdn2.hubspot.net/hubfs/5246303/Asia%20Pacific%20eCommerce%20and%20Payments%20Guide%202020.pdf

Ren, T., & Tang. Y. (2020). Accelerate the promotion of mobile payments during the COVID-19 epidemic. *The Innovation, 1*(2). https://doi.org/10.1016/j.xinn.2020.100039

Setor, T. K., Senyo, P. K., & Addo, A. (2021). Do digital payment transactions reduce corruption? Evidence from developing countries. *Telematics and Informatics, 60*. https://doi.org/10.1016/j.tele.2021.101577

Singh, N. K., Sahu, G. P., Rana, N. P., Patil, P. P., & Gupta, B. (2019). Critical success factors of the digital payment infrastructure for developing economies. In A. Elbanna, Y. Dwivedi, D. Bunker, & D. Wastell (Eds.), *Smart working, living and organising*. TDIT 2018. IFIP Advances in Information and Communication Technology (Vol. 533). Springer. https://doi.org/10.1007/978-3-030-04315-5_9

SoftBank. (2018). *SoftBank and Yahoo Japan JV to launch "PayPay". Barcode-based smartphone payment services in collaboration with India's Paytm in the fall*. https://www.softbank.jp/en/corp/news/press/sbkk/2018/20180727_01/

South China Morning Post. (2021). Japan's digital payments rise as people avoid touching cash amid coronavirus pandemic. https://www.scmp.com/news/asia/east-asia/article/3122319/japans-digital-payments-rise-people-avoid-touching-cash-amid

Statista. (2021). *Most popular e-payment services used among respondents in South Korea 2020*. https://www.statista.com/statistics/1106308/south-korea-leading-e-payment-services/

Staykova, K. S., & Damsgaard, J. (2015). The race to dominate the mobile payments platform: Entry and expansion strategies. *Electronic Commerce Research and Applications, 14*(5), 319–330. https://doi.org/10.1016/j.elerap.2015.03.004

Steven, M. (2017). *WeChat sees bigger spenders as China goes cashless*. https://www.techinasia.com/wechat-cashless-china-data

Summers, B. J. (1994). Banking and the payment system. In *The payment system: Design, management, and supervision*. International Monetary Fund. https://doi.org/10.5089/9781557753861.071

Tangit, T. M., & Law, R. (2021) Mobile payments, Chinese tourists, and host residents: Are destination stakeholders prepared to facilitate mobile payments? In W. Wörndl, C. Koo, & J. L. Stienmetz (Eds.), *Information and Communication Technologies in Tourism 2021*. Springer. https://doi.org/10.1007/978-3-030-65785-7_18

Telecommunications Carriers Association. (2020). *Number of subscribers by Carriers 2020*. https://www.tca.or.jp/english/database/

Téllez, J., & Zeadally, S. (2017). *Mobile payment systems: Secure network architectures and protocols.* Springer.

Tencent. (2021). *Tencent 2020 Fourth Quarter and Annual Results Announcement.* https://static.www.tencent.com/uploads/2021/03/24/b02a6670e499fa9b1fac9a3e09753de7.pdf

Tiago, O., Manoj, T., Goncalo, B., & Filipe, C. (2016). Mobile payment: Understanding the determinants of customer adoption and intention to recommend the technology. *Computers in Human Behavior, 61*, 404–414. https://doi.org/10.1016/j.chb.2016.03.030

Torre, D., & Xu, Q. (2019). La Chine aux avant-postes de la digitalisation des paiements. *Revue d'économie financière, 2019/3 (N° 135)*, 99–114.

Torre, D., & Xu, Q. (2020). Digital payment in China: adoption and interactions among applications. *Revue d'Economie Industrielle, 2020/4 (N° 172)*, 55–82. https://doi.org/10.4000/rei.9471

Waverman, L., Meloria, M., & Melvyn, F. (2005). The impact of telecoms on economic growth in developing countries. *The Vodafone Policy Paper, Series, 3*(2), 10–23.

World Travel & Tourism Council. (2019). *Mobile payments in travel & tourism: Unlocking the potential.* https://wttc.org/Portals/0/Documents/Reports/2019/Security_and_Travel_Facilitation_Seamless_Travel_Journey_Mobile_Payments_in_Travel_and_Tourism_Mar_2019.pdf?ver=2021-02-25-182803-757

Wu, R. Z., Lee, J. H., & Tian, X. F. (2021). Determinants of the intention to use cross-border mobile payments in Korea among Chinese tourists: An integrated perspective of UTAUT2 with TTF and ITM. *Journal of Theoretical and Applied Electronic Commerce Research, 16*(5), 1537–1556. https://doi.org/10.3390/jtaer16050086

Yan, L. Y., Tan, G. W. H., Loh, X. M., Hew, J. J., & Ooi, K. B. (2021). QR code and mobile payment: The disruptive forces in retail. *Journal of Retailing and Consumer Services, 58*. https://doi.org/10.1016/j.jretconser.2020.102300.

Yano Research Institute. (2018). *Survey on mobile payment market.* https://www.yano.co.jp/press-release/show/press_id/2031

Yiping, H., Xue, W., & Xun, W. (2020). Mobile payment in China: Practice and its effects. *Asian Economic Papers, 19*(3), 1–18. https://doi.org/10.1162/asep_a_00779

Zhao, X., & Sun, Y. (2012). A study of third-party online payment: Risk control and supervision analysis. In *Eleventh Wuhan International Conference on e-Business 95.*

10

Digitalization and the Transition to a Cashless Economy

Paweł Marszałek and Katarzyna Szarzec

Introduction

Ever since the official demonetization of gold in 1978 (and in practical terms since 1971), money has had no formal ties with any commodity, and has been in individual countries a purely fiat unit. At that time, the last ties between gold and the national monetary units were removed, and the monetary system of central banking, with independent, fiduciary money, became the dominant type of monetary system. At the same time, the activity of national monetary systems was formally freed from international factors—in international terms, the so-called multi-exchange system emerged. For the first time in history, the majority of

P. Marszałek (✉) · K. Szarzec
Poznań University of Economics and Business, Poznań, Poland
e-mail: pawel.marszalek@ue.poznan.pl

K. Szarzec
e-mail: katarzyna.szarzec@ue.poznan.pl

M. Ratajczak-Mrozek and P. Marszałek (eds.), *Digitalization and Firm Performance*,
https://doi.org/10.1007/978-3-030-83360-2_10

countries introduced the non-convertible paper money standard not as a temporary solution, but as a systemic mechanism.

In such systems, money is fully fiat, non-backed and not exchanged for any commodity, and there are fixed or floating exchange rates between national monetary units. Within a given monetary system, money, created in the banking system, is used as a legal tender and a unit of account. It is predominantly endogenous, and its dominant form is non-cash (Handa, 2000; Ingham, 2004; Wolman, 2012).

Such features of contemporary monetary systems reflect and result in certain trends that have long been noticeable in the monetary sphere—actually for centuries. These trends are: (1) the continuous dematerialization of money; (2) the strengthening of the state monopoly in the monetary sphere; and (3) changes in the institutional foundations of money creation. All these processes have consequences for the structure of the money supply and its circulation.

These trends have been fuelled by many phenomena and processes taking place in the economies of individual countries, as well as in the international sphere. Among them, the most important are globalization, deregulation and the liberalization of financial activity, changes in the structure and directions of financial institutions, the emergence of new forms and types of money, financialization and, finally, technological progress.

These factors directly and indirectly influenced the individual elements of monetary systems—the monetary unit, banks, and monetary authorities, and at the same time forced changes both in the regulatory environment of these systems and in the principles of conducting economic policy (mainly monetary). Importantly, their impact also had—apart from the economic component—a social and cultural dimension, which is not surprising, given that money is clearly a social phenomenon (Lietaer & Belgin, 2012; Ingham, 2020; Zelizer, 1989).

The significance of the indicated factors has changed in recent years, and thus their impact on the monetary sphere has been different. Among them, of special importance have been factors related to digitalization, modern technologies and the transition to the so-called *Economy 4.0* (Gordon, 2000; Rifkin, 2011; Schwab, 2016). New technologies (along with the deregulation of banks) have changed the forms and features of money itself, the ways of using it, the behaviour of money issuers, and the relations between financial and non-financial agents.

The rapid technological development also resulted in much thought being devoted to the potential reconstruction of the contemporary monetary systems and their functioning in the future. Such reconstruction, in the face of many theoretical and practical flaws of the systems (see e.g. Bernholz, 2003; Jurek & Marszałek 2015; Lavoie, 2016), has been the subject of many works, offering various, sometimes contradictory solutions (e.g. local vs supranational money, digital vs commodity, etc.). But, in fact, digitalization and new technologies (connected mainly with blockchain, cryptocurrencies and massive use of various payment instruments other than cash and cheques) play a key role in each of the potential directions of changes in the monetary system formulated in the literature: progressive dematerialization and digitalization of money, identified with the situation of the so-called cashless economy, a return to some form of commodity money, returning to free banking solutions, the development of private money issued by global corporations (e.g. Diem, planned by Facebook), interest groups or local communities, monetary unification (the creation of new common, supranational monetary units), or the increase in the number and importance of local currencies.

All the scenarios entail serious consequences and the necessity of making adjustments to all the involved entities—monetary authorities, governments, financial institutions, firms and households. It is worth noticing that some of these scenarios are rather gradual developments, while the others mean the dramatic reconstruction of social and economic life. One of these 'revolutionary' solutions is the (potential) development of the cashless economy. Such a situation is already occurring in some economies (e. g. Sweden, the United Kingdom, China), where the share of cash in monetary circulation is negligible, and the border between cash and non-cash assets has become blurred.

Full transition to an economy without cash will certainly have specific—economic and social—consequences for policymakers, financial systems and society as a whole. The aim of the chapter is to characterize the impact that a cashless economy would have on the economic/financial behaviour of economic agents, connected with the potential benefits and disadvantages of a situation in which cash disappears in the economy. We also try to shed some light on the essential meaning of the cashless economy, and to identify the determinants of the transition to non-cash environment.

To this end, first we discuss the definitions of the cashless economy, its origins, features, and the way it is understood—from both the micro and macroeconomic points of view. Then we classify and discuss the most important determinants of the transition to an economy without cash. In the next section, we identify key advantages and disadvantages of the cashless economy, adopting the perspectives of different stakeholders. Finally, we conclude and attempt to assess whether the transition to the cashless economy is inevitable.

The Cashless Economy—Definitions and Features

A cashless economy, perceived as an issue inherently related to the recent expansion of technological solutions, is not a new issue. Somehow paradoxically, it was considered and discussed—as will be presented in a while—already before the emergence of the fourth industrial revolution, the birth of cryptocurrencies, and the proliferation of sophisticated financial instruments and financial engineering. Still, the term is not clearly defined or understood.

First, it should be clearly emphasized that a cashless economy is not the same as a barter economy, although the latter is, obviously, also 'cashless'. A cashless economy should not be—though it often is, mistakenly—identified with the situation of an economy with no money. Money exists in a cashless economy; it just has no physical form. In other words, one might say that the cashless economy is equivalent to a situation in which there is no physical means of payment and government money is only a unit of account, but other means of payment function in the economy.[1]

[1] The relations between different functions of money and possibility of their separation are discussed e.g. by McCallum (2003).

In this context one of the earliest, most consistent conceptions of the cashless economy is the one formulated within so-called New Monetary Economics (NME). Representatives of this school, including Eugene Fama, Fischer Black, Robert Hall, Robert Greenfield and Leland Yeager, were in a way the precursors of studies on the functioning of the economy, financial markets and economic authorities in the 'world without money'. The concepts they developed and the research they conducted initially fell within the stream of a broader debate on the impact of financial innovations on the economy (Cowen & Kroszner, 1987). These economists were very radical in their recommendations for increasing the scope of economic freedom and limiting the scale of state interference in the monetary sphere (and more broadly, in the entire market mechanism): they perceived the very existence of money as dependent on such state interference. As Hall (1982, p. 1552) explicitly stated, money is 'purely the work of regulation'. It would not exist—actually, there would not even be such a need—if the economy was organized solely according to free market principles. Without the existence of state regulations, it would be a 'moneyless' economy, or more precisely, a cashless economy, because settlements and payments would take place through cashless (not necessarily state) money. In other words, as White (1987, p. 448) argued, 'separate money would disappear under laissez-faire conditions'. Importantly, authors like Black, Fama, and Yeager argue that such a solution would be effective from the point of view of the equilibrium level of the economy. Furthermore, it would not generate inflationary tensions (see Black, 1970; Cronin, 2012; Fama, 1980; Greenfield & Yeager, 1983; Yeager, 1983, 1985). Hence, according to NME theorists, the complete deregulation of the monetary system and the ensuing situation of the cashless economy would be beneficial for the economy, in both micro and macro terms.

In subsequent works on the cashless economy, this issue was defined and explained in various ways. According to Maurya (2019), the cashless economy is characterized by an exchange of funds by cheque, debit or credit cards, or by electronic methods, rather than through the use of cash. A similar definition is presented by Ejiofor and Rasaki (2012), who argued that the cashless economy means an economy where purchases and transactions are done mainly by electronic means, and rarely by cash.

Hence, neither of these authors assume the complete disappearance of money. This is consistent with the definitions of Achor and Robert (2012) and Yaqub et al. (2013), who also claim that the cashless economy does not entail the complete exclusion of cash activities from the economic system, but is rather equal to a situation in which cash-based activities are kept to a minimum.

This group of definitions has a rather microeconomic overtone. There are however also others which deal with these issues from the macroeconomic perspective. For example, according to Cochrane (2005), the cashless economy can be defined as a situation in which there is no cash in a given economy, and the traditional categories of money demand and money supply do not apply. The demand for the government's fiat money has disappeared, and thus, in turn, also its supply. Such a state is by no means a theoretical curiosity. Cochrane argues that the situation, with some approximation, has been present in some developed economies since the beginning of the twenty-first century. In modelling these issues, Cochrane presents an economy in which transactions are financed by an exchange of liabilities, consisting in the provision of a certain amount of private assets. He emphasizes that such transactions may be denominated in, for example, 'dollars', even though the 'dollars' provided by the government do not exist as such. At the same time, there is no room for monetary policy, as there are almost no mechanisms by which it could affect the economy. The central bank basically has lost its influence on the state of equilibrium because it is too small a player in the financial market. Its financial obligations no longer have any special features that would induce agents to acquire and maintain them (Cochrane, 1998).

The understanding of the cash-free economy presented by Cochrane is quite controversial, the more so as the author himself emphasized that in his model state, money still exists as a unit of account. Hence, as postulated by Woodford (1998), the concept of the so-called non-cash limit seems to be closer to reality. This is a situation in which there are few transactions, generating a demand for cash balances. The amount of cash held for making transactions is also negligible. The seigniorage is then a marginal source of state budget revenues, and changes in cash balances have only minor effects on the marginal utility of income. In this situation, this utility is only a diminishing function of total spending (governmental and private), and the government's total nominal liabilities correspond only to the value of public debt (Woodford, 1998, 2003).

A similar view is presented by B. Friedman (1999, 2000), who claims that money will not disappear, but there will be so much of it that central banks will lose the ability to effectively shape aggregate demand. Therefore, also in the macroeconomic perspective, the situation of the cashless economy is not necessarily linked with the complete absence of money.

For Buiter also (2000), a cashless economy does not have to mean a situation in which money does not exist as a physical object. In his opinion, this is only one of two possible scenarios. The second is a situation in which cash does exist, but has become redundant as a means of payment, and has been replaced as a measure of value by money-denominated securities that bring income.

Sometimes the term 'cashless society' is used as a synonym for the cashless economy. As early as 1967, i.e. in times when the technological breakthrough was just starting, Reistad, who was probably the first to use the term 'cashless society', defined it as a society in which the transfer of electronic funds takes the place of paper currency. Worthington (1995) understands it as, a 'society where clumsy and expensive to handle coins and notes are replaced by efficient electronic payments initiated by various types of plastic cards'. The authors argued that in such a situation consumers can make payment at unmanned vending machines, manned point of sale (POS) using mobile devices, cards, non-banking intermediaries, etc.

Bringing all these threads together, a cashless economy can be treated as a situation in which economic agents use electronic means and devices of payments rather than cash. This influences not only the course of the transactions carried out and settled in a given economy, as well as the functioning of banks as creators of non-cash money and other institutions responsible for payments or creation of payment instruments. It also changes the role of the central banks, being issuers of banknotes and coins, as it undermines their monopoly in providing a specific amount of a legal tender. Yet, state money can still exist as a unit of account and even—to a very small extent—as a medium of exchanges.

Thus, the transition to the conditions of the economy without cash is a process that is difficult to grasp, as there is no precise threshold at which the amount of cash can be regarded as already small enough to constitute a cashless economy. For these reasons, the dynamics of the process are also important here, as they reflect the changing role of cash in a given economy. Moreover, the emergence of the cashless economy manifests itself on many different levels and in principle everyone is affected by the changes it generates.

Determinants of the Transition to the Cashless Economy

The determinants of the transition to an economy without cash—and determinants accelerating the process in the recent years—have been diverse, reflecting the multidimensionality and complexity of the phenomenon. In principle, they can be divided into four groups. The first includes issues connected with digitalization and new technologies. The second encompasses changes in activity and the offers of banks, as creators of cashless money and quasi-money instruments and as operators of payment systems. The third group refers to changes in the demand for cash, banking services and the payment habits of the customers. The fourth and last group consists of macroeconomic factors. One should however bear in mind that such a division is somehow artificial, as the impact of individual determinants is multidimensional and multifaceted. Moreover, individual determinants are in many cases linked and reinforce each other. A typical phenomenon here is the feedback between them, which additionally fuels the expansion of the cashless economy.

Without a doubt, a crucial determinant in spreading non-cash money and cashless payments has been the process of digitalization. According to Bofinger (2018), there are four major areas where digitalization modifies the traditional forms of money and credit (and, consequently, also changes monetary policy and the construction of monetary systems): (1) the replacement of cash with electronic money; (2) the replacement of traditional bank deposits and banknotes with cryptocurrencies; (3) the replacement of bank deposits with central bank deposits for everyone ('universal reserves'); and (4) the replacement of bank lending with peer-to-peer lending on the basis of digital platforms.

Among those four areas, the most important from the perspective of the subject of this chapter is the first one, as the second one is so far only a possibility, as cryptocurrencies are at the moment nothing more than a speculative asset, or, at best, a so-called 'safe haven'. This situation might change after introduction of the digital currencies by the central banks, but this scenario is only at the stage of plans and preliminary trials. The other two areas do not refer to the issue of the cashless economy, but rather to disintermediation processes.

Rapid technological progress (mainly in the area of the IT sector) and digitalization, being very complex and dynamic processes, completely changed the face of the contemporary economies in both their macro and microeconomic aspects, as well as the social life and behaviour of individuals. Phenomena and factors like automation and data exchange in manufacturing technologies and processes which include cyber-physical systems (CPS), the internet of things (IoT), Big Data, cognitive computing, high-speed (5G) internet, machine learning and Artificial Intelligence, found broad application in different branches of the economy and society, reshaping people's everyday lives and business models. In addition to its influence on the sale and distribution of products and services, the role of information in economic processes is also emphasized.

The role and behaviour of financial institutions are characteristic here, as the entities reacted very flexibly and quickly to these changes, by adjusting their services and activity patterns and adapting to the new environment. Without a doubt, financial institutions (mainly banks) have been pioneers in the practical application of new technologies in their operation, which have led to deep changes in their organizational structures, and their offer and distribution channels, which resulted in the 'Bank 4.0' construct (King, 2018). This specific fusion of technological and financial entities and factors is identified with emergence of so-called Fintech (Gimpel et al., 2018). Examples of such entities from the area of payments include fintech platforms like PayPal, Stripe, WeChat Pay and Alibaba's Alipay (see e.g. Chapter 9).

An area of financial system, on which the technological progress has had an extraordinary impact was the area of payments and, money circulation in general. New technologies contributed here to the emergence of the so-called electronic money and the application of new, non-cash forms of payment and different private financial instruments, perceived as quasi-money, with cryptocurrencies being their newest exemplification. These instruments have been significantly and rapidly exploited in transactions between economic agents (micro aspect) and have started to be considered as a factor that is changing the whole monetary system.

However, the changes are not just limited to the new instruments. As Alonso et al. (2018) stress, traditional non-cash payment methods—direct debits, bank transfers or credit cards—had long been electronic in the interbank space, but for clients they were only available in the offline mode, for decades. The initiation of these transactions did not require any technological input from users: direct debits were accepted by users when signing a contract, bank transfers were ordered by consumers in branches and only credit cards required a basic physical device (a plastic card) to be initiated.

It is argued that it was the advent of the internet, mobile phones and smart devices that qualitatively changed the situation. Due to these new technological devices, users are able to make transfers in online banking, authorize direct debit through electronic means, and pay with cards with enhanced functionalities (instant debit, reinforced security, etc.). Moreover, new technologies have made it possible to leverage the existing interbank infrastructures to offer new payment methods (e- and m- payments, virtual cards or p2p payments), which has changed the business model of banks and created circumstances in which the role of cash is diminished (Alonso et al., 2018, Hakkarainen, 2021).

This was only a part of broader processes occurring in the economy, which generated specific feedback, as non-cash payments and digital money subsequently reinforced further digitalization of the economy. Both elements support the growth of e-commerce and connected lifestyles, satisfying people's demand for immediacy and seamless integration between payments and digital services. This leads to the third group of cashless economy determinants: those connected with changes in the behaviour of banks clients.

The changes in banks' operations largely reflected changes in customer preferences (which, however, were often induced by banks themselves), evident in the reduced demand for cash and payment on the part of bank clients. Alongside the popularity of banking services, like internet and mobile banking, payment cards, POS terminals and digital wallets, the almost universal availability and popularity of the technological solutions (smartphones, e-commerce and internet access) introduced by banks (and also non-bank intermediaries) in response to the conditions of the new economy contributed to the situation existing in many countries, in which cash is no longer the unique, or even dominant, possibility of making a payment. At the same time, paper-based payments (like 'traditional' transfers or cheques) have become obsolete.

Moreover, entrepreneurs have been somehow forced to use non-cash payments as a result of regulations introduced in many countries to prevent money laundering and terrorism (a limit on the maximum amount that can be paid in cash). These changes in consumer preferences and the options open to entrepreneurs (voluntary or enforced) have opened the way to the increasing dematerialization of money. As Goczek and Witkowski (2015) stress, the importance of this process lies in the fact that the payment process is not only a mechanical act carried out every day by consumers or businesses. It is the possibility of payment that allows for the existence of markets. Therefore, the act of payment is the basis for society to reap gains from exchanges in the economy. In this context, the process of transitioning to a cashless payment method has profound, far-reaching consequences.

The last group of factors which determine the transition to a cashless economy is quite heterogeneous, as it includes different macroeconomic factors, connected mainly with such vast areas as monetary policy, financial stability, the general growth of variability and uncertainty in the economy, and so-called monetary disorder (Bernholz, 2003). These factors, being to a large extent the aftermath of the global financial crisis of 2007–2009, shed light on the necessity of making reforms in monetary and financial systems. The cashless economy and private digital currencies have been considered as potential solutions to the problems in the monetary system—ones that could provide a more stable monetary environment (Marszałek, 2016).

Among other macro factors contributing to expanding the non-cash environment, one might point to the increasing role of the government in individual economies, resulting in stricter control over economic processes, stricter supervision over financial markets and institutions, continuous financialization processes in the most developed countries, changes of a cultural and social character, and even demographical changes, since for the younger generations who enter markets and institutions, the nexus between technology and financial services is something obvious. Moreover, they do not know other types of money than the fiduciary one, which by its very nature is not bound up with any physical form.

An additional, unprecedented and unexpected factor, which can be treated as a macroeconomic one, and one that gave a rapid boost to non-cash forms of payments and transactions, was the COVID-19 pandemic. One might say that it significantly accelerated the trend towards the use of non-cash money within modern societies. The social distance caused by COVID, together with changes in the organization of economic life and the payment habits of societies, constituted an additional factor that made the abandonment of cash even faster (Auer et al., 2020; Deloitte, 2020).

The tendencies in this regard, as they occur in selected countries, will be discussed more thoroughly in Section "Conclusions". Here it must be noticed, however, that the first impact of the pandemic on the structure of the money supply was rather expressed in depositors' increased interest in cash. As is typical in periods of high uncertainty, the outbreak of the COVID-19 pandemic was accompanied by increased cash withdrawals. They were made not for a transactional purpose, but rather for precautionary reasons, as a consequence of concerns about the condition of the financial system, its stability in crisis conditions, and the continuity of financial operations and settlements. Customers who were afraid, inter alia, of the closure of bank branches and a deepening of the crisis situation, withdrew cash to be prepared for the worst-case scenarios (King & Shen, 2020).

With time, as the situation became more predictable, this short-lived hype for additional cash ended. The pandemic intensified contact between banks and customers through remote channels at the cost of a decline in the role of bank branches. It also changed the picture of the payments market, as the closure of the economy accelerated the digitization of payments and contributed to the widespread popularity of e-commerce. The crisis situation (lockdowns) has contributed to a very rapid increase in the popularity of different non-cash payments, such as mobile payments, internet payments, etc. An additional factor in favour of non-cash payments has been the concerns connected with paper money and coins as potential vectors of transmissible disease. Wiśniewski et al. (2021), using a survey of 5,504 respondents from 22 European countries, showed that consumers preferred cashless transactions as they believed that handling cash presents a higher risk of infection. In some cases, it even led to a refusal to accept cash payments (Auer et al., 2020; Chen et al., 2021). This, in turn, triggered a reaction from central banks that launched a campaign to restore confidence in cash and to promote universal acceptance (see e.g. King & Shen, 2020).

A separate group of reasons why contemporary economies are going cashless are the benefits from such a situation. The advantages of the economy without cash, together with potential problems connected with this situation, are described in the next section.

The Advantages and Disadvantages of the Economy Without Cash

A discussion on the benefits and costs of the cashless economy is in fact a discussion about the advantages and disadvantages of cash, as both issues constitute the opposite sides of the same coin. In trying to assess the positive and negative aspects of the transition to the economy without cash, one should take into account different aspects of a given economy, as the replacement of cash by other means of exchange, brings not only purely economic consequences, but also has repercussions in social, cultural and even health areas. Moreover, the costs and benefits of the cashless economy can be considered with reference to different groups of actors involved.

From the point of view of central banks and governments, consideration should mainly be given to macroeconomic aspects, connected with economic policy and the functioning of the whole economy. The benefits from going cashless are especially visible here, taking into consideration the tax system and law enforcement, conducting monetary policy, the reduced costs of printing cash, and the previously mentioned potential reconstruction of monetary system.

Traditionally, it is argued that the cashless economy reduces the shadow (or grey) economy and thus contributes to higher revenues for the government. It is highly impossible to hide income or evade taxes if all financial records are digitized—in other words, the greater the digital economy, the higher the tax compliance. The absence of banknotes and coins would also prevent the practice of money laundering that allows criminals to spend illegally gained money. Non-cash money is easy to track and control, thus financial crimes (not to mention false banknotes) would probably become obsolete in a cashless economy, and the scale and freedom of financing crimes, terrorism and drug trafficking would shrink (see e.g. Immordino & Russo, 2016; Jakubowska, 2017; Mai, 2016; Pickhardt & Prinz, 2012; Schneider, 2013, 2019).

One of the main advantages of the cashless economy which has become apparent in recent years is connected with changes in the central banks' instruments. Namely, in the face of economic crises of the last two decades, one of the most debated issues is the possibility and purposefulness of monetary authorities employing negative interest rate policies (NIRP). This unconventional monetary policy tool boils down to a central bank setting nominal target interest rates with a negative value, below the theoretical lower bound of zero per cent. This implies—quite peculiarly somewhat paradoxically—that saving generates costs while borrowing brings in money (Altavila et al., 2019; Jobst & Lin, 2016). This controversial instrument—together with quantitative easing and forward guidance—has been used by many central banks (e.g. ECB, Sveriges Bank and Bank of Japan) after the space for conventional policy became exhausted.

However, using negative interest rates meets an obstacle in the form of cash. As long as interest rates are negative, only transactions between banks, non-banking entities are not affected by their levels. But making nominal interest rates negative also for transactions between banks and their clients would cause these entities to 'run' to cash. In this context,

Rogoff (2016, 2017) argues that the growth of electronic payment systems and the increasing marginalization of cash in legal transactions create a much smoother path to negative rate policy today than even two decades ago. The author offers four approaches to implementing negative interest rates: (1) moving to a cashless society, since paying interest (positive or negative) on electronic bank reserves is no problem, and is already a widespread practice; (2) finding a technological approach to paying interest (positive or negative) on paper currency, an idea that Keynes considered at length; (3) dispensing with the one-to-one exchange rate between electronic bank reserves and paper currency, which frees up the central bank to introduce approaches to discounting cash that mimics paying negative interest; and (4) taking steps to make a large-scale hoarding of cash much more costly—for example, by phasing out large-denomination notes—without affecting normal retail cash transactions.

Thus, although Rogoff also proposes other solutions, not necessarily connected with the rejection of cash, he considers cash as a negative factor, being a constraint for the negative interest rate policy. The transition to conditions of the cashless economy would enable the central banks to conduct unorthodox monetary policy more effectively.

However, the central banks can also face the negative sides of the cashless economy. Namely, as Friedman (2000) argues, even if cash does not completely disappear, its amount will be too small for central banks to be able to effectively shape aggregate demand. This will therefore have an impact on the possibility of conducting monetary policy—but if the cashless economy, allowing for use of NIRP, increases opportunities of central banks, in this case it reduces the room for manoeuvre. This problem was noticed at the European Central Bank when it was not as advanced as it is now (for example, cryptocurrencies were not functioning at the time, and the vast majority of technological payment solutions common today were not available). The ECB made attempts to identify the challenges faced by the central banks as a result of the development of e-money and changes in the demand for legal tender reported by non-banking entities and commercial banks (being the aftermath of financial engineering and development of financial markets and instruments). In particular, the following issues were noted (EBC, 2000): (1)

the need to protect the role of money as a unit of account in economic transactions; (2) the possibility of limiting the effectiveness of monetary policy instruments in the conditions of the ever wider diffusion of digital money; and (3) the consequences that the dissemination of electronic money may have for the informational value of monetary variables, and thus for the achievement of the overarching goal of stabilizing the price level.

It should be emphasized that such a situation is very unfavourable for a central bank. Conducting monetary policy becomes more difficult as there are almost no mechanisms by which it is able to influence the economy. The central bank has basically lost its influence on the state of equilibrium, as it is only one of many players in the financial market, according to B. Friedman and Cochrane. The smaller the share of cash in the total stock of money becomes, the more difficult the situation becomes for the monetary authorities.

While the issues related to electronic money did not turn out to be so important, the decreasing demand for cash, being, one of the determinants of cashless economy—as was described in the previous section, has become a real problem. Hence, there are those who argue that it is necessary to provide direct financial supervision over IT companies offering new payment solutions, and to even enable them to participate in open market operations. Another response of central banks to the changes taking place in the monetary sphere is the introduction of a digital currency, issued by digital banks, based—just like cryptocurrencies—on blockchain technology (Berch & Garrat, 2017; Engert & Fung, 2017, Iwańczuk-Kaliska, 2017).

Despite problems, the advantages connected with the cashless economy appear to outweigh the problems. One might also list other benefits of such a state, referring to the functioning of the economy, individual markets, and the activities of households and enterprises. Bearing in mind that money is a social construct and phenomenon, it is obvious that in order to function smoothly, the cashless economy also has to be somehow accepted by society. Without understanding the phenomenon and benefits ordinary people can gain from using non-cash methods of payments, it will not be possible. This is even more important under the conditions of digitalization, which is still somewhat mysterious process for ordinary people, or which is treated only instrumentally, without deeper reflection on its consequences.

In particular, the literature emphasizes that the cashless economy is a 'greener' and universal solution (however, one should take into account the huge cost of energy connected with cryptocurrencies, which are perceived as digital money of the future, and are one of the symbols of the non-cash economy). Next, cash-free payments are faster, which is a major issue for time-sensitive businesses operating under very short transaction time horizons in the contemporary economy. Without a doubt, when people pay by cash, the transaction becomes slower. Replacing cash with cards, for example, will speed up service, as 'tap-and-go', contactless and prepaid digital payment methods are significantly more efficient—cashiers do not have to waste time counting bills. It also eliminates a need for cash registers, which simultaneously lowers the risk of theft. At the same time, it is possible for merchants who accept only non-cash payments to save on labour time, as there is no need to count cash and then transport it to the bank (which also is connected with the risks of transporting large amounts of cash). Also accounting time and the number of employees who spend time reconciling transactions are reduced. With digital money, they can simply download a report of all transactions, and the appropriate funds are then transferred electronically to individual accounts. Cashless service also helps the merchants to avoid problems related to counting or dealing with potentially forged banknotes; it also reduces the need for spare change and helps solve the problems associated with accepting large denominations.

Cashless transactions are also more convenient and need less contact. This feature turned to be crucial during the COVID-19 pandemic, when many merchants strongly encouraged e-payment or even completely banned cash payments. As was argued in pre-COVID research, a virus could live on paper money and coins (Angelakis et al., 2014), thus paying by card or smartphone reduces the risk of transmitting disease.

Functioning without cash also implies less time and lower costs associated with handling, storing, and depositing paper money, and—in general—with the overall cash infrastructure costs, which are mostly paid directly by commercial banks that, however, pass this burden on to consumers. For example, Access to Cash Review (2019) reports that

Britain's cash infrastructure costs around £5 billion a year to run, being predominantly paid by retail banks, and run mostly by commercial operators. Maryuja (2019) highlights the very high cost of printing paper money in India (the raw material itself, ink, technology involved).

De Meijer (2010) indicates that from a social point of view cash is, compared to other payment instruments, a very expensive means of payment. According to De Meijer, the high cost of cash is primarily determined by the higher costs of production, storage, distribution and maintaining appropriate security measures, all of which create the so-called hidden cost of money. Producing coins and paper notes that cannot be counterfeited is very expensive. The transition to a cashless environment reduces the cost of producing a physical currency. The author also states that the cost of operating a cash system largely depends on the level of development of the retail payment system.

The disadvantages of the cashless economy stem, in principle, from three general groups of problems. The first is connected with the phenomenon of so-called financial exclusion and the resulting inequalities. The second group includes issues associated with citizens' personal freedom and privacy, and certain psychological issues related to the perception of money. The third group encompasses different problems that concern technological factors, especially in the context of the security of non-cash payments.

The phenomenon of financial exclusion, understood as the exclusion of individuals or households from using financial services in the realm of consumption, production and social cohesion (see e.g. Leyshon & Thrift, 1995) is one of the most important economic and social problems facing the world today. Somewhat paradoxically, the problem intensified with financialization processes and the rapid development of financial sectors worldwide. Financial exclusion has also taken on a new dimension in the light of the banking sector's increased use of new financial technologies and the introduction by banks of new services, products and channels of distributions (Warchlewska, 2020). The growing complexity of financial services translates into increased demand for technological equipment and the qualifications necessary to operate it. Under such circumstances, people who are physically and mentally separated from modern technologies encounter a barrier that prevents access to these new technological solutions and devices.

This also applies also to cashless forms of payment, as they require some specialized equipment, knowledge, and a significant level of trust. However, for people who are vulnerable to financial exclusion, meeting these requirements is difficult. At the same time, the basic condition for encouraging the development of the cashless economy is to provide sufficient and accessible infrastructure of payments, which obviously requires involvement of banks and access to banks by ordinary persons. Yet, this condition is not fulfilled in many countries, as it is typical for there to be a significant proportion of people who make up the so-called 'unbanked'. The latter can be defined as those adults or families who do not use banks or banking institutions in any manner, or, taking into account the fact that such a situation might be not voluntary, as persons or entities not having access to the services of a bank or similar financial organization (Oxford Dictionary, 2021).

The number of persons that qualify as unbanked is high. According to the Demirguc-Kunt et al. (2018), globally about 1.7 billion adults remained unbanked—without an account at any financial institutions or through a mobile money provider. This phenomenon is not equally distributed (and women are overrepresented among the unbanked in most economies), and the problem is most serious in Asia and Africa. But even in the United States, as the report of Federal Deposit Insurance Corporation (2019) shows, six and a half percent of households were unbanked in 2017.

At the same time, data shows that low-income individuals are the most likely to be unbanked and that 70 per cent of this group use cash for daily purchases. In a cashless world, millions of unbanked citizens would have difficulties buying what they need for daily life. People with no knowledge, bank accounts, or modern technological devices (like smartphones) will struggle to keep up with rapidly evolving cashless technology. Thus, if digital payments become typical or even the only option, people who are unable or unwilling (for example for privacy reasons) to use such services risk being excluded from the economy.

Cash, on the other hand is 'inclusive'. It is essential to ensure the inclusion of socially vulnerable citizens who may not have bank accounts or who lack the necessary digital skills. From these reasons, cash is regularly used by citizens of all ages, all educational levels and all income groups, taking into account all cultural differences and payment habits in individual countries. This signals some potential problems and threats with the transition to the cashless economy, as such a situation could fuel inequalities (De Meijer, 2010). Maintaining the smooth functioning of the cash circulation, including easy access to cash and wide acceptance of cash at points of sale, can be perceived in this context as something that could prevent financial exclusion.

According to some authors, these advantages entail that cash will remain widely available and accepted. One might even point out that cash is the form of money that has the most common understanding and trust. Moreover, in the symbolic layer, it is at least some reflection of commodity money, which still has—at least imaginary—importance, especially for those entities who are looking for monetary anchors and some 'tangible' assets in the contemporary systems of fiduciary money. Cash also allows anonymity, thus avoiding control and oversight by the authorities in relation to certain transactions between economic actors. For not all 'unofficial' transactions are criminal acts, and even the shadow economy has its advantages.

These arguments can already be included in the second group of critical views on the cashless economy, including arguments of a social and ideological nature. Besides the above-mentioned statements, one can also argue that the cashless economy is less personable (dehumanization of transactions by technology), that it destroys communities as it is conducive to a rather individual way of life (purchases via internet, the limited role of mutual exchange) and limits individual freedom to choose, as merchants' refusal to accept cash can be perceived as a form of discrimination against those without bank accounts and those individuals who want to use cash, having, as was mentioned, their own reasons to pay this way.

The independent choice of payment method and desirable form of money is seen as a manifestation of economic and civil rights in the market economy. At the same time, the cashless economy creates an environment in which the government is able to access a wealth of data on households, enterprises and organizations. According to advocates of free choice in the monetary sphere, the transition to digital money gives the government too much power over its citizens and raises fears of a techno-dystopia. With non-democratic states, such an ability to monitor—through a full record of transactions and the circulation of digital money—any economic activity could reinforce a dictator's ability to clamp down on dissent. And even in cashless democracies, individuals may be the subject of over control from the side of the government, as well as commercial firms that are able to track spending patterns and send targeted marketing. Thus, the transition to non-cash money, by undermining privacy, can be seen (mainly by libertarians) as a major threat to civil liberties (Fabris, 2019; Sajter, 2013).

There are also other non-economic and non-efficiency considerations with regard to the flaws and shortages of the cashless economy. Namely, it is argued that it can create bad spending habits (cash is easier to control, as its outflow is visible), it deprives the money of emotional value (different saving process and the emotional value of charity), and it increases dependence on technology at the expense of human qualities and skill.

The latter factor relates to the third strain of critique, which focuses on technological problems, connected mainly with problems with access to money and transactions, as well as their security. Certainly, the technology and procedures associated with non-cash payments are extremely well designed and secured. But even if digital payments are designed to be as robust as possible, they still remain vulnerable to potential disruptions, such as energy blackouts or technical failures. Such factors, even if only temporary, can generate severe problems, undermining trust in digital money and non-cash payments, and reducing or even completely invalidating the benefits that appear in the context of cashless payments and settlements.

Using modern technologies also tends to raise also questions about the security of such operations. The modern conditions of a highly digitalized economy, where the role of information is crucial and access to data (or the possibility of protecting it) is of the highest importance, are extremely vulnerable to cyber-attack. Moreover, hackers have gone far beyond tapping into PCs, laptops and smartphones—actually, any smart device can be hacked. This of course increases the costs of security and creates uncertainty, especially on the side of entities that, for various reasons, are not able to ensure the confidentiality and security of sensitive data. In the context of the cashless economy, a hacker attack on a bank or other financial institution can expose personal financial information to a possible data breach, disrupt the processing of payments and even limit access to money. What is important here is that without cash there will be no alternative source of money.

In such situations, cash can support resilience in payments, as it provides a crucial 'emergency exit', since it is a trusted, well-known store of value that helps to survive the suspension of payment infrastructure and to avoid losses. Thus, in this regard, cash can fulfil the traditional precautionary motive purpose of holding money that non-cash forms cannot guarantee (Panetta, 2020).

As a solution to these problems, and therefore a factor giving more resilience and stability to the cashless economy, one could refer to the introduction of digital currencies (private or issued by central banks) based on blockchain and distributed ledger technology, which is widely used in cryptocurrencies. First of all, blockchain technology ensures resistance to cyber-attacks (thanks to cryptographic security) and immunity to IT failures (thanks to its decentralized structure). It is claimed that the technology of data storage and registered systems based on blockchain technology is not decryptable or crackable. Its additional advantages are lower operating costs compared to central systems and resistance to tampering (Gupta, 2017; Strebko & Romanovs, 2018). Yet, despite these advantages, digital currencies still lack the features of traditional cash, such as being immune to any breakdowns in technology and, at the same time, being more trustworthy and familiar to the average citizen.

To summarize the considerations in this section, it should be noticed that the end result of the cashless economy is not unambiguous, and the advantages and disadvantages are distributed unevenly. The cashless economy definitely brings significant and clear benefits to the governments, supervisors, Big Techs and other big companies. These entities are essentially not burdened with the cost of transitioning to an economy without cash. The benefits, however, begin to be more doubtful, and potential problems more severe, when we look at people at risk of financial exclusion, like persons with cognitive or physical disabilities, those with financial difficulties, or those living in remote, rural areas or suburbs, where access to online banking is restricted due to temperamental broadband and mobile data coverage, small cash-based businesses (market traders and takeaway food services) or the homeless (see Access to Cash Review: Final Report 2019).

Thus, the asymmetry of winners and losers from abandoning cash is visible. However, the problems are generated not only by cashless economy itself. It would be fairer to say that the cashless economy can exacerbate some problems that already exist in a given society. And it should be also borne in mind that, as an institutional solution, it also has many advantages for regular citizens.

Conclusions

The cashless economy is a phenomenon that is receiving increasing attention in the financial, social and economic literature and that is becoming ever more present in the debate on the practical aspects of the functioning of monetary and financial systems. Without a doubt, the issue is not only a theoretical curiosity, as the COVID-19 pandemic strengthened the popularity of non-cash settlements. Additionally, it seems that some trends, like the massive increase in e-commerce, the popularity of online stores, the use of many services via the Internet that was traditionally only provided in a stationary form (like e.g. medical assistance) via the Internet, or the increasing digitization of state and local administration services, are already irreversible, opening up a further field for the dissemination of cashless payments.

Moreover, we should rather expect the further evolution of banks, as they try to compete with non-bank intermediaries. The changes will probably lead to even more intense usage of new technologies, especially those connected with gathering data on clients, further streamlining the payment process, and refinements in the functioning of distribution channels.

Furthermore, central banks are following this path towards a world without cash: preparing and designing their digital currencies and adapting instruments to new operating conditions. The People's Bank of China and its declaration on digital currency with an expiration date is probably the most obvious example here, but the Bank of England and the Bank of Sweden seem to be even more advanced in this regard.

Another group of stakeholders with interests in the cashless economy are Big Tech companies—mainly those labelled as GAFAT. The clearest example here is Facebook and its Diem (former Libra) programme, supported by the Diem Association, which includes payment (e.g. PayU and checkout.com), technology, telecommunication, an online marketplace and venture capital companies. One might expect that other companies will try to start similar initiatives, bringing other private, digital currencies into the cashless landscape of the future.

Still, it is hard to imagine the complete disappearance of cash. It still has lots to offer for households and small enterprises. Just like those who predicted the 'death' of traditional banks with the advent of electronic banking, the predictions of the death of cash, seem to be, to paraphrase the famous quote, highly exaggerated. Cash will probably survive, as long as its advantages are not limited, or until the modes of social and economic life, as well as cultural features of societies, are subject to some drastic changes under the influence of digitalization. At the same time, some of the flaws of cashless economy described in this chapter cannot be easily erased, and even more problems connected with digital money are becoming visible (e.g. with reference to cryptocurrencies—the high costs of energy).

One can imagine, however, that in the face of subsequent crises, similar to that caused by the pandemic, the increasing role of governments and specific consent to certain actions and decisions may lead to further restrictions being imposed on the use of cash, or even withdrawal from it. This seems to be a rational assumption, as crises are usually triggers for profound changes that are impossible to introduce during 'ordinary' times. On the other hand, one can expect the emergence of private currencies (even if at the beginning they are only local), not necessarily fiat ones, but perhaps referring to commodity money. However, a revival of theories and concepts claiming that any link to commodity could provide more stable a monetary system that is also noticeable in contemporary discussions on monetary reforms.

Taking all these things into account, the cashless economy is clearly not an inevitable scenario, even if it is already so advanced in many countries. In general, the very large geographic diversity is an important aspect here, as some countries are clearly 'embedded' in cash, while the others rather seek to eliminate it. Thus, the famous quotation of William Gibson, namely that 'the future is already here — it's just not evenly distributed', also applies to the cashless economy.

Acknowledgements The project is financed within the Regional Excellence Initiative programme of the Minister of Science and Higher Education of Poland, years 2019–2022, grant no. 004/RID/2018/19, financing 3,000,000 PLN.

References

Access to Cash Review: Final Report. (2019). Retrieved from: https://www.accesstocash.org.uk/media/1087/final-report-final-web.pdf

Achor, P. N., & Robert, A. (2012). Shifting policy paradigm from cash-based economy to cashless economy: the Nigeria experience. *Afro Asian Journal of Social Sciences, 4,* 1–16. Retrieved from: http://www.onlineresearchjournals.com/aajoss/art/124.pdf

Alonso, J., Ganga, H., Belio, J. L., Martín, Á., Mirón, P., Plata, C. T., Rubio, A., Santos, A., & Burke, J. V. (2018, June). *The use of cash and its determinants.* BBVA Research, Madrid. Retrieved from: https://www.bbvaresearch.com/wp-content/uploads/2018/06/2018-06-The-use-of-cash-and-its-determinants_EDI-vf.pdf

Altavilla, C., Burlon, L., Giannetti, M., & Holton, S. (2019). *Is there a zero lower bound? The effects of negative policy rates on banks and firms* (Working Paper Series 2289). European Central Bank.

Angelakis, E., Azhar, E. I., Bibi, F., Yasir, M., Al-Ghamdi, A. K., Ashshi, A. M., Elshemi, A. G., & Raoult, D. (2014). Paper money and coins as potential vectors of transmissible disease. *Future Microbiology, 9*(2), 249–261. https://doi.org/10.2217/fmb.13.161

Auer, R., Cornelli, G., & Frost, J. (2020). Covid-19, cash, and the future of payments. *BIS Bulletin* No 3. https://EconPapers.repec.org/RePEc:bis:bisblt:3.

Bech, M., & Garratt, R. (2017, September). Central bank cryptocurrencies. *BIS Quarterly Review*, 55–70. https://EconPapers.repec.org/RePEc:bis:bisqtr:1709f.

Bernholz, P. (2003). *Monetary regimes and inflation. History, economic and political relationship*. Edward Elgar.

Bindseil, U. (2019). Central bank digital currency: Financial system implications and control. *International Journal of Political Economy, 48*(4), 303–335. https://doi.org/10.1080/08911916.2019.1693160

Black, F. (1970). Banking and interest rates in a world without money: The effects of uncontrolled banking. *Journal of Bank Research, 1*, 9–20.

Bofinger, P. (2018). *Digitalisation of money and the future of monetary policy*. VoxEU. Retrieved from https://voxeu.org/article/digitalisation-money-and-future-monetary-policy

Chen, H., Engert, W., Huynh, K., Nicholls, G. & Zhu, J. (2021). *Cash and COVID-19: The effects of lifting containment measures on cash demand and use* (Discussion Papers 2021-3). Bank of Canada. Retrieved from: https://www.bankofcanada.ca/wp-content/uploads/2021/03/sdp2021-3.pdf

Cochrane, J. H. (1998). "A frictionless view of U.S. inflation," NBER chapters, In *NBER macroeconomics annual, 13*, 323–421, National Bureau of Economic Research, Inc.

Cochrane, J. H. (2005). Money as stock. *Journal of Monetary Economics, 52*(3), 501–528. https://doi.org/10.1016/j.jmoneco.2004.07.004

Costa Storti, C., & De Grauwe, P. (2001). *Monetary policy in a cashless society* (CEPR Discussion paper no. 2696). Brussels. Retrieved from https://ssrn.com/abstract=261872

Cowen, T., & Kroszner, R. (1987). The development of the new monetary economics. *Journal of Political Economy, 95*(5), 567–590.

Cronin, D. (2012). New monetary economics revisted. *Cato Journal, 32*(3), 581–594.

De Meijer, C. (2010). SEPA for cash. The single European cash area: Towards a more efficient European cash society. *EPC Newsletter*, 146.

Deloitte. (2020). *Global payments remade by COVID-19. Scenarios for resilient leader*. Retrieved from: https://www2.deloitte.com/content/dam/Deloitte/global/Documents/Financial-Services/gx-fsi-global-payments-remade-by-covid-19.pdf

Demirgüç-Kunt, A., Klapper, L., Singer, D., Ansar, S., & Hess, J. (2018). *Global Findex Database 2017: Measuring Financial Inclusion and the Fintech Revolution.* World Bank Group.

EBC. (2000, November). Issues arising from the emergence of electronic money. *Monthly Bulletin.*

Ejiofor, V. E., & Rasaki, J. O. (2012). Realising the benefits and challenges of cashless economy in Nigeria: Its perspective. *International Journal of Advances in Computer Science and Technology, 1,* 7–13.

Engert, W., & Fung, B. S. (2017). *Central bank digital currencies: motivations and implications* (Staff Discussion Paper 2017-16). Bank of Canada. Retrieved from: https://www.bankofcanada.ca/2017/11/staff-discussion-paper-2017-16/

Fabris, N. (2019). Cashless society—The future of money or a Utopia? *Journal of Central Banking Theory and Practice, 8*(1), 53–66. https://doi.org/10.2478/jcbtp-2019-0003

Fama, E. (1980). Banking in the theory of finance. *Journal of Monetary Economics, 6*(1), 39–57.

Federal Deposit Insurance Corporation (FDIC). (2020) *How America Banks: Household Use of Banking and Financial Services, 2019 FDIC Survey (October 2020).* Retrieved from: https://www.fdic.gov/analysis/household-survey/2019report.pdf

Friedman, B. M. (1999). The future of monetary policy: The central bank as an army with only a signal corps*? International Finance, 2*(3), 321–338. https://doi.org/10.1111/1468-2362.00032

Friedman, B. M. (2000). Decoupling at the margin: The threat to monetary policy from the electronic revolution in banking. *International Finance, 3*(2), 261–272.

Gimpel, H., Rau, D., & Roeglinger, M. (2018). Understanding FinTech start-ups—A taxonomy of consumer-oriented service offerings. *Electronic Markets, 28*(4), 245–264. https://doi.org/10.1007/s12525-017-0275-0

Gobble, M. A. M. (2018). Digitalization, digitization, and innovation. *Research-Technology Management, 61*(4), 56–59. https://doi.org/10.1080/08956308.2018.1471280

Goczek, Ł., & Witkowski, B. (2015). *Determinants of non-cash payment* (NBP Working Paper No. 196). Retrieved from: https://www.nbp.pl/publikacje/materialy_i_studia/196_en.pdf

Golosova, J., & Romanovs, A. (2018). The advantages and disadvantages of the blockchain technology conference. In *2018 IEEE 6th Workshop on Advances in Information, Electronic and Electrical Engineering (AIEEE) Deutsche Bank Research, Frankfurt, 2016 November.*

Gordon, R. J. (2000). Does the „new economy" measure up to the great inventions of the past? *The Journal of Economic Perspectives, 14*(4), 49–74. https://doi.org/10.1257/jep.14.4.49

Greenfield, R. L., & Yeager, L. B. (1983). A Laissez-Faire approach to monetary stability. *Journal of Money, Credit and Banking, 15*(3), 302–315.

Gupta, V. (2017, February). A brief history of blockchain. *Harvard Business Review* [online]. Retrieved from: https://hbr.org/2017/02/a-brief-history-of-blockchain

Hakkarainen, P. (2021, February 3). *Digitalisation disrupts traditional banking?* Speech by Member of the Supervisory Board of the ECB, at the 5th Afore Conference, Frankfurt am Main. Retrieved from: https://www.bankingsupervision.europa.eu/press/speeches/date/2021/html/ssm.sp210203~17a2ae3848.en.html

Hall, R. E. (1982). Monetary trends in the United States and the United Kingdom: A review from the perspective of new developments in monetary economics. *Journal of Economic Literature, 20*, 1552–1556.

Handa, J. (2000). *Monetary economics*. Routledge.

Immordino, G., & Russo F. F. (2016, June). *Cashless payments and tax evasion* (Center for Studies in Economic and Finance Working paper, 445). https://doi.org/10.12775/CJFA.2017.021

Ingham, G. (2004). *Nature of money*. Polity.

Ingham, G. (2020). *Money*. Cambridge: Polity.

Iwańczuk-Kaliska, A. (2017). Challenges for central banks in a changing payments landscape. *Financial Internet Quarterly, 13*(2), 75–86.

Jakubowska, M. (2017). The role of cashless Transactions in the process of limiting the scale of the shadow economy. *Copernican Journal of Finance & Accounting, 6*(4), 23–37.

Jobs, T. A., & Lin, H. H. (2016). *Negative interest rate policy (NIRP): Implications for monetary transmission and bank profitability in the Euro area* (IMF Working Papers). Issue 172. https://doi.org/10.5089/9781475524475.001

Jurek, M., & Marszałek, P. (2015). *Policy alternatives for the relationship between ECB monetary and financial policies and new member states* (FESSUD Working Papers, 112).

King, B. (2018). *Bank 4.0: Banking everywhere, never at bank*. Marshall Cavendish Business.

King, R., & Shen, A. (2020, March 20). Will cash survive Covid-19? *Central Banking*. Retrieved from: https://www.centralbanking.com/central-banks/currency/7509046/will-cash-survive-covid-19

Lavoie, M. (2016). Understanding the global financial crisis: Contributions of post-Keynesian economics. *Studies in Political Economy, 97*(1), 58–75. https://doi.org/10.1080/07078552.2016.1174463

Leyshon, A., & Thrift, N. (1995). Geographies of financial exclusion: Financial abandonment in Britain and the United States. *Transactions of the Institute of British Geographers, New Series, 20*(3), 312–341.

Lietaer, B., & Belgin, S. (2012). *New money for a new world*. Quiterra Press.

Mai, H. (2016). *Cash, freedom and crime: Use and impact of cash in a world going digital* (EU Monitor Global financial markets, 23). Deutsche Bank Research. Retrieved from: https://www.dbresearch.com/PROD/RPS_EN-PROD/Cash%2C_freedom_and_crime%3A_Use_and_impact_of_cash_in/RPS_EN_DOC_VIEW.calias?rwnode=PROD0000000000435631&ProdCollection=PROD0000000000441785

Marszałek, P. (2016). *Local money systems and their features* (FESSUD Working Papers Series, no. 188). Retrieved from: https://www.researchgate.net/publication/318284721_Working_Paper_Series_No_188_Local_money_systems_and_their_features_Local_money_systems_and_their_features

Maurya, P. (2019). Cashless economy and digitalization. In *Proceedings of 10th International Conference on Digital Strategies for Organizational Success*. Retrieved from: https://ssrn.com/abstract=3309307 or http://dx.doi.org/10.2139/ssrn.3309307

McCallum, B. T. (2004). Monetary policy in economies with little or no money. *Pacific Economic Review, 9*, 81–92. https://doi.org/10.1111/j.1468-0106.2004.00213.x

Nakamura, L. (2000). Economics and the new economy: the invisible hand meets creative destruction. *The Business Review*, 15–30.

Ozili, P.K. (2020). Financial inclusion and Fintech during COVID-19 crisis: Policy solution. *The Company Lawyer Journal, 8*. https://doi.org/10.2139/ssrn.3585662

Paneta, F. (2020). *From the payments revolution to the reinvention of money, Speech at the Deutsche Bundesbank conference on the "Future of Payments in Europe"*. Retrieved from: https://www.ecb.europa.eu/press/key/date/2020/html/ecb.sp201127~a781c4e0fc.en.html

Pickhardt, M., & Prinz, A. (Eds.). (2012). *Tax evasion and the shadow economy*. Edward Elgar Publishing Company.

Reis, J., Amorim, M., Melao, N., & Matos, P. (2018). Digital transformation: A literature review and guidelines for future research. In Á. Rocha, H. Adeli, L. P. Reis, & S. Costanzo (Eds.), *Trends and advances in information systems and technologies*. WorldCIST'18 2018. Advances in Intelligent Systems and Computing (Vol. 745). Springer. https://doi.org/10.1007/978-3-319-77703-0_41

Reistad, D. (1967). The coming cashless society. *Business Horizons, 10*(3), 23–32. https://doi.org/10.1016/0007-6813(67)90080-8

Rifkin, J. (2011). *The third industrial revolution: How lateral power is transforming energy, the economy, and the world*. Palgrave Macmillan.

Rogoff, K. (2016). *The curse of cash*. Princeton University Press.

Rogoff, K. (2017). Dealing with monetary paralysis at the zero bound. *Journal of Economic Perspectives, 31*(3), 47–66. https://doi.org/10.1257/jep.31.3.47

Rogoff, K. S. (2014). *Costs and benefits to phasing out paper currency* (NBER Working Paper No. 20126, NBER Macroeconomics Annual Conference, 29). https://doi.org/10.1086/680657

Sahay, R., Eriksson von Allmen, U., Lahreche, A., Khera, P., Ogawa, S., Bazarbash, M., & Beaton, K. (2020). *The promise of Fintech: Financial inclusion in the post Covid-19 era* (IMF Departmental Paper, No. 20/09). Retrieved from: https://www.imf.org/en/Publications/Departmental-Papers-Policy-Papers/Issues/2020/06/29/The-Promise-of-Fintech-Financial-Inclusion-in-the-Post-COVID-19-Era-48623

Sajter, D. (2013). *Privacy, identity, and the perils of the cashless society, conference: Culture, identity, society—European realities, Osijek, Croatia, 20–21.03.2013*. Retrieved from: https://www.researchgate.net/publication/326060290_Privacy_Identity_and_the_Perils_of_the_Cashless_Society

Schneider, F. (2013). *The shadow economy in Europe*. A.T. Kearney.

Schneider, F. (2019). *Restricting or abolishing cash: An effective instrument for eliminating the shadow economy, corruption and terrorism? Some remarks*. SUERF Conference Proceedings, Vienna.

Schwab, K. (2016). *The fourth industrial revolution*. Penguin.

Sennett, R. (2006). *The culture of the new capitalism*. Yale University Press.

Serhan, C. (2020). *Dirty money: Does the risk of infectious disease lower demand for cash?* (IMF Working Papers). https://doi.org/10.5089/9781513560892.001

Stiroh, K. (1999). Is there a new economy? *Challenge, 42*(4), 82–101.

Strebko, J., & Romanovs, A. (2018). The advantages and disadvantages of the blockchain technology. In *2018 IEEE 6th workshop on advances in information, electronic and electrical engineering (AIEEE)* (pp. 1–6). https://doi.org/10.1109/AIEEE.2018.859225

Warchlewska, A. (2020). Will the development of cashless payment technologies increase the financial exclusion of senior citizens? *Acta Scientiarum Polonorum – Oeconomia, 19*(2). https://doi.org/10.22630/ASPE.2020.19.2.21

White, L. H. (1987). Accounting for non-interest-bearing currency: A critique of the legal restrictions theory of money. *Journal of Money, Credit and Banking, 19*(4), 448–456.

Wisniewski, T. P., Polasik, M., Kotkowski, R., & Moro, A. (2021, February 28). *Switching from cash to cashless payments during the COVID-19 pandemic and beyond*. https://doi.org/10.2139/ssrn.3794790

Wolman, D. (2012). *The end of money. Counterfeiters, preachers, techies, dreamers—And the coming cashless society*. Da Capo Press.

Woodford, M. (1998). Doing without money: Controlling inflation in a post-monetary world. *Review of Economic Dynamics, 1*(1), 173–219. https://doi.org/10.1006/redy.1997.0006

Woodford, M. (2003). *Interest and prices*. Princeton University Press.

Worthington, S. (2000). Changes in payments markets, past, present and future: A comparison between Australia and the UK. *International Journal of Bank Marketing, 18*(5), 212–221. https://doi.org/10.1108/02652320010356771

Yaqub, J. O., Bell, H. T., Adenuga, I. A., & Ogundeji, M. O. (2013). The cashless policy in Nigeria: Prospects and challenges. *International Journal of Humanities and Social Science, 3*(3), 200–212.

Yeager, L. B. (1983). Stable money and free market currencies. *Cato Journal, 3*(1), 305–333.

Yeager, L. B. (1985). Deregulation and monetary reform. *American Economic Review, 75*(2), 103–107.

Zelizer, V. (1989). The social meaning of money: "Special monies." *American Journal of Sociology, 95*(2), 342–377.

11

Identifying Financial Drivers of Bitcoin Price in Times of Economic and Policy Uncertainty: A Threshold Analysis

Teodora Cristina Barbu, Iustina Alina Boitan, Raluca Crina Petrescu, and Cosmin Cepoi

Introduction

During the last decade the particularities and novelty of cryptocurrencies, especially of Bitcoin, have been topics of interest for both academics and practitioners. Subsequently, in the context of increased Bitcoin price volatility and spectacular developments during 2017 and 2018, empirical studies started to focus on identifying the key drivers of the Bitcoin price. Global interest on Bitcoin as a means of payment is confirmed

T. C. Barbu · I. A. Boitan (✉) · R. C. Petrescu · C. Cepoi
Bucharest University of Economic Studies, Bucharest, Romania
e-mail: iustina.boitan@fin.ase.ro

T. C. Barbu
e-mail: teodora.barbu@fin.ase.ro

R. C. Petrescu
e-mail: raluca.petrescu@fin.ase.ro

C. Cepoi
e-mail: cosmin.cepoi@fin.ase.ro

M. Ratajczak-Mrozek and P. Marszałek (eds.), *Digitalization and Firm Performance*,
https://doi.org/10.1007/978-3-030-83360-2_11

by recent events, such as the announcement of PricewaterhouseCoopers on accepting Bitcoin for payments made by customers. Also, Facebook's announcement regarding the launch of Diem, which seeks to connect 1.7 billion users worldwide to a cheaper and more transparent payment network, has generated broader concerns for regulators, banks, and other decision-makers who need to find creative solutions to these new challenges.

In this regard, two distinct strands of literature can be mentioned, namely the official positions adopted by the European Central Bank board members and the International Monetary Fund during several conferences and workshops, and then the analytical/empirical approaches developed in economic literature.

For instance, Coeure (2018) argues that Bitcoin is a smart but risky innovation, given the impact exerted by the new technologies on which it is based. He argues that it is imperative that more interdisciplinary research is conducted by joint teams of macroeconomists, payment experts and IT developers, in order to catalyze the benefits of these new technologies and to support central banks, regulators and standard-setting bodies in designing new policies and regulations to maintain the safety and resilience of the financial system.

A World Bank (2018) report complements the above statement with an argument in favour of the increased interest and preference for cryptocurrencies: the ease and rapidity of new means of payment that do not involve central banks, and the ability to make transactions without the need for financial institutions to play an intermediary role. The emergence of cryptocurrencies is associated with the aftermath of the financial crisis, being part of a broader wave of new technologies that facilitate peer-to-peer commerce and lending and the individualization of products. The report also enumerates a series of new challenges driven by the use of cryptocurrencies and of the block chain technologies they rely on, such as: the development of new strategies and measures for improving financial supervision, consumer protection and tax administration; maintaining a balance between the strength of the regulations and the process of financial innovation; tailoring strategies for managing the massive volume of electricity used to mine cryptocurrencies; and establishing whether governments and central banks can use block chain technologies to improve their services.

A more granular study published by the World Economic Forum in collaboration with Statista (Buchholz, 2021) reveals that cryptocurrencies have become a popular and cheaper solution for sending money across borders, especially in African countries, followed by several countries in Southeast Asia and Latin America. According to their survey, Switzerland and Greece exhibit the highest cryptocurrency adoption rate in Europe (11 per cent each). However, the general picture is that European countries record very low levels of cryptocurrency adoption.

Lagarde (2020) adopts a different perspective and focuses on the historical evolution recorded by the nature of money, as a result of the various socioeconomic changes. Although the traditional functions of money—as a means of exchange, a unit of account and a store of value—have remained unchanged for centuries, nowadays regulators are witnessing a process of dematerialization through digitalization and technological innovation. Block chain technology, on which crypto-assets rely, offers the opportunity for transactions to be performed directly between peers. There is, however, the risk of relying purely on technology, without any identifiable issuer or claims, while the trust between counterparties is replaced by cryptographic proofs and the security and integrity of records. A persistent drawback of crypto-assets is the lack of a stable value, increased volatility, illiquidity and their speculative nature. These intrinsic features do not allow crypto-assets to successfully fulfil all the functions of conventional money.

The second strand of the literature is related to the diverse analytical and empirical approaches and outcomes obtained by researchers.

An attempt to explain the preference for Bitcoin is made by Harold (2018), who argues that Bitcoin is perceived as a plausible alternative currency, mainly due to the attractive idea that it is based on an inherently superior and more secure payment technology that reconciles anonymity and un-traceability with security. Also, the author associates Bitcoin with a twenty-first century version of gold, because of the specific mining process which requires large amounts of computer power. Deloitte (2014) also explains that Bitcoin may be assimilated with gold due to the broad-scale investments in sophisticated "mining" equipment and the expanding ecosystem supporting the block chain protocol.

The idea that Bitcoin is gaining increasing relevance to businesses and the broader economy is supported by a number of authors, including Neves (2020), who highlights the widespread use of Bitcoin as an alternative investment or as a safe haven in financial markets. Bitcoin has a number of intrinsic features that can help investors and governments find new mechanisms for conducting transactions. A singular study is that of Wang (2020), who shows that Bitcoin has frequent uses in the air transport industry, to reduce the processing time and facilitate operations, as well as in the real estate sector. The author also expresses concerns about Bitcoin interference in the sphere of governmental institutions. The importance of the Bitcoin in the economy is also approached from the perspective of environmental impact. Thus, according to Badea and Mungiu-Pupazan (2021), given the energy consumption and CO_2 emissions, Bitcoin has a negative impact on the environment, but despite these effects Bitcoin continues to be used in the economy.

The trade-off between the risks and benefits presented by cryptocurrencies and their underlying technologies are extensively discussed by Bouveret and Haksar (2018). The category of benefits often includes the reduced cost and time for performing international payments or transferring remittances, the stimulus for financial inclusion. However, a major drawback is the pseudo-anonymity of many cryptocurrencies, which increases the likelihood of their being used in money laundering and to finance terrorism, unless an intermediary entity checks the integrity of these transactions or the identity of the people making them. A radical opinion belongs to Carstens (2018), who summarizes the manifold deficiencies of Bitcoin as "a combination of a bubble, a Ponzi scheme and an environmental disaster".

From a macroeconomic perspective, Panetta (2020) emphasizes that retail payments play a fundamental role for the European economy, thus Eurosystem's role is to safeguard the resiliency and soundness of the payment system. The large-scale digital transformation is already triggering a major shift in the functioning of the financial sector, which is a source of innovation but also of new types of risks. The author warns about both the pros and cons of new technologies, such as block chain, which could disrupt the European financial system by altering competition, privacy of data, financial stability, and even monetary sovereignty, while at the same time providing convenient and efficient payment solutions. The aim of European regulators is hence to shape new policies that can contain any digital shock, in order to establish the premises for an innovative, diverse and competitive payments landscape in the service of the evolving needs of European people and businesses.

The paper of Adachi et al. (2020) advocates for stablecoins as an alternative to more volatile crypto-assets, as they may curb price volatility and function as a potential means of payment and a store of value. The main feature of stablecoins is that they are backed by funds, traditional assets or even crypto-assets, or they may simply rely on expectations. It is generally agreed that Bitcoin is exposed to ample price volatility and limited scalability, which makes it more a risky asset than a reliable means of making payments. In comparison, stablecoins have the ability to reduce price volatility by anchoring the coin to a "safe" low-volatility reference asset or basket of assets.

Regardless of the perspective from which Bitcoin is analyzed—as currency, as means of payment or as an investment assetfor portfolios diversification, the most frequently asked questions focus on the factors that may explain the Bitcoin price dynamics. With that in mind, our study aims to test the extent to which the evolution of Bitcoin price is due to some specific variables such as stock market indexes, commodity, foreign exchange rates and monetary rates.

The novelty of our approach resides in identifying the financial determinants of Bitcoin price dynamics, which are conditioned by changes in decision-makers' economic policies that may alter the strength of this relationship. Although a few other studies have considered various measures of uncertainty (the trade policy uncertainty is tested by Gozgor et al. (2019, pp. 75–82); the Economic Policy Uncertainty is tested by Demir et al. (2018, pp. 145–149) and Panagiotidis et al. (2018, pp. 235–240); geopolitical risks are tested by Aysan et al. (2019, pp. 228–234); equity market uncertainty index and VIX are used by Wang et al. (2018, forthcoming), they used them as explanatory variables and obtained mixed, inconclusive and even contradictory results.

Instead, our study builds on the informational content brought by the Economic Policy Uncertainty Index and treats it not as an explanatory variable but as a threshold variable. Therefore, to uncover the determinants of Bitcoin price we treat the Economic Policy Uncertainty Index for USA (EPU) as a benchmark variable, while the remaining set of explanatory variables comprises the equity market, the monetary market, and the foreign exchange market, along with commodity market variables, and a composite index for measuring the global financial stress. The peculiarity of the threshold regression is that it generates two distinct sets of coefficients, for each type of effect, namely below and above the identified threshold. Moreover, the present study brings additional evidence regarding Bitcoin's hedging or diversifier role.

The chapter has been structured in five sections. Following the introduction, section two provides a summary of the most recent and influential papers that have examined various determinants of Bitcoin price. The description of the variables included in the study, as well as methodological details of the threshold regression analysis, is developed in section three. Section four describes the empirical results obtained under the baseline model and the robustness check performed in order to validate the stability of the initial results. Concluding remarks are provided in section five.

Literature Review

Investigating Bitcoin determinants is challenging and controversial, as the recent literature in this field shows. A bibliometric study of the Bitcoin literature performed by Merediz-Sola and Bariviera (2019) revealed that the first paper on this topic was published in 2012, and by 2019 at least 1162 studies had been published. However, the literature devoted to investigating the key drivers of Bitcoin price presents inconclusive results. For example, Kristoufek (2015) found no correlation between Bitcoin price and gold, while increases in financial stress fuel the further rise of Bitcoin price. Panagiotidis et al. (2018) and Das and Kannadhasan (2018) assessed whether stock market returns, exchange rates, gold and oil, FED's and ECB's interest rates exhibit an influence on Bitcoin price. These findings are relevant only in a short time-frame; long-term developments may also be attributed to endogenous factors interconnected with the economic and financial environment.

The goal pursued by Kjærland et al. (2018) was to highlight the factors that affected Bitcoin price during the period with the highest volatility, namely the end of 2017 and the beginning of 2018. They show that Bitcoin price was influenced by the return on the capital market, reflected in the S&P 500 index and by the investors' sentiment, reflected in the number of Google searches. Furthermore, Dirican and Canoz (2017) aimed to identify, by means of the ARDL boundary test method, relationships between the price of Bitcoin and capital market transactions, reflected in most representative stock market indices. In this respect, the authors identified a cointegration relationship between Bitcoin and stock market indices from the USA and China, which means that in the long run, stock investment decisions are subject to Bitcoin price developments. However, they fail to reveal any correlation between Bitcoin price and the FTSE 100 and Nikkei 225 stock indices.

Also of importance is the comparative approach of the USD/EUR and USD/YEN exchange rates highlighted by Baur and Dimpfl (2021), which shows that Bitcoin has 10 times higher volatility than these currency pairs, which limits its possibility to fulfil the traditional role of currency, namely providing a medium of exchange, while at the same time being able to fulfil the function of storing value.

Regarding the impact of information and statements on Bitcoin quotations, the study of Kjærl and et al. (2018) examined the explanatory factors of Bitcoin fluctuation and identified that political statements and events are important, relevant drivers. The concerns and interest of Bitcoin investors, reflected in the number of Google hits, are in a significantly positive relationship with the price of Bitcoin. Despite that, the authors' opinion is that Bitcoin is not a safe investment. More to the point, Dastgir et al. (2019) examined the existence of causality between Bitcoin returns and the public attention paid to it (measured by them using Google Trends search queries). They focused on the period January 1, 2013 to December 31, 2017 and tested the dates using Copula-based Granger Causality in Distribution. The results highlighted the existence of a bi-directional causal relationship in the left tail (poor performances) and right tail (higher performances).

Bitcoin's price sensitivity in respect of large events was studied by Fenga et al. (2018) who found out, through a new indicator, that trades of cryptocurrency related to these events are very profitable in such a new market. Comparing to the regulated stock markets, the lack of supervision over the Bitcoin market induces an increase of informed trading in that market. That specific behaviour is also encouraged by the availability of the market worldwide, the informed traders being able to build positions anytime and anywhere, in direct connection with privately received information, which puts them at an advantage with regard to uninformed investors. The authors also analyzed the importance of the timing of large events on informed traders regarding their investment decision-making and profits. Their final conclusion is similar to that reached by other authors (Bacilar et al., 2017): Bitcoin prices are more volatile than other similar assets, and are more sensitive to regulatory and market events.

Also related to Bitcoin prices, Conlon and McGeeet (2019) even measured the gambling appetite of Bitcoin holders by tracking gaming transactions data. They found out that the changes in the volume spent as lottery-like gambling had an important impact on Bitcoin price movements before 2016 (32% from the changes in returns can be explained by it) and the effects are not present after 2016, and even the proportion and not the volume of gambling transactions decreased.

Another research direction has investigated the similarities between Bitcoin and other commodities in terms of prices, supply and demand. By using linear and non-linear GARCH models, Gronwald (2019) made an empirical comparison between Bitcoin, crude oil and gold markets. The conclusion of the study is that large movements in prices are stronger in the Bitcoin market due to the different characteristics of the supplies: the short-term supply for gold and crude oil is uncertain while the supply for Bitcoin has no uncertainties. Wang et al. (2019) were also preoccupied with the correlation of Bitcoin with other major financial assets (stock, commodities futures, gold, foreign exchange, monetary assets and bonds in China) and about the possibility of using it as a hedging asset or a safe haven. Their conclusions, which are also offered as advice for investors, based on their empirical results, are that Bitcoin has a profoundly speculative nature, meaning a higher volatility than other assets, high returns but also significant risks, being weakly correlated with other assets. They might confirm the capability of Bitcoin as a hedging asset, safe haven, or means of diversification, but at the same time the presence of Bitcoin in a portfolio in which it also plays multiple roles will have an impact in terms of risks in portfolio management.

An analysis of Bitcoin in terms of the supply and demand of money was conducted by Horra et al. (2019), who explain the main factors that determine the demand for Bitcoin, despite the increased volatility of its price, and highlight whether the demand for this cryptocurrency is due to its role as a medium of exchange, as a speculative asset or as a safe-haven commodity. Thus, Bitcoin behaves like a short-term speculative asset, but in the long term the demand is not influenced by speculation but by the prospect of using it as a currency functioning as a means of exchange.

The degree of interest in Bitcoin is reflected in the level of demand, which depends on the macroeconomic conditions, as stated in the paper of Ifigeneia et al. (2015). When considered as an asset or as an investment opportunity, the demand for Bitcoin may be affected by speculative behaviours and investors' sentiment, which are captured by indicators such as Google queries and searches. The degree of public interest in Bitcoin is directly related to the price of Bitcoin. Regarding the correlation between the price of Bitcoin and the foreign exchange market, the authors highlight a negative relationship between cryptocurrency quotations and the exchange rate of US dollar/euro on short term. The stock price developments on the US capital market, according to the Standard and Poor's index, have a negative impact on the longer term, which means that investors consider stocks and Bitcoin to be interchangeable assets.

In this respect, Erdas and Caglar (2018) tested the causal relationship between the S&P 500 index and the Bitcoin price and confirmed the relationship identified in the previous paper. The results indicate that capital market investors have sufficient information about Bitcoin due to technological advances and computer applications that track them, but there is no causal relationship between S&P 500 and Bitcoin price, only a one-way relationship between Bitcoin and the S&P 500 index. For this reason, the authors recommend that investors should maintain active positions in the capital market to follow the evolution of Bitcoin prices. Negative Bitcoin shocks generate positive and negative shocks in the S&P 500 index, while Bitcoin positive shocks generate negative shocks on the S&P 500 index.

Another strand of literature recently emerged which insufficiently explored attempts to answer the question of whether Bitcoin may be used as a hedging asset. Dyhrberg (2016a) concludes that Bitcoin may be used for hedging risks generated by the FTSE stock exchange index, or for contracts having gold as an underlying asset. Demir et al. (2018) share the same idea, while Liu and Tsyvinski (2018) argue that cryptocurrencies behave similarly with shares or gold, so their future return may be explained by factors specific to these markets.

The safe haven, hedge or diversifier features of Bitcoin are also the focus of attention of Kliber et al. (2019) in connection with the economic situation of some countries and with the currency trading. They choose five countries with different economic environments (Venezuela, Japan, China, Sweden and Estonia) and estimated the correlations between main stock indices and the Bitcoin price in the local currency, and respectively the correlations between the main stock indices and the Bitcoin price in US dollar. The conclusions were different, depending on whether it was a local or global Bitcoin exchange. In the case of investments in the local currency, Bitcoin was treated as a diversifier in Japan and China, as safe haven asset in Venezuela, and in Sweden and Estonia as a hedging instrument. At the same time, for USD trade the results for all the analyzed countries are that Bitcoin is a weak hedge. A similar study was conducted by Musialkowska et al. (2020), which revealed that gold is a better safe haven than oil for Venezuelan investors, while Bitcoin turns out to be a weaker safe haven, although it can perform limited money functions in a crisis-driven country.

Recent Deutsche Bank research (Kaya, 2018) highlights a temporary divergence between the uncertainty of the financial markets and the uncertainty associated with economic policy, which proved in the past to be interconnected, in close co-movement. Given the striking impact of the uncertainty associated with economic policies on financial markets and the business cycle, we relied on a novel methodology called threshold regression, in order to capture the effect exerted by a series of explanatory variables on Bitcoin price, conditioned by fluctuations in the level of the uncertainty surrounding policymakers' economic decisions (regulatory measures, structural reforms and fiscal policy).

Other authors have tried to establish if a connection can be inferred between the returns and price volatility of Bitcoin and political risks. Aysan et al. (2019), using a Bayesian Graphical Structural Vector Autoregressive technique on daily returns and price volatility for July 18, 2010-May 31, 2018, concluded that global geopolitical risks exert predictive power on both of them. In that respect, we may consider Bitcoin as an important hedging tool against global geopolitical risks, due to its positive effects on returns and volatility at the higher quartiles. A complementary perspective is provided by Dina el Mahdy (2021), who launches a series of questions in a study mainly related to the capability of Bitcoin to reduce transaction costs, market frictions, cyber-attacks and fraudulent activities.

Among the studies considering the hedging capabilities of Bitcoin, we highlight the contribution of Sebastião and Godinho (2019, available online) which studied the capabilities of Bitcoin futures during the initial months of trading. Their conclusion is that Bitcoin futures are able to mitigate the losses in the spot market and also to hedge the price risk for other cryptocurrencies.

On the same subject, namely the newly launched Bitcoin futures, is also addressed in the paper of Ruozhou et al. (2019), which measured their impact on Bitcoin and other 7 non-Bitcoin cryptocurrencies returns. They came to the conclusion that after a peak in the price a few days from the launch, Bitcoin suffered losses in the next year almost equal to 80% (26.5% loss in the first 45 days). At the same, time other cryptocurrencies kept their positive returns trend, meaning that there is a positive (or an insignificant negative) relationship between them and Bitcoin futures, and a negative relationship between the introduction of Bitcoin futures and Bitcoin prices.

The topic of Bitcoin futures is a relatively new one among the authors who were involved in research topics on cryptocurrencies from different perspectives (safe haven, hedge or diversifier); in this respect we may cite Kim et al. (2019), who investigated the results of the introduction of Bitcoin futures on the intraday volatility of Bitcoin. Their results show that immediately after the introduction, the market became more volatile, before switching to a stable one, even when compared with the market before the introduction of futures.

Chevapatrakul and Mascia (2019) investigated the investors' reaction to Bitcoin price movements in connection with the return distribution. For this, they used the quantile autoregressive model and concluded that, at the level of daily frequency, investors overreact to sharp declines in Bitcoin price, supporting the conclusion that the Bitcoin market is inefficient. The same conclusion was reached by Al-Yahyaee et al. (2018); Charfeddine and Maouchi (2018), Yonghong and Ruan Weihua (2017), and Vidal and Analbanez (2018). Also, it is emphasized that there is a need for increasing the supervision of Bitcoin trading, despite the fact that it is considered a small part of the financial markets. The argument is that we face a highly complex digital currency with significant potential to destabilize the financial markets, mainly due to little understanding and an increased potential of risk spreading from the cryptocurrency markets.

Urquhart (2016) also studied the market efficiency of Bitcoin, using a battery of tests. The conclusion was that today we are witnessing a process of moving towards an efficient market, the past evidence showing that previous returns were inefficient.

Cheah and Fry (2015) studied the movements of Bitcoin prices and their impact on specific markets and found that the price has an important speculative component. They also found empirical evidence that the fundamental price of Bitcoin is zero.

Al-Yahyaee et al. (2018) examined and compared, in terms of efficiency, gold, currency and stock markets, with the Bitcoin market, using an MF-DFA approach. The conclusions of the study were that Bitcoin is more inefficient than gold, stock and currency markets because they found evidence that the multifractality of the Bitcoin market is stronger when compared with the rest of the markets included in the study.

The multifractality of Bitcoin was also studied by Takaishi (2018) using 1 min returns on Bitcoin prices and an MF-DFA analysis. The study also investigated daily volatility asymmetry with GARCH, GJR and RGARCH models, resulting in the conclusion that there is no evidence on such a component. At the same time, the Bitcoin time series presents multifractality, the sources of it being both the temporal correlation and fat-tailed 1-min return distribution. The multifractal properties of Bitcoin were measured in connection with the influence of Brexit on the GBP-USD exchange rate (on June 23, 2016), concluding that Bitcoin was resilient to Brexit.

Academics who were of the view that Bitcoin is an efficient asset studied whether it may be used for portfolio diversification. Kajtazi and Moro (2019) developed a study in that respect, measuring the effects of including Bitcoin in an optimal portfolio of US, European and Chinese assets. The measure was performed using the CVaR approach on both portfolios with and without Bitcoin. Their conclusion was that Bitcoin may be used in portfolio management and diversification because the performance is improving with Bitcoin mainly due to the increase in returns and not to decreases of volatility.

To sum up, the above-mentioned papers emphasize various aspects of Bitcoin, which complement each other, namely: a currency with limited functions, an asset with increased volatility, a security asset comparable to other financial assets or commodities, and an alternative investment and risk hedging tool contributing to portfolio diversification. As Settle (2018) explains, although cryptocurrencies have become one of the most controversial topics in relation with the financial services industry at a global level, in order to remain a successful product another step is required, namely institutionalization through banks, stock exchanges, payment providers and Fintechs' access on the crypto-assets market.

Data and Methodology

The Data

We consider Bitcoin price alongside stock market indexes, foreign exchange rates, and commodity and monetary market variables, from October 2013–November 2018, each series containing 1.122 observations. We intentionally decided that our analysis would only cover data till the end of 2018 because we did not want the results to be impacted by the manifestation of the pandemic crisis, but to identify the determinants of the Bitcoin price in stable periods. Table 11.1 presents the description of the data series used for the subsequent analysis.

Methodology

To investigate the nonlinear behaviour of Bitcoin price, we used a threshold regression analysis in line with Tong (1983) and Hansen (2011, pp. 123–127). These threshold approaches are suitable alternatives to linear regression methods when it comes to capturing sudden breaks or asymmetries noticeable in financial time series. Formally, a threshold regression model with two regions can be described by Eq. (11.1):

$$y_t = \begin{cases} x_t\beta + z_t\delta_1 + \varepsilon_t, & -\infty < w_t \leq \gamma \\ x_t\beta + z_t\delta_2 + \varepsilon_t, & \gamma < w_t \leq \infty \end{cases}. \tag{11.1}$$

The dependent variable y_t, is represented by the Bitcoin price, the set of covariates are given by x_t and might also include lagged values of y_t, while z_t is a matrix of independent variables (bond yields, gold price, oil price, interest rates, capital market indexes alongside exchange rates) characterized by some region-specific coefficients included in vectors marked with δ_1 and δ_2. Moreover, β is a vector containing region-invariant estimates (in our case we include only independent variables with region-specific coefficients so β will be set to zero), w_t is the threshold variable given by EPU index while ε_t is an IID error term having constant variance σ^2 and zero mean. Region 1 consists of those observations in which the value of w_t is less than the threshold γ. Similarly, Region 2 is limited to the subset of observations in which the value of w_t is greater than γ.

Inference on the nuisance parameter γ is a challenging task, mainly due to its nonstandard asymptotic distribution. In this respect, to identify the threshold value ($\hat{\gamma}$) we need to apply the least square optimization to the following regression with T observations and two

Table 11.1 Bitcoin and covariates

Variables	Description and Source
Bitcoin Price	Daily sport closing price of Bitcoin. *Source:* https://Bitcoin.org/en/ (accessed on December 13, 2020)
EPU Index	The economic and policy uncertainty index based on media news for United States of America. *Source:* http://www.policyuncertainty.com/ (accessed on December 13, 2020)
Stress Index	A daily market-based snapshot of stress in global financial markets. It is constructed from 33 financial market variables, such as yield spreads, valuation measures, and interest rates. *Source:* https://www.financialresearch.gov/ (accessed on December 13, 2020)
Bond yields USA	United States 5-Year Bond Yield. *Source*: Bloomberg (accessed on December 13, 2020)
Bond yields CHN	China 5 Year Bond Yield. *Source*: Bloomberg (accessed on December 13, 2020)
Bond yields JAP	Japan 5 Year Bond Yield. *Source*: Bloomberg (accessed on December 13, 2020)
Bond yields GER	Germany 5 Year Bond Yield. *Source*: Bloomberg (accessed on December 13, 2020)
Bond yields UK	United Kingdom 5 Year Bond Yield. *Source*: Bloomberg (accessed on December 13, 2020)
Gold Price	Daily sport closing price of gold. *Source*: Bloomberg (accessed on December 13, 2020)
Oil Price	Daily sport closing price of oil. *Source*: Bloomberg (accessed on December 13, 2020)
EONIA	The Euro Overnight Index Average is the average interest rate at which a selection of European banks lend one another funds denominated in euros whereby the loans have a maturity of 1 day. *Source*: ECB—Statistical Data Warehouse (accessed on December 13, 2020)
SONIA	The Sterling Overnight Index Average is based on actual transactions and reflects the average of the interest rates that banks pay to borrow sterling overnight from other financial institutions. *Source*: Bank of England (accessed on December 13, 2020)
S&P Index	Is a market-capitalization-weighted index of the 500 largest U.S. listed firms. *Source*: Bloomberg (accessed on December 13, 2020)

(continued)

Table 11.1 (continued)

Variables	Description and Source
Nikkei 225 Index	Is a market-capitalization-weighted index of Japan's top 225 companies listed on the Tokyo Exchange. *Source*: Bloomberg (accessed on December 13, 2020)
DAX Index	Is a market-capitalization-weighted index of German's top 30 blue-chips listed on the Frankfurt Stock Exchange. *Source*: Bloomberg (accessed on December 13, 2020)
FTSE100 Index	Is a market-capitalization-weighted index including the largest 100 companies which list on the London Stock Exchange. *Source*: Bloomberg (accessed on December 13, 2020)
SHANGHAI Index	Is a market-capitalization-weighted index including all the A-shares and B-shares listed on the Shanghai Stock Exchange. *Source*: Bloomberg (accessed on December 13, 2020)
EUR/USD	The currency pair indicates how many U.S. dollars are needed to purchase one euro. Source: Bloomberg (accessed on December 13, 2020)
USD/JPY	The currency pair indicates how many Japanese Yens are needed to purchase one U.S. dollar. *Source*: Bloomberg (accessed on December 13, 2020)
EUR/JPY	The currency pair indicates how many Japanese Yen are needed to purchase one euro. *Source*: Bloomberg (accessed on December 13, 2020)
EUR/GBP	The currency pair indicates how many British Pounds are needed to purchase one euro. *Source*: Bloomberg (accessed on December 13, 2020)

regions:

$$\begin{aligned} y_t = x_t\beta + z_t\delta_1 I(-\infty < w_t \leq \gamma) \\ + z_t\delta_2 I(\gamma < w_t \leq \infty) + \varepsilon_t \end{aligned} \tag{11.2}$$

The threshold is obtained based on the following minimization algorithm:

$$\hat{\gamma} = \arg\min_{\gamma \in \Gamma} S_{T_1}(\gamma) \tag{11.3}$$

where $\Gamma \in (-\infty, \infty)$, T_1 is a sequence of values in w_t, with $T_1 < T$ and corresponds to the number of observations between two certain quantiles of w_t distribution (in Stata 15 the default is 10% meaning that T_1 corresponds to 10th to 90th percentiles). Furthermore, $S_{T_1}(\gamma)$ is given by:

$$S_{T_1}(\gamma) = \sum_{t=1}^{T} [y_t - x_t\beta - z_t\delta_1 I(-\infty < w_t \leq \gamma\ ) \\ -z_t\delta_2 I(\ \gamma < w_t \leq \infty)]^2 \tag{11.4}$$

and represents a $T_1 x_1$ vector of sum of squared residuals while γ is a $T_1 x 1$ vector of potential thresholds for Eq. (11.1).

In general, a $m-$ thresold regression model has $m + 1$ regions and can de described by Eq. (11.5):

$$y_t = x_t\beta + z_t\delta_1 I_1(\gamma_1, w_t) + \ldots + z_t\delta_{m+1} I_{m+1}(\gamma_{m+1}, w_t) + \varepsilon_t \tag{11.5}$$

where $\gamma_1 < \gamma_2 < \ldots < \gamma_m$ and $\gamma_{m+1} = \infty$. Moreover, $I_k(\gamma_k, w_t) = I(\gamma_{k-1} < w_t < \gamma_k)$ is an indicator function for kth regime. The estimation procedure for localizing the first threshold $(\hat{\gamma}_1)$ implies estimating a model with two regions in line with Eq. (11.2). Furthermore, the second threshold $(\hat{\gamma}_2)$ estimation depends on $(\hat{\gamma}_1)$ since it is computed by minimizing the total sum of squares over the entire sample excluding the first threshold. The ith threshold minimizes the sum of squared residual and is given by:

$$\hat{\gamma}_i = \arg min_{\gamma_i \in \Gamma_i} S_{T_i}\left(\hat{\gamma}_i | \hat{\gamma}_1, \ldots, \hat{\gamma}_{i-1}\right) \tag{11.6}$$

where $\Gamma_i = (\gamma_0 = -\infty, \gamma_{m+1} = \infty)$ excluding $\hat{\gamma}_1, \ldots, \hat{\gamma}_{l-1}$.

Empirical Results

The Baseline Model

This section carries out an extensive assessment of the key determinants of Bitcoin price during normal times, with the help of the Threshold Regression approach. We considered Kristoufek's statement (2015) that Bitcoin behaves independently from economic and financial developments, which may be further correlated with the findings obtained by Chen et al. (2021) claiming that during times of extreme uncertainty or risk, such as crisis events, Bitcoin provides significant diversification benefits for the investors.

We show that the EPU Index for the USA can act as a powerful threshold variable when explaining Bitcoin dynamics. More to the point, we identified a threshold for the EPU Index at around 112, a value that divides the sample into two extreme regimes which can be seen in Fig. 11.1. When EPU is higher than 112 i.e., the uncertainty is persistent, we can observe that Bitcoin has lower values, suggesting that the trading activity on cryptocurrencies market intensifies during times of economic stability.

However, we are interested in how Bitcoin price reacts to different financial drivers, determined by economic and policy uncertainty. This

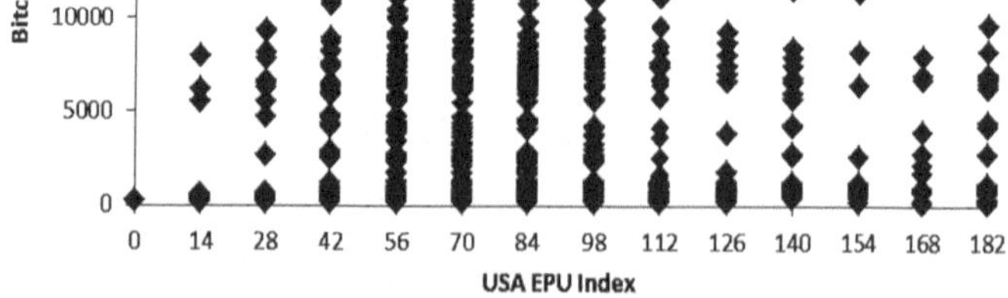

Fig. 11.1 Bitcoin price and estimated threshold

type of analysis provides a bigger picture on Bitcoin evolution and can be helpful for both investors and regulators to accurately understand the Bitcoin—financial markets nexus.

The full-sample estimates in Table 11.2 indicate that 10 out of 19 variables preserve their statistical significance irrespective of the level of the EPU threshold. Hence they exert a stable, persistent influence on Bitcoin price, no matter the kind of economic policies. However, most variables trigger an impact on Bitcoin price in times of low economic

Table 11.2 All samples (2013–2018)

	Low information Regime (EPU < 112)		High information regime (EPU > 112)	
	Estimates	*p*-Value	Estimates	*p*-Value
Stress index	**0.0304**	0.0890	0.0576	0.2060
Bond yields USA	**0.6100**	0.0000	**0.6073**	0.0180
Bond yields CHN	**0.4721**	0.0000	**0.6387**	0.0000
Bond yields JAP	**−1.5824**	0.0000	**−3.0219**	0.0000
Bond yields GER	**−0.7887**	0.0000	**−0.9291**	0.0010
Bond yields UK	**−0.1408**	0.0670	−0.0751	0.7240
Gold Price	**−1.4376**	0.0000	**−3.4437**	0.0010
Oil Price	**−0.3132**	0.0010	−0.1805	0.4850
EONIA	−0.1784	0.2160	**1.3404**	0.0120
SONIA	**0.3275**	0.0090	−0.5692	0.1330
S&P Index	**−0.7487**	0.1000	1.6656	0.2260
Nikkei 225 Index	**4.0107**	0.0000	**2.9581**	0.0010
DAX Index	**4.3773**	0.0000	**3.4771**	0.0000
FTSE100 Index	**−4.2527**	0.0000	**−4.4669**	0.0030
SHANNGHAI Index	**−0.5480**	0.0000	−0.2351	0.5590
EUR/USD	**6.3004**	0.0040	**−19.3048**	0.0010
USD/JPY	−0.0338	0.1480	**−0.3071**	0.0000
EUR/JPY	−0.0001	0.9960	**0.2422**	0.0000
EUR/GBP	**5.4866**	0.0000	**5.0638**	0.0000
Intercept	**−24.8353**	0.0000	17.7490	0.2010

uncertainty (EPU < 112). The global financial stress index, as a measure of the disruptions in the normal functioning of financial markets, shows a positive and significant impact on Bitcoin price only in environments with low economic policy uncertainty. This finding suggests that financial stress and economic uncertainty act as equivalents, each one being able to trigger, independently, a further impact on Bitcoin price. In other words, the perception that there is a background of economic uncertainty is per se to lead a movement in Bitcoin price; this is also true for financial stress: even in times of low economic uncertainty, signals of financial markets' distress determine a Bitcoin price rise.

The relationship between Bitcoin price and the US and Chinese bond yields is positive and significant irrespective of the level of the policy-related uncertainty index. The explanation may reside in the fact that the US and Chinese financial markets are mature and developed, and the broad array of conventional and new investment opportunities seem to co-exist rather than to compete. However, the relationship with Japanese bond yields is negative and significant, being amplified in times of increased EPU volatility. The same negative influence is present for German and UK bond yields. Investors on large European bond markets are mostly driven by optimizing their earnings. In times of bond yields decreases, investments in Bitcoin are more attractive, and thus its price increases. Under those circumstances, investments in bonds are substituted by those in Bitcoin. This conclusion also holds for the Japanese case.

Gold price exerts a negative impact on Bitcoin price. Increases in the gold price are followed by lower attractivity of holding Bitcoin, as its price decreases. This effect is more pronounced in times of increased uncertainty due to economic policy. This result may be due to investors' financial behaviour: risk-averse ones will prefer gold investments, as the value of gold is more stable and the risks incurred are lower. The negative relation is even stronger during periods characterized by the high unpredictability of fiscal, regulatory, monetary or trade policies implemented by policymakers. Our result is consistent with the previous findings of Das and Kannadhasan (2018) and Zwick and Syed (2019). Furthermore, the oil price exhibits behaviour similar to that of gold, but only in times of low economic uncertainty.

The two major interbank interest rates with an overnight maturity—EONIA for the Eurozone, and SONIA for the UK banking system—show a positive but mixed influence on Bitcoin price, only at a probability level of 10%.

Fluctuations recorded by major stock market indexes trigger mixed influence on Bitcoin price, in terms of EPU levels. DAX and Nikkei indexes always exhibit statistical significance and the same sign, no matter the sample employed. Improvements in the performance of German and Japanese stock market indexes generate a positive and significant impact on Bitcoin price, suggesting investors' preference for portfolio diversification in order to offset a potential loss with a gain from holding multiple financial assets. As regards British, Chinese and US stock market indexes, most of the time they record a negative relationship with Bitcoin price. Rising indexes performance determines a fall in Bitcoin price, as investors seem to prefer investing more in the equity market than in a speculative asset.

The results obtained by Dyhrberg (2016b) are confirmed by our study, revealing that Bitcoin exhibits hedging capabilities and may be used as a hedge against the FTSE index and US dollar fluctuations. In addition, we found that investments in Bitcoin can hedge against the S&P and Shanghai indexes, too.

The strength of the relationship between Bitcoin and the foreign exchange market is determined by the economic policy uncertainty level. Decreases of the USD/JPY exchange rate are followed by increases in Bitcoin price. Therefore Bitcoin acts as a short-term hedge against exchange rate volatility. On the other hand, increases of the EUR/GBP and EUR/JPY exchange rates fuel a further rise in Bitcoin price, hence suggesting a diversifier role of Bitcoin, as investors are willing to trade both currencies and Bitcoin. As regards the EUR/USD exchange rate, its impact on Bitcoin is mixed: in times of low economic uncertainty it exhibits a positive influence and Bitcoin acts as a diversifier, meanwhile during increased regulatory uncertainty it has a negative effect on Bitcoin price, which acts as a hedge.

The Robustness of the Results

In this section we validate our results with a robustness check. The analysis had been performed again (see Table 11.3 for an output summary), by including an autoregressive term of Bitcoin price so as to test whether past evolutions of Bitcoin price are able to trigger an influence on the current price.

Table 11.3 All samples (2013–2018)

	Low information Regime (EPU < 124.5)		High information regime (EPU > 124.5)	
	Estimates	*p*-Value	Estimates	*p*-Value
Bitcoin price (-1)	**0.9462**	0.0000	**0.9722**	0.0000
Stress Index	0.0071	0.1850	−0.0038	0.6260
Bond yields USA	−0.0021	0.9240	0.0002	0.9960
Bond yields CHN	**0.0505**	0.0000	−0.0186	0.3990
Bond yields JAP	**−0.1553**	0.0060	0.0395	0.7020
Bond yields GER	0.0123	0.6580	**−0.1013**	0.0220
Bond yields UK	−0.0254	0.2510	−0.0013	0.9710
Gold Price	**−0.2241**	0.0240	−0.0573	0.7500
Oil Price	0.0297	0.3000	0.0167	0.6990
EONIA	**−0.0716**	0.0780	**0.1527**	0.0940
SONIA	−0.0225	0.5440	0.0029	0.9630
S&P Index	0.0365	0.7880	−0.1288	0.5610
Nikkei 225 Index	**0.2234**	0.0240	**0.3582**	0.0290
DAX Index	**0.2559**	0.0190	**0.4038**	0.0280
FTSE100 Index	−0.2344	0.1300	**−0.5266**	0.0310
SHANNGHAI Index	**−0.0582**	0.0830	−0.0642	0.3160
EUR USD	0.7360	0.2450	1.0225	0.3200
USD JPY	0.0035	0.6060	0.0047	0.6790
EUR JPYY	−0.0044	0.4170	−0.0081	0.3860
EUR GBP	0.2526	0.1180	0.3307	0.1910
Intercept	−1.4873	0.2670	−1.4447	0.5050

The estimated threshold for the EPU Index, of around 124.5, represents a value that is not far away from the initial one. However, the results show a significant decrease in the number of explanatory variables which kept their statistical significance and hence preserve their influence on Bitcoin price. When assessing the significance of the estimates against different benchmark levels of economic uncertainty (EPU), we uncover that 7 variables exert an impact on Bitcoin price in times of low uncertainty, as opposed to only 5 in times of above-threshold uncertainty, for the 2013–2018 sample. The lagged Bitcoin price positively determines its current level irrespective of the economic uncertainty level. Bond yields, gold, euro area interbank interest rate and stock market indexes still influence Bitcoin price in times of low uncertainty, while in times of increased economic uncertainty the main impact comes from fluctuations in the stock market indexes, EONIA and gold price.

Conclusions

The analytical approach developed in this chapter is justified by the ongoing interest in cryptocurrencies in times of both stability and turmoil, and the manifold and diverse official opinions and empirical findings that have emerged so far. Our specific research aim was to identify the key determinants of Bitcoin price during normal times, conditioned by the level recorded by a pre-established threshold variable, namely the Economic Policy Uncertainty. In this respect, we obtain distinct estimates for the two regions positioned above and below the cut-off level of the threshold variable, to account for the specific changes in the amplitude and significance of the impact exerted by the stock market, foreign exchange, commodity and monetary market variables. The particularities of the methodological framework employed in this study allowed us to perform a granular, detailed analysis of the leading determinants of Bitcoin, while discriminating between times of increased economic unpredictability and sound and stable times.

Our findings are in line with those generated by previous literature in this field, confirming that most financial market variables included in the sample preserve their statistical significance irrespective of the level of the EPU threshold. Consequently, they exhibit a persistent influence on Bitcoin price in periods characterized by both increased economic uncertainty and respectively stable economic environments. Also, our findings confirm that Bitcoin exhibits hedging capabilities as well as a diversifier role in relation to various financial market variables.

Based on the reported results, we can highlight several contributions to the existing literature: first of all, the relationships between Bitcoin price and bond yields from China and Japan respectively are robust and statistically significant only in times of low economic or political uncertainty, unlike German bond yields, which negatively influence the Bitcoin price in periods of economic or political turbulence. Second, gold price exerts a negative impact on Bitcoin price; however, this result is valid only in an environment characterized by low economic or political uncertainty. Third, the higher the interbank interest rates for the Eurozone i.e., EONIA, the higher Bitcoin price is, but only in times of high uncertainty. Finally, an important result highlighted by the empirical study is that Bitcoin is a versatile financial product, which may act either as a diversifier or as a hedge asset, depending on investors' behaviour and risk appetite. Also, it has a dual nature, being perceived as an asset whose future path is determined by other assets (such as bonds, stock market indices, gold or oil) but also as a currency with limited functions, which is influenced by the main exchange rates or interbank interest rates.

As a future research direction, we intend to expand the analytical framework developed within this chapter for a dataset covering exclusively the onset of the pandemic crisis and its containment phase, in order to establish whether the correlations found in normal times are also maintained during severely distressed times. In addition, we intend to make estimates by setting several COVID-19 related variables as a threshold, so as to reveal the changes that occurred in the statistical relationship between Bitcoin and the various financial market indicators.

The findings may be of interest also for policymakers, because they reveal the degree of interconnectedness between Bitcoin and the various traditional financial indicators, and can support the development of appropriate regulation. Obviously, the key issues that will determine the future of crypto-assets are represented by new regulations on crypto-assets' taxonomy and adoption, regulatory compliance, cybersecurity, accounting and tax compliance.

References

Adachi, M., Cominetta, M., Kaufmann, C., & van der Kraaij, A. (2020). A regulatory and financial stability perspective on global stablecoins. *Macro-prudential Bulletin Articles* - No. 10

Al-Yahyaee, K. H., Mensi, W., & MinYoon, S. (2018). Efficiency, multifractality, and the long-memory property of the Bitcoin market: A comparative analysis with stock, currency, and gold markets, *Finance Research Letters, 27*(C), 228–234. https://doi.org/10.1016/j.frl.2018.03.017.

Aysan, A. F., Demir, E., Gozgor, G., & Lau, C. K. M. (2019). Effects of the geopolitical risks on Bitcoin returns and volatility. *Research in International Business and Finance, 47*(C), 511–518. https://doi.org/10.1016/j.ribaf.2018.09.011.

Bacilar, M., Bouri, E., Gupta, R., & Roubad, R. (2017, August). Can volume predict Bitcoin returns and volatility? A quantiles-based approach. *Economic Modelling, 64,* 74–81. https://doi.org/10.1016/j.econmod.2017.03.019

Badea, L., & Mungiu-Pupazan, M. C. (2021). The economic and environmental impact of Bitcoin. *IEEE Access* (99), 1–1. https://doi.org/10.1109/ACCESS.2021.3068636

Baur, D. G., & Dimpfl, T. (2021). The volatility of Bitcoin and its role as a medium of exchange and astore of value. *Empir Econ* (2021). https://doi.org/10.1007/s00181-020-01990-5 https://link.springer.com/article/10.1007/s00181-020-01990-5#citeas

Bouveret, A., & Haksar, V. (2018, March). What are cryptocurrencies? A potential new form of money offers benefits while posing risks. *Finance & Development, 55*(2). https://www.imf.org/external/pubs/ft/fandd/2018/06/what-are-cryptocurrencies-like-bitcoin/basics.htm

Buchholz, H. (2021). *These are the countries where cryptocurrency use is most common.* https://www.weforum.org/agenda/2021/02/how-common-is-cryptocurrency/

Carstens, A. (2018, February 6). *Money in the digital age: What role for central banks?* Speech at House of Finance, Goethe University, Frankfurt.

Charfeddine, L., & Maouchi Y. (2018). Are shocks on the returns and volatility of cryptocurrencies really persistent? *Finance Research Letters, 28,* 423–430 (March 2019). https://doi.org/10.1016/j.frl.2018.06.017

Cheah, E. T., & Fry, J. (2015). Speculative bubbles in Bitcoin markets? An empirical investigation into the fundamental value of Bitcoin. *Economics Letters, 130,* 32–36. https://doi.org/10.1016/j.econlet.2015.02.029

Chevapatrakul, T., & Mascia, D. (2019). Detecting overreaction in the Bitcoin market: A quantile autoregression approach. *Elsevier Finance Research Letters, 30*(C), 371–377. https://doi.org/10.1016/j.frl.2018.11.004

Chen, T., Lau, C. K. M., Cheema, S., & Koo, C. K. (2021). Economic policy uncertainty in China and Bitcoin returns: Evidence from the COVID-19 period. *Frontiers in Public Health, 9.* https://www.frontiersin.org/article/10.3389/fpubh.2021.651051, https://doi.org/10.3389/fpubh.2021.651051, ISSN=2296-2565.

Coeure, B. (2018, November 15). *The new frontier of payments and market infrastructure: on cryptos, cyber and CCPs.* Welcome remarks by Benoît Cœuré, Chair of the Committee on Payments and Market Infrastructures of the Bank for International Settlements and Member of the Executive Board of the ECB, at the Economics of Payments IX conference, Basel. https://www.ecb.europa.eu/press/key/date/2018/html/ecb.sp181115.en.html

Conlon, T., & McGee, R. (2019). Betting on Bitcoin: Does gambling volume on the blockchain explain Bitcoin price changes? *Economics Letters.* Available online 30 September 2019, 108727, https://doi.org/10.1016/j.econlet.2019.108727

Das, D., & Kannadhasan, M. (2018). Do global factors impact Bitcoin prices? Evidence from Wavelet approach. *Journal of Economic Research, 23,* 227–264. https://www.researchgate.net/publication/329308550_Do_global_factors_impact_Bitcoin_prices_evidence_from_wavelet_approach

das Neves, H. R. (2020). Bitcoin pricing: Impact of attractiveness variables. *Financial Innovation, 6*(21). https://doi.org/10.1186/s40854-020-00176-3

Dastgir, S., Demir, E., Downing, G., Gozgor, G., Keung, C., & Lau, M. (2019). The causal relationship between Bitcoin attention and Bitcoin returns: Evidence from the Copula-based Granger causality test. *Finance Research Letters, 28*, 160–164. https://doi.org/10.1016/j.frl.2018.04.019

Deloitte. (2014). *Bitcoin. The new gold rush?* Deloitte Center for Financial Services. https://www2.deloitte.com/content/dam/Deloitte/us/Documents/financial-services/us-fsi-bitcoin-the-new-gold-rush-031814.pdf

Demir, E., Gozgor, G., Lau, C. K. M., & Vigne, S. A. (2018). Does economic policy uncertainty predict the Bitcoin returns? An empirical investigation.

Finance Research Letters, 26, 145–149. https://doi.org/10.1016/j.frl.2018.01.005

Dina El Mahdy. (2021). *The economic effect of Bitcoin halving events on the U.S. Capital Market* [Online First]. IntechOpen. https://doi.org/10.5772/intechopen.96791. Available from: https://www.intechopen.com/online-first/the-economic-effect-of-bitcoin-halving-events-on-the-u-s-capital-market

Dirican, C., & Canoz, İ. (2017). The cointegration relationship between Bitcoin prices and major world stock indices: an analysis with ARDL model approach. *Journal of Economics, Finance and Accounting (JEFA), 4*(4), 377–392. https://doi.org/10.17261/Pressacademia.2017.748

Dyhrberg, A. H. (2016a). Hedging capabilities of Bitcoin. Is it the virtual gold? *Finance Research Letters, 16*(C), 139–144. https://doi.org/10.1016/j.frl.2015.10.025

Dyhrberg, A. H. (2016b). Bitcoin, gold and the dollar—A GARCH volatility analysis. *Finance Research Letters, 16*(C) 85–92. https://doi.org/10.1016/j.frl.2015.10.008

Erdas, M. L., & Caglar, A. E. (2018). Analysis of the relationships between Bitcoin and exchange rate, commodities and global indexes by asymmetric causality test. *Eastern Journal of European Studies, 9*(2), 27–45. http://ejes.uaic.ro/articles/EJES2018_0902_ERD.pdf

Fenga, W., Wang, Y., & Zhangb, Z. (2018). Informed trading in the Bitcoin market. *Finance Research Letters, 26,* 63–70. https://doi.org/10.1016/j.frl.2017.11.009

Gozgor, G., Tiwari, A. K., Demir, E., & Akron, S. (2019). The relationship between Bitcoin returns and trade policy uncertainty. *Finance Research Letters, 29*, 75–82. https://doi.org/10.1016/j.frl.2019.03.016

Gronwald, M. (2019). Is Bitcoin a commodity? On price jumps, demand shocks, and certainty of supply. *Journal of International Money and Finance, 97*, 86–92. https://doi.org/10.1016/j.jimonfin.2019.06.006

Hansen, B. E. (2011). Threshold autoregression in economics.*Statistics and Its Interface, 4,* 123–127. https://www.ssc.wisc.edu/~bhansen/papers/saii_11.pdf

Harold, J. (2018, June). Lucre's Allure. Throughout time, new currency has been associated with mystical qualities, and Bitcoin is no exception. *Finance & Development, 55*(2). https://www.imf.org/external/pubs/ft/fandd/2018/06/bitcoin-blockchain-history-of-money/james.htm

Horra, L. P., de la Fuente, G., & Perote, J. (2019). The drivers of Bitcoin demand: A short and long-run analysis. *International Review of Financial Analysis, 62,* 21–34. ISSN 1057–5219, https://doi.org/10.1016/j.irfa.

2019.01.006, https://www.sciencedirect.com/science/article/pii/S1057521918307208

Ifigeneia, G., Pournarakis, D., Bilanakos, C., Sotiropoulos D., & Giaglis, G. (2015). *Using time-series and sentiment analysis to detect the determinants of Bitcoin prices*. SSRN: https://ssrn.com/abstract=2607167 or http://dx.doi.org/10.2139/ssrn.2607167.

Kajtazi, A., & Moro, A. (2019). The role of Bitcoin in well diversified portfolios: A comparative global study. *International Review of Financial Analysis, 61,* 143–157. https://doi.org/10.1016/j.irfa.2018.10.003

Kaya, O. (2018). Economic policy uncertainty in Europe Detrimental to capital markets and bank lending. *Deutsche Bank Research, EU Monitor - Global Financial Mar*kets. https://www.dbresearch.com/PROD/RPS_EN-PROD/PROD0000000000460235/Economic_policy_uncertainty_in_Europe%3A_Detrimental.pdf.

Kjærland, F., Meland, M., Oust, A., & Øyen, V. (2018). How can Bitcoin Price fluctuations be explained? *International Journal of Economics and Financial Issues, 8*(3), 323–332. https://www.econjournals.com/index.php/ijefi/article/view/6446

Kliber, A., Marszałek, P., Musiałkowska, I., & Świerczyńska, K. (2019). Bitcoin: Safe haven, hedge or diversifier? Perception of Bitcoin in the context of a country's economic situation—A stochastic volatility approach. *Physica A: Statistical Mechanics and Its Applications, 524*(C), 246–257.

Kristoufek, L. (2015). What are the main drivers of the Bitcoin price? Evidence from wavelet coherence analysis. *PLoS ONE, 10*(4), e0123923, pp. 1–15. https://doi.org/10.1371/journal.pone.0123923

Kim W., Lee J., & Kang K.(2019). The effects of the introduction of Bitcoin futures on the volatility of Bitcoin returns. *Finance Research Letters*. https://doi.org/10.1016/j.frl.2019.06.002

Lagarde, C. (2020, November 30). *The future of money—Innovating while retaining trust*. Article by Christine Lagarde, President of the ECB, in L'ENA hors les murs magazine, Paris. https://www.ecb.europa.eu/press/inter/date/2020/html/ecb.in201130~ce64cb35a3.en.html

Liu, Y., & Tsyvinski, A. (2018). *Risks and returns of cryptocurrency* (NBER Working Paper Series, 24877). National Bureau of Economic Research, Inc. https://www.nber.org/papers/w24877. https://doi.org/10.3386/w24877

Merediz-Solà, I., & Bariviera, A. F. (2019). A bibliometric analysis of Bitcoin scientific production. *Research in International Business and Finance, 50,* 294–305. https://doi.org/10.1016/j.ribaf.2019.06.008

Musialkowska, I., Kliber, A., Świerczyńska, K., & Marszałek, P. (2020). Looking for a safe-haven in a crisis-driven Venezuela: The Caracas stock exchange vs gold, oil and bitcoin. *Transforming Government: People, Process and Policy, 14*(3), 475–494. https://doi.org/10.1108/TG-01-2020-0009

Panagiotidis, T., Stengos, T., & Vravosinos, O. (2018). On the determinants of Bitcoin returns: A LASSO approach. *Finance Research Letters, 27*(C), 235–240. https://doi.org/10.1016/j.frl.2018.03.01627

Panetta, F. (2020, November 27). *From the payments revolution to the reinvention of money.* Speech by Fabio Panetta, Member of the Executive Board of the ECB, at the Deutsche Bundesbank conference on the "Future of Payments in Europe", Frankfurt am Main. https://www.ecb.europa.eu/press/key/date/2020/html/ecb.sp201127~a781c4e0fc.en.html

Ruozhou, L., Shanfeng, W., Zili, Z., & Xuejun, Z. (2019). Is the introduction of futures responsible for the crash of Bitcoin? *Finance Research Letters.* https://doi.org/10.1016/j.frl.2019.08.007

Sebastião, H., & Godinho, P. (2019). *Bitcoin futures: An effective tool for hedging cryptocurrencies.* Available online, 4 July 2019, In Press, Corrected Proof, https://doi.org/10.1016/j.frl.2019.07.003

Settle, P. (2018). *What does the future hold for crypto*? https://info.kpmg.us/news-perspectives/industry-insights-research/uncertain-outlook-for-crypto assets.html

Takaishi, T. (2018). Statistical properties and multifractality of Bitcoin. *Physica A: Statistical Mechanics and Its Applications, 506*(C), 507–519.

Tong, H. (1983). *Threshold models in non-linear time series analysis* (Vol. 21). Springer-Verlag New York, eBook, ISBN 978-1-4684-7888-4. https://doi.org/10.1007/978-1-4684-7888-4

Urquhart, A. (2016). The inefficiency of Bitcoin. *Economics Letters, 148*, 80–82. https://doi.org/10.1016/j.econlet.2016.09.019

Vidal, D., & Analbanez, T. (2018, December). Semi-strong efficiency of Bitcoin. *Finance Research Letters, 27,* 259–265. https://doi.org/10.1016/j.frl.2018.03.013

Wang, G. J., Tang, Y., Xie, C., & Chen, S. (2019). Is Bitcoin a safe haven or a hedging asset? *Evidence from China, Journal of Management Science and Engineering,.* https://doi.org/10.1016/j.jmse.2019.09.001

Wang, G. J., Xie, C., Wen, D., & Longfeng Z. (2018). When Bitcoin meets economic policy uncertainty (EPU): Measuring risk spillover effect from EPU to Bitcoin. *Finance Research Letters* – Forthcoming.

Wang, M. (2020). *Bitcoin and its impact on the economy.* Cornell University. arXiv:2010.01337v1 [econ.GN].

World Bank. (2018, May). *Cryptocurrencies and blockchain. Europe and Central Asia economic update*. World Bank. https://doi.org/10.1596/978-1-4648-1299-6

Yonghong, J., & Ruan Weihua, N. H. (2017). Time-varying long-term memory in Bitcoin market. *Finance Research Letters, 25*, 280–284 (June 2018). https://doi.org/10.1016/j.frl.2017.12.009

Zwick, H. S., & Syed S. A. S. (2019). *Bitcoin and gold prices: A fledging long-term relationship* (MPRA Paper), vol. 92512, pp. 1–12. https://mpra.ub.uni-muenchen.de/92512/1/MPRA_paper_92512.pdf

Index

M. Ratajczak-Mrozek and P. Marszałek (eds.), *Digitalization and Firm Performance*, https://doi.org/10.1007/978-3-030-83360-2

The manufacturer's authorised representative in the EU is Springer Nature Customer Service Centre GmbH, Europaplatz 3, 69115 Heidelberg, Germany. If you have any concerns regarding our products, please contact ProductSafety@springernature.com

Printed and bound by CPI Group (UK) Ltd, Croydon, CR0 4YY
22/09/2026
02221066-0010